Communications in Computer and Information Science 953

Commenced Publication in 2007
Founding and Former Series Editors:
Phoebe Chen, Alfredo Cuzzocrea, Xiaoyong Du, Orhun Kara, Ting Liu,
Dominik Ślęzak, and Xiaokang Yang

More information about this series at http://www.springer.com/series/7899

Michail Salampasis · Thomas Bournaris (Eds.)

Information and Communication Technologies in Modern Agricultural Development

8th International Conference, HAICTA 2017
Chania, Crete, Greece, September 21–24, 2017
Revised Selected Papers

 Springer

Editors
Michail Salampasis
TEI of Thessaloniki
Thessaloniki, Greece

Thomas Bournaris
Aristotle University of Thessaloniki
Thessaloniki, Greece

ISSN 1865-0929   ISSN 1865-0937 (electronic)
Communications in Computer and Information Science
ISBN 978-3-030-12997-2   ISBN 978-3-030-12998-9 (eBook)
https://doi.org/10.1007/978-3-030-12998-9

Library of Congress Control Number: 2019931958

This Springer imprint is published by the registered company Springer Nature Switzerland AG
The registered company address is: Gewerbestrasse 11, 6330 Cham, Switzerland

Preface

Agriculture is continuously faced with crucial problems along with new challenges and opportunities. These new challenges stretch over many issues among which is the globalization of food markets, which intensifies the competition in the agricultural sector, the productivity and competitiveness of small farms, the rise of both producer and input prices, climate change etc. In this context, effective interventions in agriculture are essential for the fulfillment of its vital role, which is to maintain economic and social stability and provide the environment for sustainable development. The use of information and communication technologies (ICTs) can be, among others, one major intervention that can reduce consumer prices, support farmers to increase their production, and contribute to "smarter," more efficient and sustainable agriculture.

But what exactly are ICTs and how can they be applied in agriculture? The definition of ICT in Wikipedia is: "Information and communications technology or ICT, is often used as an extended synonym for information technology (IT), but is a more specific term that stresses the role of unified communications and the integration of telecommunications (telephone lines and wireless signals), computers as well as necessary enterprise software, middleware, storage, and audio-visual systems, which enable users to access, store, transmit, and manipulate information." A more comprehensive definition of ICT in agriculture is given by an overview published by the World Bank's Agriculture and Rural Development division:

"First, an ICT is any device, tool, or application that permits the exchange or collection of data through interaction or transmission. ICT is an umbrella term that includes anything ranging from radio to satellite imagery to mobile phones or electronic money transfers. Second, these ICTs and others have gained traction even in impoverished regions. The increases in their affordability, accessibility, and adaptability have resulted in their use even within rural homesteads relying on agriculture. New, small devices (such as multifunctional mobile phones and nanotechnology for food safety), infrastructure (such as mobile telecommunications networks and cloud computing facilities), and especially applications (for example, that transfer money or track an item moving through a global supply chain) have proliferated. Many of the questions asked by farmers (including questions on how to increase yields, access markets, and adapt to weather conditions) can now be answered faster, with greater ease, and increased accuracy. Many of the questions can also be answered with a dialogue—where farmers, experts, and government can select best solutions based on a diverse set of expertise and experience."

This volume contains selected papers from the 8th International Conference on ICTs in Agriculture, Food, and Environment (HAICTA 2017) that took place in Crete, Greece, in September 2017, on the premises of the Mediterranean Agronomic Institute of Chania (CIHEAM). The conference was organized by the Hellenic Association for Information and Communication Technologies in Agriculture Food and Environment (HAICTA), CIHEAM, and the University of Macedonia, Greece.

The papers in their initial version were peer reviewed by the members of the scientific committee of the HAICTA 2017 conference in order to be published in the conference proceedings. From the 55 submissions accepted as full papers, 15 papers were invited to submit a new, extended and revised, version to be considered for publication in this volume. The selection of the works appearing in this volume was based on three criteria: their relevance to the scope of the CCIS conference series, the evaluation score of the conference papers (each paper was reviewed by at least two reviewers), and finally the diversity of ICT in agriculture research that the volume should collectively present. All manuscripts underwent a new round of single-blind review by at least two additional reviewers before being accepted for publication. The number of reviewers who participated in this second round review was 29, and we would like to acknowledge their contribution to this volume. Based on reviewer's scores and comments, 14 papers were finally accepted to appear in this volume.

The papers span across various subjects, from ICT innovations and smart farming, to decision support systems, as well as precision farming, disease diagnosis using mobile devices, IoT for monitoring and controlling animal production, sensor-based solutions, GIS-based water management, environmental planning, information systems for monitoring of fish stocks and fisheries, information management in the agri-food sector and, forestry planning and management.

HAICTA (Hellenic Association of Information and Communication Technology in Agriculture, Food and Environment) is the Greek Branch of the European Federation for Information Technology in Agriculture (EFITA). The series of HAICTA conferences is an international venue for research and development in ICT in agriculture.

The main goal of the conferences is to bring together professional, experts, and researchers working on ICTs in agriculture. Furthermore, emphasis is put on the applicability of ICT solutions to real industry cases and the respective issues, problems, and challenges.

The HAICTA conference in 2017 received 124 paper submissions, out of which 55 (44.4%) were accepted as full papers. Submissions were received from authors coming from 45 countries. The top five countries in terms of accepted papers (according to contact author affiliation) were Greece, Poland, Italy, Czech Republic, and Spain. The top scientific areas covered by the submitted papers (as indicated by the primary keyword assigned by the authors) were decision support systems, information systems, environmental impact assessment, precision farming systems, environmental design and policy. We hope you will find the selected papers presented in this book interesting and that it will provide you with a valuable starting point to know better the field of ICT in agriculture.

Organization

Organizing Committee Co-chairs

Konstantinos Parisis   Technological Educational Institute of Western Macedonia, Greece

Athanasios Ragkos   Alexander Technological Educational Institute of Thessaloniki, Greece

Organizing Committee

Christos Batzios   Aristotle University of Thessaloniki, Greece

Thomas Bournaris   Aristotle University of Thessaloniki, Greece

Evangelos Grigoroudis   Technical University of Crete, Greece

Katerina Karapataki   Mediterranean Agronomic Institute of Chania, Greece

Michail Salampasis   Alexander Technological Educational Institute of Thessaloniki, Greece

Vagis Samathrakis   Alexander Technological Educational Institute of Thessaloniki, Greece

Alexandros Theodoridis   Aristotle University of Thessaloniki, Greece

Argyro Zervou   Mediterranean Agronomic Institute of Chania, Greece

Secretarial Support

Elias Tsourapas   Hellenic Open University, Greece

Maria Botsiou   University of Macedonia, Greece

Nikoleta Mazaraki   Aristotle University of Thessaloniki, Greece

Georgia Trikoupi   Aristotle University of Thessaloniki, Greece

Alexandra Tsistilianou   Aristotle University of Thessaloniki, Greece

Program Committee

Oleksandr Chernyak   Taras Shevchenko National University of Kyiv, Ukraine

Pavlos Delias   Eastern Macedonia and Thrace Institute of Technology, Greece

Vania V. Estrela   Universidade Federal Fluminense, Brazil

Sebastien Ferre   Université de Rennes 1, France

Ioannis Fotidis   Technical University of Denmark, Denmark

Nuno Garcia   Universidade da Beira Interior, Portugal

Theofanis Gemtos   University of Thessaly, Greece

Contents

ICT Innovations and Smart Farming 1
Claus Aage Grøn Sørensen, Dimitrios Kateris, and Dionysis Bochtis

Methods and Tools for Supporting the Integration of Stocks and Fisheries ... 20
Yannis Tzitzikas, Yannis Marketakis, Nikos Minadakis,
Michalis Mountantonakis, Leonardo Candela, Francesco Mangiacrapa,
Pasquale Pagano, Costantino Perciante, Donatella Castelli,
Marc Taconet, Aureliano Gentile, and Giulia Gorelli

Semiotic-Sociological Textures of Landscape Values. Assessments
in Urban-Coastal Areas 35
Salvatore Giuffrida, Maria Rosa Trovato, and Annalaura Giannelli

A Systematic Review on Collective Awareness Platforms 51
Thomas Kappas, Thomas Bournaris, Evangelia Economou,
and Christina Moulogianni

Using Geostatistics and Multicriteria Spatial Analysis to Map Forest
Species Biogeophysical Suitability: A Study Case for the Centro Region
of Portugal.. 64
Luís Quinta-Nova, Natália Roque, Isabel Navalho, Cristina Alegria,
and Teresa Albuquerque

CAP 2020 Regionalization Design: A Decision Support System 84
Dimitris Kremmydas, Michael Malliapis, Leyteris Nellas,
Apostolos Polymeros, Stelios Rozakis, and Kostas Tsiboukas

Strategic Decision Making and Information Management
in the Agrifood Sector.. 97
Maria Kamariotou, Fotis Kitsios, Michael Madas, Vicky Manthou,
and Maro Vlachopoulou

Water Data Sharing in Italy with SIGRIAN WebGIS Platform 110
Raffaella Zucaro, Gianfranco Giannerini, Antonio Gerardo Pepe,
Fabrizio Luigi Tascone, and Marco Martello

Towards the Commercialization of a Lab-on-a-Chip Device for Soil
Nutrient Measurement 118
Georgios Kokkinis, Guenther Kriechhammer, Daniel Scheidl,
Bianca Wilfling, and Martin Smolka

SheepIT, an IoT-Based Weed Control System....................... 131
Luís Nóbrega, Paulo Pedreiras, and Pedro Gonçalves

Techniques for Plant Disease Diagnosis Evaluated
on a Windows Phone Platform   148
    Nikos Petrellis

Different Remote Sensing Data in Relative Biomass Determination
and in Precision Fertilization Task Generation for Cereal Crops   164
    *Jere Kaivosoja, Roope Näsi, Teemu Hakala, Niko Viljanen,
    and Eija Honkavaara*

Unmanned Ground Vehicles in Precision Farming Services: An Integrated
Emulation Modelling Approach   177
    *Dimitrios Bechtsis, Vasileios Moisiadis, Naoum Tsolakis,
    Dimitrios Vlachos, and Dionysis Bochtis*

Precision Poultry Farming: Software Architecture Framework and Online
Zootechnical Diary for Monitoring and Collaborating on Hens' Health   191
    Magdalena Stefanova

Author Index   207

ICT Innovations and Smart Farming

Claus Aage Grøn Sørensen[1](✉), Dimitrios Kateris[2],
and Dionysis Bochtis[2]

[1] Department of Engineering, Aarhus University,
Finlandsgade 22, 8700 Aarhus N, Denmark
claus.soerensen@eng.au.dk
[2] Institute for Bio-Economy and Agri-Technology (IBO),
Center for Research and Technology Hellas (CERTH),
6th km Charilaou – Thermi Road, 57001 Thermi, Thessaloniki, Greece
{d.kateris,d.bochtis}@certh.gr

Abstract. Agriculture plays a vital role in the global economy with the majority of the rural population in developing countries depending on it. The depletion of natural resources makes the improvement of the agricultural production more important but also more difficult than ever. This is the reason that although the demand is constantly growing, Information and Communication Technology (ICT) offers to producers the adoption of sustainability and improvement of their daily living conditions. ICT offers timely and updated relevant information such as weather forecast, market prices, the occurrence of new diseases and varieties, etc. The new knowledge offers a unique opportunity to bring the production enhancing technologies to the farmers and empower themselves with modern agricultural technology and act accordingly for increasing the agricultural production in a cost effective and profitable manner. The use of ICT itself or combined with other ICT systems results in productivity improvement and better resource use and reduces the time needed for farm management, marketing, logistics and quality assurance.

Keywords: Agriculture · Information and Communication Technology · Robotic · FMIS · Precision Farming Management

1 Introduction

ICT in agriculture is a highly innovative and rapidly advancing field of practice that aims to promote the development of remunerative agriculture using innovative applications that provide the farmers with accurate, relevant and timely information and services.

The ICT contribution to agriculture includes cost reduction, increase of efficiency and productivity improvement. But first the information requirements should be analyzed and documented and then adequate information systems (IS) should be developed taking into account the new challenges arising from the deregulation and the globalization of agriculture [1].

Having accurate and timely information about the seed, the water, the nutrients and protection of the plant plays a significant role for the success of the farming.

© Springer Nature Switzerland AG 2019
M. Salampasis and T. Bournaris (Eds.): HAICTA 2017, CCIS 953, pp. 1–19, 2019.
https://doi.org/10.1007/978-3-030-12998-9_1

Information-intensive and precise techniques of farming based on knowledge will be the leading factors of sustainable agricultural production. Thus, referring to the agricultural production management it is crucial that the benefits from the information providers such as the internet and other information and communication technologies (ICT) are made clear to farmers. Nevertheless, the use of ICT in the agricultural sector is not widespread and its economic potential is not utilized to the fullest. For instance, ICT could offer great support to managers but also policy makers when making a decision related to precision farming and livestock management [2].

An area of application for ICT lies in the improvement, through a better management, of the efficiency and sustainability in using inputs—land, soil nutrients, feed and fodder, water, energy, pesticides, labour and most importantly information—in agriculture. ICT also contribute to the reduction of the negative effects of pests and disease and to the aversion and mitigation of risks coming for example from inclement weather, droughts, floods and long-term change of climate. For the small farmers, these applications of ICT have not become yet mainstream. The economic returns from agriculture and access to affordable technology, useful in small farm operations, are the main constraints to a more widespread use of ICT in small holder agricultural production.

Information means empowerment through resources control and decision-making processes. An effective and efficient delivery system of basic information and technology services facilitates the end users critical role in decision-making towards improved agricultural production and processing trading. In the agricultural sector, with appearance of sustainable agricultural systems, information becomes a major input for agricultural production because sustainable agriculture is more information-intensive rather than technology-intensive.

However, the use of ICT in agriculture does have some weaknesses; among the most common problems is the fact that farmers do not know how to use such technology applications to their full potential, not to mention the non-availability of information sources in different languages, the considerable cost of the technology, plus the denial of the farmers to adopt a positive approach towards the use of ICT. Last but not least comes the human factor which transmits the Information Knowledge to farmers and their groups, having the ICT in the end to depend heavily on this unpredictable factor and its changes. Thus, it is crucial to find out to which extent ICT meets the farmers needs, in order to promote the ICT usage by satisfying most of their needs.

2 ICT Use in Agricultural

The use of ICT itself or combined with other ICT systems results in productivity improvement and better resource use and reduces the time needed for farm management, marketing, logistics and quality assurance. As time goes by, ICT improves the access of the farmers to information, knowledge, skills and technology, improves the productivity of the farm and its ability to take part in the markets, not to mention its contribution to increased sustainability and to the resilience of the farming systems while changing them to face the new challenges. Next figure shows the impact of ICT on agriculture section (Fig. 1).

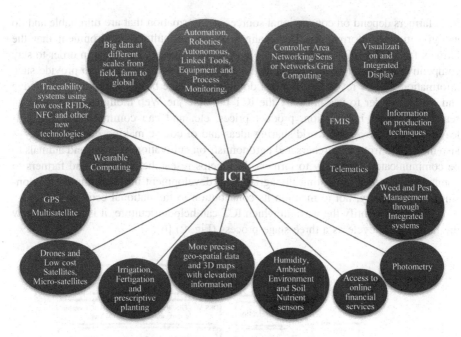

Fig. 1. ICT impact in agriculture section.

2.1 Role of ICT in Agriculture

In agricultural sector, ICT can be used in two ways: (a) Directly, where ICT is used as a tool that contributes directly to productivity of agricultural production, and (b) Indirectly, where ICT is used as a tool that provides information to farmers for making quality decisions in efficient management of their enterprises [3–5].

(a) Direct contribution of ICT to agricultural production

In direct contribution of ICT to agricultural production, the intensive use of ICT characterizes precision farming and subsequently smart farming. In order to increase the agricultural production, remote sensors techniques with support of geographic information systems (GIS), satellite technology, soil science and agronomics are used. ICT gives to the farmers the ability to track and react to weather condition changes on a daily basis. Meteorological stations on a field can be connected to farmers' computers in order to send information about current air temperature, relative air humidity, rainfall, soil moisture, wind speed and solar radiation. All these technologies of crop monitoring require substantial capital investments. Thus, mostly larger farms will make use of such technologies and also can afford to pay for them. Smaller farm enterprises cannot usually cope with such technologies.

(b) Indirect contribution of ICT to agricultural production

Most indirect benefits of ICT have to do with the facilitation and supporting of the decision-making. Farmers need timely and reliable information sources. Currently, most farmers depend on conventional sources of information that are unreliable and do not give timely information. The changes of the agricultural environment that the farmers face make information not only useful but necessary for them in order to stay competitive and survive on a globalized market. However, the efforts to provide such information will be revoked if farmers do not have some basic computing knowledge and skills in order to use not only the ICT but also the Web though which they can search for useful information, product prices, etc. and can communicate with colleagues from all over the world sharing ideas and of course making questions. Key is also the advice from researchers and agronomists on cultivation of crops and animals to be communicated efficiently to farmers. ICT helps researchers/adviser and farmers to communicate better promoting the agricultural development but also human relationships in the society, not to mention its contribution to the national economy.

In order to identify the ways in which ICT can help agriculture, it is useful to view the farming life cycle as a three-stage process (Fig. 2) [6]:

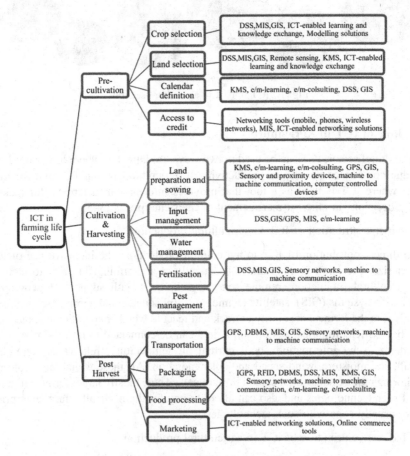

Fig. 2. ICT contribution in farming life cycle.

3 ICT and Automation

During 1990–2010 extensively changes in automated technology, plant varieties and livestock with improved genetic potentials lead to an evolution of the agriculture and other bio-production types increasing the scale and degree of specialization of farm operations. Consequently, agricultural production is mainly done by large, specialised units, which management is complex enough and therefore an important issue to deal with, especially when it comes to work operations. What is more, the technology used, including the machinery, is of high cost which tends to raise faster than returns to the point that an increase in efficiency results merely in the maintenance of the productivity and not in its improvement. In conclusion, the profit of the enterprise coming from development is solely contained within the marginal earnings of the production. In order this profit to be secured a rise in production and in operations management will be required based on an unprecedented level of flexibility and precision.

Concurrently farming operations need to comply with several regulations and standards in order for example to ensure food security, labour conditions, reduce environmental impact etc. This means that concerning the farming systems there should be considerations referring to efficiency, economy, environment and society. Thus, sustainability has become a key factor for bio-production meaning that the very nature of farm planning has changed in the last years. In the past farmers worked the traditional way of planning what crops to grow and which machines to use whereas nowadays there are implementation and scheduling issues to be solved using different production strategies and organizations of the farming system [7–9], giving more emphasis to the ability of the decision maker (or automation system) to do the right thing at the right time. The goal has become first to present the activities or operations needed to achieve a predefined goal, and next to set a timetable for execution as well as the resources to the operations in question. At the same time, it is necessary to comply with a number of temporal resource constraints. In the next years more, automation in bio-production operations is expected, which will certainly raise the demand for advanced management tools, like fleet management and logistics tools, for mobile units' scheduling, monitoring and on-line coordination etc. Also, system analyses and integration will be on the focus raising the need for operational data. The processing of stochastic planning system as a basis when making a decision requires a much more comprehensive description and quantification of labour and machinery data than in the past.

Due to the development of agriculture the scope of operations management has changed significantly from manual work operations to automated work operations, where the operator merely monitors the process. Sørensen [10], lists some of the most important developments of operations management in agriculture (Fig. 3).

The development mentioned above is clearly reflected in the topics of the last 2 decades. The topics have moved from the more classical work science developments to more comprehensive management systems using the methods of work science and ergonomics combined with advanced information technology system for automatic data acquisition and data processing. What is more the last years there is a strong focus on how technology and management can ensure sustainability of the bio-production development.

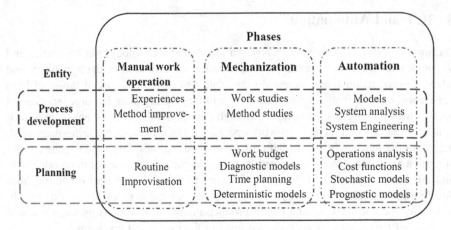

Fig. 3. The evolution of operations and system management in agriculture.

Apart from the hardware implementation also the software, this is to say the automation technologies for field operations, requires that new management techniques is implemented (e.g. site specific management systems, including precision spraying systems, precision irrigation systems, and monitoring on site of the processes auto-steering systems).

The management of the activities relates to:

- Open environment (arable farming and forestry domain),
- Semi-structured environments (controlled traffic farming systems, open air horticulture, vineyards, orchards etc.),
- Controlled environments (greenhouses, urban farming, animal production units, processing plants for agro-food, wineries, which are also in need of a task and operation management).

Last but not least, a form of internet application including some of the tools mentioned above could share the knowledge over specific sectors with the end users. Such an application could provide a real cost estimation as well as an environmental impact estimation of the agricultural operations. It could also be used planning activities, running and stopping the equipment, or simulating the activity of field robots. In general terms, the usage of the internet has the following pros [11]:

- The results obtained among different users could be standardizes using the same calculation method and with the same coefficients,
- Studies carried out in different conditions and locations could be compared because of the same coefficients,
- Standard data for non-expert users could be available for free,
- Installation and distribution costs for the software and the updates would not exist since the application would reside only in one server,

- Variant techniques referring to the environmental impact and the enterprise net return could be compared via several scenarios,
- A great range of scenarios would be available, due to the great number of users on the web,
- Worldwide farms and crop scenarios could be compared anonymously.

4 ICT and Agricultural Production

In order to improve the agricultural production, the farmers should be aware of the following information (Fig. 4) [3]:

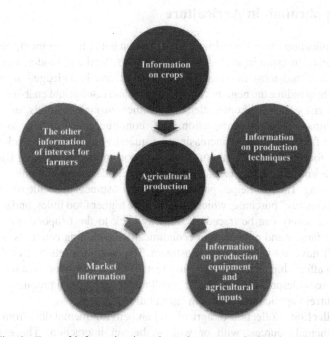

Fig. 4. Type of information in order to improve agricultural production.

Information on the crops: Field information can be collected and transferred via the Web or other types of telematics and be analyzed into reviews and statistics to which farmers may get electronical access to planning adapted to their own production. Such information may be over seeded crop categories, area of land with specific crops, time of dropping seed, time of harvest, yields etc.

Information on the production techniques: Production techniques developed by experimental institutes of agriculture and stations for agricultural improvement are also available to farmers via the internet.

Information on production equipment and agricultural inputs: Such information is provided by companies selling agricultural equipment. And may be accessible to the farmers via the Web as well.

Information on the market: Such information makes the farmers aware of the worldwide food market including product prices helping them to be more competitive and -why not- to address to markets where the products are valued higher. Furthermore, Information Technology may forecast the product demand and prices in the future helping the farmer (and trader) to plan not only the next season's crops, but also the selling price and the time of selling (now or later in an expecting high season).

Other information: Such information refers to weather forecast, availability of credit, expert advice over the crops, etc.

5 ICT Application in Agriculture

An area of application for ICT is in improving, through better management, the efficiency and sustainability in using inputs—land, soil nutrients, feed and fodder, water, energy, pesticides, labor, and most importantly, information and knowledge—in agriculture. The ICT also help reduce the negative effects of pests and disease and enable aversion and mitigation of risks such as from inclement weather, droughts, floods, and long-term change in climate. Through innovation, ICT continue to contribute to improving throughput of farming systems, increasing the quantity, quality, and marketability of outputs (e.g., food, energy, and biomaterials), supporting their marketing and enabling their effective and efficient consumption by households and communities and their ultimate recycling. The ICT helped pave the way for consumers to decide which products they can "responsibly" purchase, which seem to have higher food miles, and those whose production and safety can be traced all the way back to the fishpond. For the small, resource-poor farmer and producers in economically developing countries, these applications of ICT have not yet become mainstream. The economic returns from agriculture and access to affordable technology useful in small-farms operations are the main constraints in more widespread use of ICT in smallholder agricultural production. Figure 5 present the current application of ICT in agriculture [12].

Data Collection. Collection of agricultural and environmental data from biological and environmental sources, with or without human interaction. These data, after analysed and manipulated will feed auxiliary applications.

Number Crunching. Process of large datasets, modelling and simulation, image processing and visualization that helps plant and animal breeding, plant and animal epidemiology, management and market chain analysis agricultural meteorology, bioinformatics, farming systems research, etc.

Robotics and DSS. Data and information combined with the human factor are organized in order to help especially in semantical searching, diagnosis and farm and agricultural process automation.

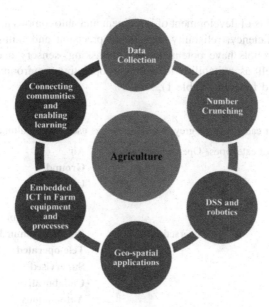

Fig. 5. Application of ICT in agriculture.

Embedded ICT in farm equipment and processes. Farm equipment and agricultural processes are more efficient as well as the transportation and marketing of the agricultural products, for example the use of RFIDs, Cellular Telephony and Wireless Internet in labelling, traceability and identity preservation.

Geo-spatial applications. Data and information related to geography and space to be managed contributes to planning of the land and water usage, to the utilization of the natural resources, the agricultural input supply and the commodity marketing, to the elimination of poverty etc.

Connecting communities and enabling learning. ICT helps researchers and farmers but also the communities of researchers to interact and communicate better promoting the agricultural development and the scientific research and publication. Furthermore, ICT promotes the cooperation between farmers and producers with the exchange of knowledge and technology which is very useful especially when problems arise.

5.1 Robotics

Robotics in agriculture is known from the past; it's been over 20 years that it is used in controlled environments. However, as computational power rises and costs are reduced robotics is spreading. Recently autonomous machines are developed in agriculture by researchers gaining serious interest. As a matter of fact a case scenario was to use many small efficient autonomous machines replacing tractors of large size [13–15]. Such vehicles are on duty 24 h a day, 7 days a week, whatever the usual weather conditions. Plus, they work normally (sensibly) in a natural/semi-natural environment for long periods, unattended, while carrying out a useful task.

The main benefits of development of intelligent and autonomous agricultural robots are to improve efficiency, reliability, repeatable precision and minimization of soil compaction. The robots have potential for multitasking, sensory acuity, operational consistency as well as suitability to different operating environment, interaction, physical format and function (Table 1).

Table 1. Robot categories. In grey the robotic types used in agricultural production.

Robot categories	Operating environment	**Air**
		Ground
		Underwater
		Space
		Living organism
	Interaction	**Pre-programmed**
		Tele-operated
		Supervised
		Collaborative
		Autonomous
	Physical format	**Arm**
		Platform
		Exo-skeletal
		Humanoid
		Micro-Nano
		Metamorphic
	Function	Assembly
		Area process
		Interaction
		Exploration
		Transporting
		Inspection
		Manipulation

In agriculture, researchers focus on the design of specialized autonomous agricultural vehicles using various farming operational parameters since conventional farm machinery is crop and topological dependent.

A lot of field operations can be executed by specialized autonomous agricultural robots, offering more benefits than conventional machines. These platforms would be used for cultivation and seeding, irrigation, weeding, fertilizing, scouting and harvesting.

When it comes to harvesting, researchers develop rational and adaptable robotics for picking Cucumber [16], Tomato [17], Pepper [18, 19], Strawberry [20, 21], Egg-plant [22], Melon and Watermelon [23], Other vegetables (Asparagus, Cabbage, Radish) [24], Rice and paddy fields [25] and Mushrooms [26], Cherry [27], Apples [28] and Citrus [29].

When it comes to robotic weed control a difficult task for the robots is to diversify between weed and crops. Researchers are developing autonomous robotic platforms for weed destruction [30, 31].

Last but not least when it comes to transplanting and seeding production, robotics apply to some of the operations (seeding, thinning, grafting, cutting sticking, transplanting etc.) [32].

5.2   Precision Farming Management

Agriculture bio-production systems in the future are expected to be of an unprecedented high precision during their operation. Thus, a high degree of embedded machinery intelligence is required combined with advanced operations management systems connected with mobile units, automated systems, advanced updated decision support systems, automatic data acquisition as an integral part of the machine operations at a total for traceability/documentation, production process with economic and environmental concerns. The above are included in precision agriculture (PA) and more recently Smart Farming, which shows the future of agricultural development and other types of bio-production.

In general terms precision agriculture (PA) shows what is the right thing to be done, the right place, the right time, and the right way; so the implementation of PA is based on technologies that define the term "right" [33]. In scientific terms, precision agriculture is an agricultural production management system that uses information and communication technologies (ICT) in order to take into account the spatial and temporal variability in fields and crops [34].

Precision agriculture as a management system is a closed-loop operation system, including data collection, interpretation, decision making, the performance of the designated actions, and last but not least the evaluation of the outcome, coming from the decisions application, and the reconsideration of the decisions that have been taken. During every cropping cycle the above data are recorded and stored in databases (libraries) as historical data for further use in the future (Fig. 6).

Precision farming is considered to contribute to the efficiency and the sustainability of the farming system in the future. The reduction of the environmental impact of the production – due to the input material reduction–, and the generation of valuable information for product traceability are the main two recognizable side benefits deriving from the implementation of PA. Precision farming promotes the development of a new integrated concept including advanced planning and control system and automated smart and robust machinery applicable for biosystems [7]. This will include production units that comply with a number of sustainability indicators such as minimized resource input, product quality and environmental impact. Consequently, precision farming focuses on the development of techniques and technologies which improve production efficiency, and on the environmental impacts measurement, modelling, and of course minimization. In detail, this includes integration of site-specific application of pesticides, fertilizers, and water and operations management (e.g. decision support systems, farm management information systems, web-based approaches and so on).

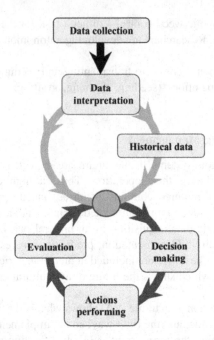

Fig. 6. The concept of precision agriculture as a management system.

PA originates from the first years of organized agricultural production. However, this concept was implemented to small-sized farms, all over which the farmer was able to walk on foot and observe any changes to crop growth or emergency, taking instant actions such as to place locally more seeds or fertilizers. The decision leading to the actions was based on direct observation and included limited "stored" knowledge from previous observations. During the mechanization phase of agricultural production, it was more difficult to store and organize this knowledge especially as the size of the field area increased. To the above phase the economies of scale lead to a homogenous treatment of the large field areas, although there could be significant variations of yield and soil properties in large fields. Last but not least, the technology of that time could not support any type of PA application.

The global positioning system (GPS) was the first technology applied in agricultural operations. Next the yield mapping technologies followed initially in arable farming and in a stepwise manner in open air horticulture and in orchards.

Studies have demonstrated that usefulness and ease of use are crucial for technology adoption, provided that these aspects do not cause a significant increase in the production cost [35, 36]. Other adoption drivers include total income, familiarity with computers, land tenure, farm size, farmers' education, costs reduction or higher revenues to acquire a positive benefit/cost ratio, location and access to information (via extension services, service provider, technology sellers). Also, another key for the adoption of PA is the quantified cost-benefits derived from the use of technologies, such as auto-section control, remote sensing, areas of machine control, guidance, nutrient management, and variable seed rate.

Although during the recent decades there has been a fast development of technologies applied to PA, the adoption by the farmers, if any, was rather slow [37].

In order for a new technology to be implemented one or more of the following points need to be met:

- There is a proven economic benefit,
- There are significant advantages compared to the existing technology to be replaced,
- The new technology is less complicated that the old one,
- The new technology is reliable and robust,
- The new technology is supported by servicing and repair satisfactory enough.

Among the reasons of this low rated adoption lies the initial establishment cost of this new technology. This led to a new generation of third parties that provide site-specific technologies (yield mapping and variable rate applications) [38].

Roughly speaking, the cost of PA technologies depends on the followings 3 points:

- Equipment Depreciation
- Training Cost
- Variable annual data analysis Cost.

5.3   Satellite Navigation

The main navigation satellite navigation systems are:

- The NAVSTAR GPS (Navigation System with Time and Ranging–Global Positioning System). This system was created by the U.S. Department of Defence and the US Department of Transportation. It is composed of a network of 24 satellites placed into orbit. This system can be accessed anywhere. Near the earth can be accessed where there is an unobstructed line of more than four GPS satellites.
- The GLONASS (GLObal NAvigation Satellite System). This system was developed by the Soviet Union and is operated by the Russian Aerospace Defence Forces. It is also composed of a network of 24 satellites placed into orbit. GPS and GLONASS are both available worldwide both for private and commercial use.
- The GNSS (Global Navigation Satellite System). This is a civilian satellite navigation system (Europe).

Nowadays, there is a huge development in the applications of GPS in various domains. Selected applications include:

a. Vehicle navigation systems. This application improves the in-vehicle experience [39], increases safety [40] and helps the driver to orientate in unfamiliar environments. Based on a satellite navigation system the location of the vehicle is identified in relation to the destination provided by the driver. Both visual and auditory directions are offered in almost real-time.

b. Fleet management. This section regards the use of GPS to reach and store locations of origins, location of destinations, trip length and duration, various time stamps during travelling, travel modes and activities. All the traditional methods of activity diaries can be potentially replaced completely by this system. Also, this system can provide the data that can be used for further analysis of the transport systems [41–45].
c. Offshore drilling research.
d. Bridge deformation monitoring.
e. Aircraft approach and landing.
f. Agricultural machinery navigation.

5.4   FMIS (Farm Management Information Systems)

During the last decades, there is an incremental change of the agricultural productivity development from scaling of assets to optimization of assets; for example, there is a strong focus to the maximisation of profit and not to production. Agricultural machines as well as the farm units get bigger and more expensive over the years to the point that a higher degree of input/output management is necessary. However, any efforts towards this direction focus more or less to a single operations management rather than having an overall systems approach.

Recent advances in agricultural RTD (ICT, robotics, processing and operations management tools) and their application has raised dramatically the efficiency in production and the sustainability using integrated processing, planning and control systems. Managers or automated decision-making systems (FMIS) control or give instructions to machine systems or production units based on internet meteorological data, history data of the management system or other information sources. The generation and the execution of a plan gets into a system, having this way the effects of actions, unexpected incidents and new information that attributes to a plan validation, refinement, or reconsideration monitored.

Information has many sources including sites, raising the expectations from the information systems. McCown stated that when an information system, the focus should be on learning the farmers behaviour [46]. Software developers should interact with farmers in a user-centric approach.

The enhancement of FMIS is apparently influenced more by business factors rather than specific farming activities [47]. Plans should be conditional using data from observations, databases, sensors and tests. Management information systems (MIS) are an integral part of a management system and supports several tools such as for example enterprise resource planning (ERP), information systems (IS) etc. ERP, which is an industry concept, involves management activities that support business processes within the production system. The management systems support multiple levels planning processes and identify any key performance indicators (KPI's) [48]. Typically, ERP is connected directly to information systems using databases and including applications for the finance and human resources of an enterprise.

MIS analyses other systems that deal with the operational activities in the production system. Thus, MIS becomes a part of the total planning and control activities covering the management of human resources, technologies, and procedures of the enterprise. As part of scientific management, MIS relates to the automation or support of human decision making [49].

Sørensen et al. refers to the structure of the various management systems in an enterprise or a production system [50] (Fig. 7).

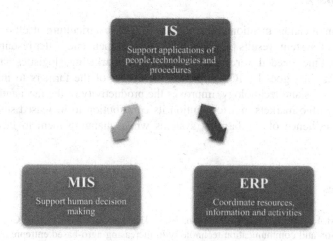

Fig. 7. Concept of management information systems.

Thus, a Farm Management Information System (FMIS) is considered as a system for the data collection, processing, storing and disseminating in order the operations functions of the farm to be executed.

Machinery have increased greatly agricultural productivity in the last decades. This development integrates with advanced automation and extensive use of embedded Information and Communication Technology systems. Such technologies allow the collection of site-specific information in detail during operation of field machinery, conventional, e.g. tractor with implement, or non-conventional autonomous vehicles, e.g. robots. Through targeted decision support systems or directly bearing an online control the resource input is reduced and the production is of high quality and, what is more, environmentally friendly. Task planning and formulation involves a time schedule referring to the predicted crop development, weather forecasts, etc. The task settings are transferred to the tractor/implement for control or implements' adjustment. In case of a difference between the executed work and the formulated plans, there will be corrections. The final result is recorded, documented and the data are stored for future projects or learning.

The task management function helps the farmer to schedule and control the field operations. When the operation and task plan are formulated, they are transferred to the machinery. The task plan give the guidelines for the machine field movements and control the agronomic operations. In case of no knowledge attained within the estimated time of a task plan, it should be reformulated in order for an optimal operation to be maintained (dynamic task plan). Concurrently with above planning, the system analyses and predicts the evolution of the system status (for example field and crop development, machine performance etc.).

6 Conclusion

In conclusion, it can be mentioned that the use of ICT in agriculture, itself or combined with other ICT systems results in productivity improvement and better resource use and reduces the time needed for farm management, marketing, logistics and quality assurance. As time goes by ICT improves the access of the farmers to information, knowledge, skills and technology, improves the productivity of the farm and its ability to take part in the markets, not to mention its contribution to increased sustainability and to the resilience of the farming systems while changing them to face the new challenges.

References

1. Samah, B.A., Shaffril, H.A.M., Hassan, M.S., Hassan, M.A., Ismail, N.: Contribution of information and communication technology in increasing agro-based entrepreneurs productivity in Malaysia. J. Agric. Soc. Sci. **5**, 93–98 (2009)
2. Kaaya, J.: Role of information technology in agriculture. In: Proceedings of the Fourth Annual Research Conference of the Faculty of Agriculture, Sokoine University of Agriculture, pp. 315–328 (1999)
3. Milovanović, S. (Faculty of Economics, N. (Serbia)): The role and potential of information technology in agricultural improvement. Економика пољопривреде/Econ. Agric. **61**, 471–485 (2014)
4. Sørensen, C.G., Bochtis, D.D.: Conceptual model of fleet management in agriculture. Biosyst. Eng. **105**, 41–50 (2010). https://doi.org/10.1016/j.biosystemseng.2009.09.009
5. Sørensen, C.G., Pesonen, L., Bochtis, D.D., Vougioukas, S.G., Suomi, P.: Functional requirements for a future farm management information system. Comput. Electron. Agric. **729**(2), 266–276 (2011). https://doi.org/10.1016/j.compag.2011.02.005
6. Van Zyl, O., Alexander, T., De Graaf, L., Mukherjee, K., Kumar, V.: ICTs for agriculture in Africa (2014)
7. Sørensen, C.G., et al.: Conceptual model of a future farm management information system. Comput. Electron. Agric. **72**, 37–47 (2010). https://doi.org/10.1016/j.compag.2010.02.003
8. Sorensen, C.G., et al.: A user-centric approach for information modelling in arable farming. Comput. Electron. Agric. **73**, 44–55 (2010)
9. Bochtis, D.D., Sørensen, C.G.C., Busato, P.: Advances in agricultural machinery management: a review. Biosyst. Eng. **126**, 69–81 (2014). https://doi.org/10.1016/j.biosystemseng.2014.07.012
10. Sørensen, C.G.C.: Decision support systems as a part of agricultural operational management. In: CIOSTA - CIGR V XXVIII International Congress, Horsens, Denmark (1999)
11. Busato, P., Berruto, R., Cornelissen, R.: Bioenergy farm Project: economic and energy analysis of biomass by web application. In: 19th European Biomass Conference (2011)

12. Ballantyne, P., Maru, A., Porcari, E.M.: Information and communication technologies—opportunities to mobilize agricultural science for development. Crop Sci. **50**, S-63 (2010). https://doi.org/10.2135/cropsci2009.09.0527

13. Bisgaard, M., Vinther, D., Ostergaard, K.Z.: Modelling and Fault-Tolerant Control of an Autonomous Wheeled Robot. Group (2004)

14. Bochtis, D., Griepentrog, H.W., Vougioukas, S., Busato, P., Berruto, R., Zhou, K.: Route planning for orchard operations. Comput. Electron. Agric. **113**, 51–60 (2015). https://doi.org/10.1016/j.compag.2014.12.024

15. Bochtis, D.D., Vougioukas, S.G., Griepentrog, H.W.: A mission planner for an autonomous tractor. Trans. ASABE **52**(5), 1429–1440 (2009). https://doi.org/10.13031/2013.29123

16. Van Henten, E.J., Schenk, E.J., van Willigenburg, L.G., Meuleman, J., Barreiro, P.: Collision-free inverse kinematics of the redundant seven-link manipulator used in a cucumber picking robot. Biosyst. Eng. **106**, 112–124 (2010). https://doi.org/10.1016/j.biosystemseng.2010.01.007

17. Zhao, Y., Gong, L., Huang, Y., Liu, C.: Robust tomato recognition for robotic harvesting using feature images fusion. Sensors (Switzerland). 16 (2016). https://doi.org/10.3390/s16020173

18. Schor, N., Bechar, A., Ignat, T., Dombrovsky, A., Elad, Y., Berman, S.: Robotic disease detection in greenhouses: combined detection of powdery mildew and tomato spotted wilt virus. IEEE Robot. Autom. Lett. **1**, 354–360 (2016). https://doi.org/10.1109/LRA.2016.2518214

19. Vitzrabin, E., Edan, Y.: Changing task objectives for improved sweet pepper detection for robotic harvesting. IEEE Robot. Autom. Lett. **1**, 578–584 (2016). https://doi.org/10.1109/LRA.2016.2519946

20. Hayashi, S., et al.: Evaluation of a strawberry-harvesting robot in a field test. Biosyst. Eng. **105**, 160–171 (2010). https://doi.org/10.1016/j.biosystemseng.2009.09.011

21. Xu, Y., Imou, K., Kaizu, Y., Saga, K.: Two-stage approach for detecting slightly overlapping strawberries using HOG descriptor. Biosyst. Eng. **115**, 144–153 (2013). https://doi.org/10.1016/j.biosystemseng.2013.03.011

22. Blanes, C., Ortiz, C., Mellado, M., Beltrán, P.: Assessment of eggplant firmness with accelerometers on a pneumatic robot gripper. Comput. Electron. Agric. **113**, 44–50 (2015). https://doi.org/10.1016/j.compag.2015.01.013

23. Mann, M., Zion, B., Shmulevich, I., Rubinstein, D.: Determination of robotic melon harvesting efficiency: a probabilistic approach. Int. J. Prod. Res. **54**, 3216–3228 (2016). https://doi.org/10.1080/00207543.2015.1081428

24. Irie, N., Taguchi, N., Horie, T., Ishimatsu, T.: Asparagus harvesting robot coordinated with 3-D vision sensor. In: Proceedings of the IEEE International Conference on Industrial Technology (2009)

25. Choi, K.H., Han, S.K., Han, S.H., Park, K.H., Kim, K.S., Kim, S.: Morphology-based guidance line extraction for an autonomous weeding robot in paddy fields. Comput. Electron. Agric. **113**, 266–274 (2015). https://doi.org/10.1016/j.compag.2015.02.014

26. Reed, J.N., Miles, J.S., Butler, J., Baldwin, M., Noble, R.: Automation and emerging technologies for automatic mushroom harvester development. J. Agric. Eng. Res. **78**, 15–23 (2001)

27. Tanigaki, K., Fujiura, T., Akase, A., Imagawa, J.: Cherryharvesting robot. Comput. Electron. Agric. **63**, 65–72 (2008)

28. Nguyen, T.T., Kayacan, E., De Baedemaeker, J., Saeys, W.: Task and motion planning for apple harvesting robot. In: IFAC Proceedings Volumes (IFAC-PapersOnline), pp. 247–252 (2013)

29. Hannan, M.W., Burks, T.F., Bulanon, D.M.: A real-time machine vision algorithm for robotic citrus harvesting. Written for Presentation at the 2007 ASABE Annual International Meeting Sponsored by ASABE (2007). Am. Soc. Agric. Biol. Eng. Ann. Int. Meet. **0300**, 1–12 (2007). https://doi.org/10.13031/2013.23429

30. Yoon, B., Kim, S.: Design of paddy weeding robot. In: 2013 44th International Symposium on Robotics, ISR 2013 (2013)

31. Bochtis, D.D., Sørensen, C.G., Jørgensen, R.N., Nørremark, M., Hameed, I.A., Swain, K.C.: Robotic weed monitoring. Acta Agric. Scand. Sect. B Soil Plant Sci. **61**(3), 202–208 (2011). https://doi.org/10.1080/09064711003796428

32. Haibo, L., Shuliang, D., Zunmin, L., Chuijie, Y.: Study and experiment on a wheat precision seeding robot. J. Robot. **2015** (2015). https://doi.org/10.1155/2015/696301

33. Pierce, F.J., Nowak, P.: Aspects of precision agriculture. Adv. Agron. **67**, 1–85 (1999). https://doi.org/10.1016/S0065-2113(08)60513-1

34. Fountas, S., Aggelopoulou, K., Gemtos, T.A.: Precision agriculture: crop management for improved productivity and reduced environmental impact or improved sustainability. In: Supply Chain Management for Sustainable Food Networks, pp. 41–65. Wiley, Chichester (2015)

35. Pierpaoli, E., Carli, G., Pignatti, E., Canavari, M.: Drivers of precision agriculture technologies adoption: a literature review. Proc. Technol. **8**, 61–69 (2013). https://doi.org/10.1016/J.PROTCY.2013.11.010

36. Bochtis, D.D., Sørensen, C.G., Busato, P., Berruto, R.: Benefits from optimal route planning based on B-patterns. Biosyst. Eng. **15**, 389–395 (2013). https://doi.org/10.1016/j.biosystemseng.2013.04.006

37. Bechar, A., Vigneault, C.: Agricultural robots for field operations. Part 2: operations and systems. Biosyst. Eng. **153**, 110–128 (2017). https://doi.org/10.1016/j.biosystemseng.2016.11.004

38. Kutter, T., Tiemann, S., Siebert, R., Fountas, S.: The role of communication and co-operation in the adoption of precision farming. Precis. Agric. **12**, 2–17 (2011). https://doi.org/10.1007/s11119-009-9150-0

39. Knapper, A., Nes, N.V., Christoph, M., Hagenzieker, M., Brookhuis, K.: The use of navigation systems in naturalistic driving. Traffic Inj. Prev. **17**, 264–270 (2016). https://doi.org/10.1080/15389588.2015.1077384

40. Bryden, K.J., Charlton, J.L., Oxley, J.A., Lowndes, G.J.: Acceptance of navigation systems by older drivers. Gerontechnology **13**, 21–28 (2014). https://doi.org/10.4017/gt.2014.13.1.011.00

41. Joubert, J.W., Meintjes, S.: Repeatability & reproducibility: implications of using GPS data for freight activity chains. Transp. Res. Part B Methodol. **76**, 81–92 (2015). https://doi.org/10.1016/J.TRB.2015.03.007

42. Hameed, I.A., Bochtis, D., Sørensen, C.A.: An optimized field coverage planning approach for navigation of agricultural robots in fields involving obstacle areas. Int. J. Adv. Robot. Syst. **10**, 231 (2013). https://doi.org/10.5772/56248

43. Jensen, M.A.F., Bochtis, D., Sorensen, C.G., Blas, M.R., Lykkegaard, K.L.: In-field and inter-field path planning for agricultural transport units. Comput. Ind. Eng. **63**(4), 1054–1061 (2012). https://doi.org/10.1016/j.cie.2012.07.004

44. Zhou, K., Leck Jensen, A., Sørensen, C.G., Busato, P., Bothis, D.D.: Agricultural operations planning in fields with multiple obstacle areas. Comput. Electron. Agric. **109**, 12–22 (2014). https://doi.org/10.1016/j.compag.2014.08.013

45. Jensen, M.F., Sørensen, C.G., Bochtis, D.: Coverage planning for capacitated field operations, Part II: optimisation. Biosyst. Eng. **139**, 149–164 (2015). https://doi.org/10.1016/j.biosystemseng.2015.07.002

46. McCown, R.L.: Changing systems for supporting farmers' decisions: problems, paradigms, and prospects. Agric. Syst. **74**, 179–220 (2002). https://doi.org/10.1016/S0308-521X(02)00026-4
47. Lewis, T.: Evolution of farm management information systems. Comput. Electron. Agric. **19**, 233–248 (1998). https://doi.org/10.1016/S0168-1699(97)00040-9
48. Folinas, D.: A conceptual framework for business intelligence based on activities monitoring systems. Int. J. Intell. Enterp. **1**, 65 (2007). https://doi.org/10.1504/IJIE.2007.013811
49. O'Brien, J.: Management Information Systems – Managing Information Technology in the Internetworked Enterprise. Irwin McGraw-Hill, Boston (1999)
50. Sørensen, C., et al.: System Analysis and Definition of System Boundaries. FutureFarm (2009)

Methods and Tools for Supporting the Integration of Stocks and Fisheries

Yannis Tzitzikas[1,2]([⊠]) [iD], Yannis Marketakis[1] [iD],
Nikos Minadakis[1] [iD], Michalis Mountantonakis[1,2] [iD],
Leonardo Candela[3] [iD], Francesco Mangiacrapa[3], Pasquale Pagano[3] [iD],
Costantino Perciante[3] [iD], Donatella Castelli[3], Marc Taconet[4],
Aureliano Gentile[4], and Giulia Gorelli[4]

[1] Institute of Computer Science, FORTH-ICS, Heraklion, Greece
{tzitzik,marketak,minadakn,mountant}@ics.forth.gr
[2] Computer Science Department, University of Crete, Heraklion, Greece
[3] Consiglio Nazionale delle Ricerche, Pisa, Italy
{leonardo.candela,francesco.mangiacrapa,
pasquale.pagano,costantino.perciante,
donatella.castelli}@isti.cnr.it
[4] Food and Agriculture Organization of the United Nations, Rome, Italy
{marc.taconet,aureliano.gentile,
giulia.gorelli}@fao.org

Abstract. The collation of information for the monitoring of fish stocks and fisheries is a difficult and time-consuming task, as the information is scattered across different databases and is modelled using different formats and semantics. Our purpose is to offer a unified view of the existing stocks and fisheries information harvested from three different database sources (FIRMS, RAM and FishSource), by relying on innovative data integration and manipulation facilities. In this paper, we describe the building blocks in terms of methods and software components that are necessary for integrating stocks and fisheries data from heterogeneous data sources.

Keywords: Fish stock · Fishery · Semantic data integration ·
Data publication · Data normalization

1 Introduction

Fish Stocks are groups of individuals of a species occupying a well-defined spatial range independent of other stocks of the same species, e.g. swordfish in the Mediterranean Sea[1]. A *Fishery* is a unit determined by an authority or other entity that is engaged in raising and/or harvesting fish. Typically, the unit is defined in terms of some or all of the following: people involved, species or type of fish, area of water or seabed, method of fishing, class of boats and purpose of activity, e.g. Fishery for Atlantic cod in

---

[1] http://firms.fao.org/firms/resource/10025/en.

© Springer Nature Switzerland AG 2019
M. Salampasis and T. Bournaris (Eds.): HAICTA 2017, CCIS 953, pp. 20–34, 2019.
https://doi.org/10.1007/978-3-030-12998-9_2

the area of East and South Greenland[2]. Information about Fish Stocks and Fisheries is widely used for the monitoring of their status, and to identify appropriate management actions [1], with the ultimate goal of sustainable exploitation of marine resources. For these reasons completeness, adequacy and validity of information is crucial. Despite this key role, there is no "one stop shop" for accessing stocks and fisheries data. Such information is usually collected (and produced as a result of data analysis) by the fishery management authorities at local, regional and national level. Therefore, the overall information is scattered across several databases, with no standard structure due to the specific local needs of the different bodies. Furthermore, the guidelines for populating existing registries are therefore heterogeneous, and every registry is actually a "database silo" that is not expected to interoperate with others to offer a global view on existing information.

Our objective (in the context of the ongoing BlueBRIDGE EU project[3]) is to construct a Global Record of Stocks and Fisheries (for short GRSF) capable of containing the corresponding information categorized into uniquely and globally identifiable records. Instead of creating yet another registry, we focus on producing GRSF records by using existing data. This approach does not invalidate the process being followed so far, in the sense that the organizations that maintain the original data are expected to continue to play their key role in collecting and exposing them. In fact, GRSF does not generate new data, rather it collates information coming from the different database sources, facilitating the discovery of inventoried stocks and fisheries arranged into distinct domains.

The advantages of this approach include: (a) increased data coverage compared to the single sources of information, (b) integrating information and identifying unique stocks and fisheries coming from the different database sources, and (c) answering queries that would be impossible to be answered from the individual database sources. These characteristics meet the needs of the main business cases that are: (i) supporting the compilation of stock status summaries at regional and global level and (ii) providing services for the traceability of sea-food products.

In this paper, we extend our previous work, described in [2]. In that work we described the methodology and the software components that were used for constructing GRSF, and presented some first results of the registry. In the current paper we focus on the methodology and the processes that were carried out for integrating heterogeneous information from the remote data sources. In addition, we describe the activities that were performed for normalizing the harvested and transformed data.

The rest of this paper is organized as follows. Section 2 describes the background information. More specifically, it describes the main requirements and the data sources that were used as input. Section 3 describes the structure of a GRSF record and elaborates with the steps that are used for constructing GRSF. Section 4 discusses the data normalization activities, while Sect. 5 describes the technical framework that was used. Finally, Sect. 6 concludes and identifies directions for future work and research.

---

[2] https://www.fishsource.org/stock_page/688.

[3] BlueBRIDGE Project website http://www.bluebridge-vres.eu/.

2   Background

In this section, we summarize the basic information of GRSF, as they have been described in detail in our previous work [2]. More specifically we discuss about the data sources that were exploited (Sect. 2.1) and the main requirements (Sect. 2.2).

2.1   The Data Sources

Below we describe the three database sources that have been used so far to harvest stocks and fisheries information. These sources are (a) Fisheries and Resources Monitoring System (FIRMS), (b) RAM Legacy Stock Assessment database, and (c) FishSource. The rationale for the selection of these sources, is that they contain complementary information (both conceptually and geographically). More specifically FIRMS is mostly reporting at regional level, while RAM is reporting at national or subnational level, and FishSource is more focused on the fishing activities. All of them contribute to the overall aim to build a comprehensive and transparent global reference set of stocks and fisheries records that will boost regional and global stocks and fisheries status and trend monitoring as well as responsible consumer practices. Since the construction of GRSF is an iterative process, we will support integrating contents from these three sources in early releases of GRSF, and in the future we will investigate exploiting new ones (i.e. FAO Global Capture Production Statistics database[4]).

FIRMS (FIsheries and Resources Monitoring System)[5] provides access to a wide range of high-quality information on the global monitoring and management of stocks and fisheries. It collects data from 14 intergovernmental organizations (that are partners of FIRMS) and contains information on the status of more than 860 stocks and 270 fisheries. The information provided by the organizations is organized in a database and published in the form of XML backboned fact sheets.

RAM (RAM Legacy Stock Assessment Database)[6] provides information exclusively on the fish stocks domain. It is a compilation of stock assessment results and time series of stock status indicators for commercially exploited marine populations from around the world. The assessments were assembled from 21 national and international management agencies for approximately one thousand stocks. RAM contents are stored in a relational database and are publicly available by releasing versions of the database in MS Access and Excel format.

FishSource[7] compiles and summarizes publicly available scientific and technical information about the status of fish stocks and fisheries. It includes information about the health of stocks, the quality of their management, and the impact of fisheries on the rest of the ecosystem. It is mainly exploited from seafood industry for assisting in taking the

---

[4] http://www.fao.org/fishery/statistics/global-capture-production/en.

[5] http://firms.fao.org/firms/en.

[6] http://ramlegacy.org.

[7] http://www.fishsource.com/.

appropriate actions for improving the sustainability of the purchased seafood. Information in FishSource is organized into fishery profiles associated with the exploited stocks. The database contains information for more than 2,000 fishery profiles.

2.2   Requirements

The selected database sources were constructed to fulfil different requirements and needs. Furthermore, they have been developed and are maintained from different initiatives. As a result, they are using different standards, data models, conceptualizations and terminologies for capturing similar information. As an example consider the fish species that are included in a particular stock or fishery; they can be identified either using: (a) their scientific name (e.g. Thunnus albacares), (b) their common name in any language (e.g. Yellowfin tuna in English), or (c) standard codes for identifying them (e.g. YFT). Furthermore, the different data sources use diverse criteria for identifying the uniqueness of a stock or fishery, as well as diverse conventions for naming their records.

GRSF aims at harmonizing the harvested information by adopting a set of standards that have been discussed and agreed with representatives of the database sources. In particular, these standards have been identified by two technical working group meetings that have been organized with the support of the BlueBRIDGE project. The working groups have defined which are the international standards that will be used (e.g. FAO 3Alpha codes for species, ISO3 country codes for flag states), which values define the uniqueness of a stock or a fishery record, which values are mandatory to accept a record as a complete one, as well as guidelines for generating unique and global identifiers (both human and machine interpretable) and names for the GRSF records. A detailed description of a GRSF record with respect to those guidelines can be found in Sect. 3.1.

The main challenge for the construction of the GRSF is the ability to semantically integrate data coming from different data sources. To tackle this challenge, we decided to rely on semantic web technologies and use top level ontologies. The best candidate is the MarineTLO [3] which provides (a) consistent abstractions or specifications of concepts included in all data models or ontologies of marine data sources and (b) the necessary properties to make GRSF a coherent source of facts relating observational data with the respective spatiotemporal context and categorical domain knowledge. The rationale is that we map attributes from different data sources into classes and properties of the top level ontologies. To this end we could also mention works like [4] that automate the mapping process using machine learning techniques.

3   Construction of the GRSF

In this section, we describe the building blocks (in Sect. 3.1) and the processes for constructing GRSF (in Sect. 3.2).

3.1 The GRSF Record

Each GRSF record is composed of several fields to accommodate the incoming information and data. The fields can be functionally divided into time-independent and time-dependent. The first group contains the identification information which uniquely defines a stock or fishery, the latter contains the stocks and fishery indicators. In general, there are two types of GRSF records: (a) stocks and (b) fishery GRSF records. Both types of records share some common metadata like their identification details, and descriptive information. Furthermore, records are assigned information about areas and their original sources. Finally, each record is assigned several time-dependent information modeled as dimensions. In the case of stock GRSF records, the dimensions refer to abundance levels, fishing pressures and biomasses. In the cases of fishery GRSF records, the dimensions refer to catches and landings indicators. We could say that a GRSF record resembles a data item in a database and as such we are describing its corresponding details in the schema shown in Fig. 1.

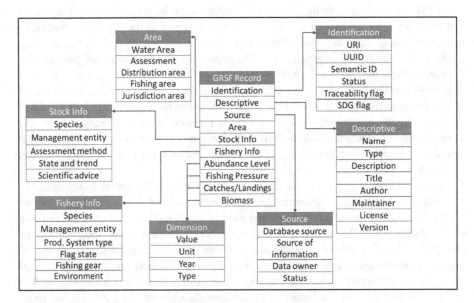

Fig. 1. The STAR schema of a GRSF record

3.2 The Process

The process for constructing GRSF adopts the ETL [10] pattern, and consists of a sequence of steps which are shown in Fig. 2. Below we describe these steps in detail. More information about particular parts of the process (i.e. the data normalization and cleaning steps) are described in Sect. 4. The technical components that carry out each step of the process are described in detail in Sect. 5.

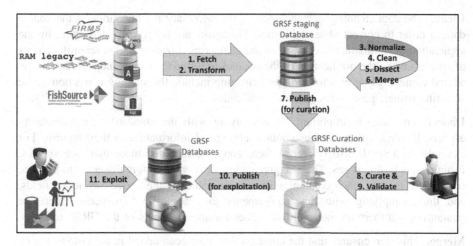

Fig. 2. The steps required for constructing and exploiting GRSF

Fetch. GRSF does not affect the data from the remote database sources. This means that the maintainers of the database sources will continue to update them in their own systems. For including the providers' data in the GRSF it is important to periodically fetch the raw data (in their original form) or view if they are exposed using particular services (i.e. in other formats like JSON or XML). In particular FIRMS offers a set of services that exposes their contents in XML format, RAM publish their MS Access database in their website, and FishSource exposes specific parts of their relational database as JSON data through a set of services. The periodicity for fetching raw data depends on the rate new data are added to each data source.

Transform. After fetching the data it is important to transform them so that they have a similar structure and semantics. At this stage data are transformed from XML, JSON and MS Access to RDF format. Specifically, data are transformed into instances of the MarineTLO ontology with respect to the identified GRSF requirements. Information harvested from the database sources will be mapped to the agreed GRSF standards, when not already compliant. Furthermore, during this step a set of proximity rules are applied (using the species, area and gear fields) for identifying similar records. This creates groupings of similar records that are being used in subsequent phases (during the curation & validation phase).

Normalize. The normalization step applies a set of normalization filters to the transformed data so that they are compliant with the GRSF standards. These filters may alter or add information to assist the instance matching functionalities of the merging process. Examples of normalization filters include the addition of the corresponding FAO 3Alpha code that is associated with the scientific name of a species, the addition of ISO3 codes to a country or the specification of a water area standard regarding to a specific code. More information about the key normalization activities that are carried out are described in Sect. 4.

Clean. The data cleaning step includes all the necessary modifications of the source data in order to correct observed errors. The errors are being corrected either by the application of automatic filters (such us the genus capitalization for the scientific names of species) or by the notification of the sources to refine their data and re - harvest the altered content. More examples of data cleaning include the spelling correction in the scientific names, gear codes or water area codes.

Dissect. This step is important for complying with the standards, for traceability aspects. In some cases, sources contain aggregated information in their records. For example, in a single fishery record there could be included more than one species, fishing gears or flag states. These aggregated records are therefore dissected to produce new GRSF records, each containing one single value for the above-mentioned fields, and thus complying with the requirements for traceability. Dissection, therefore guarantees that there are not multiple values for specific fields of the GRSF record.

Merge. This step ensures that the contents that have been added in the GRSF staging database are properly connected based on a set of criteria. This is achieved by linking records that have the same values on particular fields (specifically time-independent values) for producing a new single GRSF record. For example, if there are stock records having the same species and water area we can merge them into a single stock. During this process, we also use external knowledge to detect similarities among different names and terminologies used in the database sources (i.e. species names). The time-dependent information for the merged records will be kept distinct although collated and associated to the final merged GRSF record, with clear indication of the database source that provided it and the reference year.

Publish (for curation). The contents of the GRSF staging database are being replicated into a GRSF database, which is actually a triple-store. The triple-store can be used as a reference endpoint for answering complex queries about stocks and fisheries records. Furthermore the contents are published in a data catalogue offered through the D4Science [5] infrastructure. These resources allow the experts to inspect the contents of the GRSF and curate them appropriately. During this step, Universally Unique Identifiers (UUID) and human readable semantic identifiers are generated and associated to each GRSF record. The former are generated based on RFC 4122[8] and are used to uniquely identify records. The latter are generated using various GRSF fields and populated with standard codes and allow the identification and interpretation of records by humans, and are described in detail in Sect. 4.3.

Curate & Validate. During this step, a community of experts browse over the GRSF records and curate them in various ways. At this stage, the GRSF records are in a pending status waiting for approval by a human expert. During this process, the experts are able to either approve or reject a record, as well as to suggest alternative processes for merging records and to attach annotations with a narrative text. To do so the curators use the GRSF catalog (described in Sect. 5).

---

[8] https://tools.ietf.org/html/rfc4122.

Publish (for exploitation). The GRSF records that have been approved during the previous phase are being published into public and read-only catalog as final GRSF products[9] that can be exploited from the communities of interest.

4   Data Normalization Activities

Two of the most important steps of the process, are the steps of data normalization and cleaning. During these steps we carry out several activities for guaranteeing that the resulted data are compliant with the set of GRSF standards. The GRSF standards has been created as the result of three technical working groups, with the participation of the owners of the data sources that provide their contents, the technical partners that are responsible for the construction and maintenance of the GRSF, as well as representatives of stocks and fisheries authorities from around the world. The standards describe several aspects of the information contained in GRSF from very basic ones (i.e. the proper capitalization of management entities names, use of international standards, etc.), to much more complex ones (i.e. identify similarities of records based on the marine species and the water area). Below we describe these standards as well as the activities that were carried out for complying with them. We call the latter as Data Normalization activities.

4.1   Compliance with Standards

The key for interoperability is standardization, and GRSF is being constructed by exploiting international standards as much as possible. The use of these standards has been agreed in three dedicated technical working group meetings, with the participation of representatives of the used data sources. At this point, we should also describe that standards are being partially used for the underlying sources as well (i.e. FIRMS uses FAO 3Alpha codes for identifying marine species, while other source do not). Below we describe in detail the standard schemes that are exploited in GRSF.

Marine Species. There are various ways for identifying a marine species; usually we use their common names (e.g. yellowfin tuna), however it is not the best alternative since there are multiple common names (with values in several different languages and multiple names used even for single countries). One alternative for identifying species is their scientific name (or binomial name) which is composed of two parts, the first being the genus name and the second is the specific species name (e.g. Thunnus albacares). Another alternative for identifying species is their FAO 3Alpha code. FAO 3Alpha codes have been introduced by ASFIS[10], and consist of three letters that uniquely identify the species. In most of the cases, the codes have been derived either from the scientific name of the species, or by their common name in English (e.g. YFT is the FAO 3Alpha code for yellowfin tuna). In all other cases, the three letters are

---

[9] The approved records of GRSF are available at https://services.d4science.org/group/grsf.

[10] http://www.fao.org/fishery/collection/asfis.

assigned at random. In the absence of FAO 3Alpha codes GRSF has adopted the aphia ID[11] as an alternative standard.

Water Areas. Similarly to marine species, water areas can have commonly used names. However they are not adequate for identifying the area itself, since the boundaries of the area are not clearly defined. A more accurate method is to describe them using polygons that are formulated using a list of geographic coordinates. A polygon is an accurate description of an area, since it can take any shape. A simpler abstraction is to use bounding boxes for modeling a water area. Compared to the polygons the bounding boxes are less detailed, however it is much simpler to perform geographic calculations using them (i.e. find overlapping or adjacent areas). Apart from the above there is also a coding system[12] from FAO that allows identifying water areas using codes (e.g. the aegean sea has the FAO water area code 37.3.1). The FAO area codes are the primary standard used by GRSF but eligible standards can be as well.

Countries/States. Countries can be described using their ISO 3166-1 Alpha-3 codes. These codes are composed of three letters and represent countries, dependent territories and special areas of geographical interest (e.g. the ISO Alpha-3 code for Greece is GRC).

Fishing Gear. The Coordinating Working Party on fishery statistics (CWP)[13] provides a mechanism to coordinate fishery statistical programmes of regional fishery bodies and other inter-governmental organizations with a remit of fishery statistics. CWP adopted in 1980 a labeling and classification standard for fishing gears [6] that led to the creation of the International Standard Statistical Classification of Fishing Gears (ISSCFG). The standard assigns an acronym and a classification code that can be used for identifying gears of the same type. For example portable lift nets are identified using the acronym LNP, while boat-operated lift nets are identified using the acronym LNB. The former has the classification code "05.1.0" while the latter has the code "05.2.0". The common prefix of the classification codes (e.g. "05") allow us identifying that they are similar types of fishing gears, in this case lift nets. The most recent revision of the standard has been carried out in 2016 and contains new classification codes fishing gears.

4.2 Identification of Unique Records

A crucial step for the proper integration of stocks and fisheries data from heterogeneous sources is the identification of unique records (single records that are co-references in different sources). The identification of a single record will allow carrying out merging activities in the sequel. For example, this would allow merging the time-dependent information of records coming from different sources and deliver a single GRSF record. To this end, it is important to define which are those fields that make a record unique.

---

[11] http://www.marinespecies.org/aphia.php?p=webservice.

[12] http://www.fao.org/fishery/area/search/en.

[13] http://www.fao.org/fishery/cwp.

The GRSF standard methodology defines the uniqueness of a stock record using: (a) the fish species it contains and (b) the water area it occupies. As regards fisheries their uniqueness is defined using: (a) the fish species it contains, (b) the water area it occupies, (c) the management entity that operates the fishery, (d) the flag state under which the fishery is operated, and (e) the fishing gear that has been used.

To avoid potential disambiguation and naming issues, since different sources could use different names for their resources (i.e. marine species, water areas, fishing gears, etc.) which could result in errors, the identification of records is carried out after their compliance with standards that was described before.

4.3 Semantic Identifiers

In addition to the compliance with international standards and the identification of unique records, it has been decided to construct global identifiers for GRSF records that are human readable. These identifiers are called semantic identifiers in the sense that their values allow identifying several aspects of a record. The identifier is a concatenation of a set of predefined fields of the record in a particular form. The rationale is that users will be able to recognize important information about a stock or fishery record, just by inspecting the semantic identifier. To keep the length of the identifier in a reasonable number, it has been decided to use the standard values or abbreviations where applicable. For example consider the following semantic identifier of a stock "ASFIS:lub+FAO:51.6" that denotes the stock record is about the species "lub" (with respect to the 3Alpha code of the ASFIS system) and the water area with code "51.6" (with respect to the FAO coding system for areas).

The fields of the identifier following the pattern <SYSTEM:CODE>. The first field denotes the classification system that was used and the second is the actual code. In addition the fields are concatenated using the character '+' as a separator, and the fields are reported in particular order. If there are more than one values for a particular fields in the record then they are all reported, using the same pattern and they are concatenated using the character ';'. It is evident from the above example that for stock records the first field is the species and the second one is the water area of the record. For the case of fishery records the semantic identifier contains the following fields (in the given order): (1) species, (2) water areas, (3) management entity, (4) jurisdiction area (5) flag state and (6) fishing gear. An indicative semantic identifier of a fishery record is "asfis:COD+fao:21.3.M;rfb:NAFO+grsf-org:INT:NAFO+rfb:NAFO +iso3:LTU+isscfg:03.1.2". Notice that in this fishery record that are two different water areas (second field) described in the semantic identifier. Finally, if for a field there is not any information in the record then an empty string is added for that field. It becomes evident, that the absence of a field, might lead to incorrect results, especially if it is used for identifying the uniqueness of a record. In such cases, records will be merged and it is a duty of the experts to properly curate and validate them.

4.4 Multiple Values Prioritization

When we integrate data from heterogeneous sources, it is inevitable that we might end up with multiple values about a particular aspect of the same resource, each one coming from a different data source. This is also true for the case of GRSF, and it becomes an issue when there are multiple values for the time-independent information of a record. An indicative example is the name of a record (either stock or fishery); if a GRSF record is the result of merging of 3 original records (from the corresponding data sources) then we will end up with 3 different names for a record. This is usual, since the original data sources use their own policies for naming their records.

In order to resolve this issue it has been decided to adopt a prioritization policy for multiple values. This means that we prioritize the sources and whenever there are such situations, we will use the value coming from the top source. If the top source does not contribute with a value in the record then we move to the next source in the order and so on. We apply different priorities for different fields of a GRSF record. Just indicatively, we prioritize values about the names of the records and the assessment areas with the following order: (1) FIRMS (2) FishSource, (3) RAM.

4.5   Records Similarities

Apart from being a global registry, GRSF aims at supporting the experts with the stock and fishery assessment activities. Part of these activities is the identification of similar records that could potentially be merged to single records and produce new knowledge. To this end, during the merging step we carry out several comparisons between records in order to identify similarities between records. Table 1 shows the criteria that should apply for considering two records similar. For example if two records have species that have the same genus and appear on adjacent areas then they are considered as similar. The criteria are applied for fishery records as well, with the amendment that apart from the criteria shown in the table the records under comparison should appear under the same group of fishing gear with respect to the fishing gears hierarchy.

Table 1. Criteria for defining similarities between records

	Area		
	Same	Adjacent	Overlapping
Species	✓ (fisheries only)	✓	✓
Genus	✓	✓	✓

For this reason, we first identified the adjacent and overlapping areas of the records. We used the bounding boxes that represent the geographical coverage of the records as they have been derived from the original sources and used an R script[14] for defining if they are the same, adjacent or overlapping. Although, RAM data source did not contain any information about the bounding boxes for each record, it was using a name for the area of each record and a bounding box for the area, and this is what we have used for the comparisons. Of course, this means that a record occupied the entire area, instead of a smaller region and this could raise issues. However this is not a problem since we are just proposing similarities that will be validated from experts in subsequent phases.

---

[14] https://www.r-project.org/.

4.6   Data Cleaning

In order to maximize the quality of GRSF we supported data cleaning activities so that the textual information appears in a common and uniform way and observed errors are being corrected as much as possible. Below we describe some of the fields that were cleaned, as well the activities carried out.

- Scientific Names of species: whenever the scientific names of the species existed, we ensured that the first character of the genus was always a capital letter and the rest of it as well as the specific epithet use letters in lower case (i.e. Thunnus albacares).
- Management Entity: we used capital letters for the first characters of the terms of the management entity and also constructed an abbreviated acronym from the capital letters (i.e. Northwest Atlantic Fisheries Organization – NAFO).
- Water areas: the FAO water areas codes in the sources may include extra points or zeros, which must be, eliminated (i.e. FAO area 05 → FAO area 5).
- Fishing Gears: the gear ISSCFG codes may also contain extra points or zeros, which must be, eliminated (i.e. 01.2.0 → 01.2).
- Others: other possible errors that have not been predicted are reported to the maintainers of the data sources. They refined their data and the altered content was then harvested and imported in GRSF.

5   Software Components and Architecture

The D4Science infrastructure and gCube technology [5, 7] enable the development of Virtual Research Environments (VREs) that provide the users with a web-based set of facilities to accomplish various tasks. For the purpose of GRSF, we developed the appropriate VREs acting as a gateway for the "one stop shop" for stocks and fisheries records. More specifically we exploit the data cataloguing facilities of the infrastructure for manipulating and exposing GRSF records to the wide audience.

The core component for constructing GRSF is MatWare [8]. MatWare is a framework that automates the process of constructing semantic warehouses. By using the term semantic warehouse we refer to a read-only set of RDF triples fetched and transformed from different sources that aims at serving a particular set of query requirements. MatWare automatically fetches contents from the underlying sources using several access methods (e.g. SPARQL endpoints, HTTP accessible files, JDBC connections, several file format transformers). The fetched data are transformed into RDF descriptions using appropriate mappings [9], and stored in a RDF triplestore supporting several levels of description for preserving provenance information. One of its distinctive features, is that it allows evaluating the connectivity of the semantic warehouse. Connectivity refers to the degree up to which the contents of the semantic warehouse form a connected graph that can serve ideally in a correct and complete way the query requirements, while making evident how each source contributes by using a set of connectivity metrics. MatWare is a fully configurable tool and can be easily extended using plugins. Because of the aforementioned functionalities as well as the ease of configuration of the tool, we have used it and extended it with plugins for transforming the data from their original formats, plugins for supporting the merging and dissection steps, as well plugins for publishing the data into the catalogue supporting both the curation and validation phase, as well as the consumption phase. MatWare outperforms with respect to other similar tools like ODCleanStore [11], or UnifiedViews [12] since it supports the construction and maintenance of a semantic warehouse and assess its connectivity as well.

Figure 3 shows the overall technical deployment for the construction and maintenance of the GRSF. MatWare is responsible for the activities that construct the GRSF (as they are described in Sect. 3.2) and publishing them in the GRSF Knowledge (GRSF KB) and in the GRSF Catalogue. For the latter it exploits the component Data Catalogue publisher which carries out the necessary activities for ingesting GRSF records into the CKAN-based Catalogue instance offered by the D4Science infrastructure. Finally all the above components are controlled and interacted through the D4Science portal facilities of the GRSF VREs.

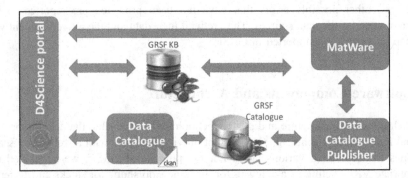

Fig. 3. The GRSF construction deployment setting

6 Conclusion – Future Work

The collation of information for the monitoring of fish stocks and fisheries is a difficult and time-consuming task, as the information is scattered across different databases and modelled using different formats and semantics. We introduced a process for providing a unified view of several stock and fisheries databases, by relying on semantic web technologies and innovative hybrid data infrastructures. The resulting Global Record of Stocks and Fisheries integrates data from three data sources, and contains more than 11,500 records about stocks and fisheries. It can be seen as a core knowledge base supporting the collaborative production and maintenance of a comprehensive and transparent global reference set of stocks and fisheries records. This is accomplished because of the processes that were applied during the construction, that guarantee the unique identification of stock and fisheries and the easy access to all the available information associated to a particular stock or fishery. In addition, during the validation step, the experts can validate the information of the GRSF records which also allows them spotting errors in their original sources, because their provenance is also preserved. We could highlight the presence of many GRSF records that have been derived from more than one sources. The added value for these records is that the GRSF record provides a more detailed view (i.e. of the time-dependent information of a stock) that exists partially in the original sources. As an example one source might contain information about catches, another about landings, however GRSF will contain both in a single record.

In order to maximize the quality of the GRSF contents, as well as their potential exploitation, we carry out a set of data normalization activities during the dissection and merging steps. These activities assert that the records and their accompanying information is valid and it is compliant with international standards where this is feasible. Table 2 summarize some statistics about GRSF. If we notice the number of fishery records in GRSF, compared with the summary of fishery records in the original sources, it becomes evident that many of the fishery records were dissected in GRSF, so that they do not contain multiple values in particular fields (e.g. species).

Table 2. Summary of the information fetched and integrated into GRSF

	FIRMS	RAM	FishSource	GRSF
Stock records	866	1294	1156	2,918
Fishery records	271	–	3,112	8,719
Species	612	349	488	1, 494
Water areas	275	803	418	1,496
Fishing gears	33	–	50	83
Dimensions	9,242	226,725	47,656	283,623
Similar records	–	–	–	18,524

The curation and validation of GRSF records is a laborious task that is carried out by domain experts. For this reason, in future we plan to investigate whether machine-learning techniques could be exploited for automating or assisting the curation and validation of GRSF records. In addition, in order to speed up the construction of GRSF, especially as soon as new data sources are included, we could include components, like [4], that automate the mapping process and reduce corresponding human effort. Another activity that is worth for further investigation is the exploitation of advanced discovery services based on spatio-temporal information.

Acknowledgments. This work has received funding from the European Union's Horizon 2020 research and innovation programme under the BlueBRIDGE project (Grant agreement No 675680).

References

1. Hilborn, R., Walters, C. (eds.): Quantitative Fisheries Stock Assessment: Choice, Dynamics and Uncertainty. Springer, Dordrecht (2013). https://doi.org/10.1007/978-1-4615-3598-0
2. Tzitzikas, Y., et al.: Towards a global record of stocks and fisheries. In: 8th International Conference on Information and Communication Technologies in Agriculture, Food and Environment (HAICTA 2017), Chania, Crete Island, Greece, pp. 328–340 (2017)
3. Tzitzikas, Y., et al.: Unifying Heterogeneous and Distributed Information About Marine Species Through the Top Level Ontology MarineTLO, vol. 50(1). Emerald Group Publishing Limited (2014). https://doi.org/10.1108/prog-10-2014-0072
4. Pham, M., Alse, S., Knoblock, C.A., Szekely, P.: Semantic labeling: a domain-independent approach. In: Groth, P., et al. (eds.) ISWC 2016. LNCS, vol. 9981, pp. 446–462. Springer, Cham (2016). https://doi.org/10.1007/978-3-319-46523-4_27
5. Candela, L., Castelli, D., Manzi, A., Pagano, P.: Realising virtual research environments by hybrid data infrastructures: the D4Science experience. In: International Symposium on Grids and Clouds (ISGC), vol. 210, p. 022 (2014)
6. Nedelec, C., Prado, J.: Definition and classification of fishing gear categories. FAO Fisheries Technical Paper 222 (1990)
7. Assante, M., et al.: The gCube system: delivering virtual research environments as-a-service. Future Gener. Comput. Syst. (2018). https://doi.org/10.1016/j.future.2018.10.035
8. Tzitzikas, Y., et al.: MatWare: constructing and exploiting domain specific warehouses by aggregating semantic data. In: Presutti, V., d'Amato, C., Gandon, F., d'Aquin, M., Staab, S., Tordai, A. (eds.) ESWC 2014. LNCS, vol. 8465, pp. 721–736. Springer, Cham (2014). https://doi.org/10.1007/978-3-319-07443-6_48
9. Marketakis, Y., et al.: X3ML mapping framework for information integration in cultural heritage and beyond. Int. J. Digit. Libr. 18(4), 1–19 (2016). https://doi.org/10.1007/s00799-016-0179-1
10. Vassiliadis, P.: A survey of extract–transform–load technology. Int. J. Data Warehouse. Min. (IJDWM) 5(3), 1–27 (2009)
11. Knap, T., et al.: ODCleanStore: a framework for managing and providing integrated linked data on the web. In: Wang, X.S., Cruz, I., Delis, A., Huang, G. (eds.) WISE 2012. LNCS, vol. 7651, pp. 815–816. Springer, Heidelberg (2012). https://doi.org/10.1007/978-3-642-35063-4_74
12. Knap, T., et al.: UnifiedViews: an ETL tool for RDF data management. Seman. Web 9(5), 661–676 (2018)

Semiotic-Sociological Textures of Landscape Values. Assessments in Urban-Coastal Areas

Salvatore Giuffrida[1(⊠)], Maria Rosa Trovato[1],
and Annalaura Giannelli[2]

[1] Department of Civil Engineering and Architecture, University of Catania,
Catania, Italy
{sgiuffrida,mrtrovato}@dica.unict.it
[2] Special Educational Department of Architecture – Syracuse,
University of Catania, Catania, Italy
annalauragiannelli@live.it

Abstract. One of the most relevant issues of planning in the most landscape valuable locations, especially along the coastal areas, is to define the assessment support to be performed in order to balance the preservation of the main landscape features, and the local economic development. By referring to the case of the waterfront of Syracuse (Italy), this contribution introduces a semiotic-sociological pattern for accounting and assessment concerning the main topics of the Sustainable Development Plan currently in force. The assessment takes into account the connection of the multiple thematic layers grouping the different functional/symbolic land units that are characterised by a semantic link, within an assessment pattern working as a syntactic field, highlighting the interactions between them. The pattern involves the social relevance of the different criteria featuring this landscape unit by making the "facts of nature" and the "narrations of culture" worth together.

Keywords: Human landscape · Social systems · Multi criteria analysis · Syntactic/semantic pattern · Qualitative accounting · Landscape assessment

1 Introduction

The water front of Syracuse is a unitary landscape identity comprising the Islet of Ortigia, the old town of Syracuse, and the peninsula of The Maddalena; they face each other closing the large inlet of the "Porto Grande" (big harbor) of Syracuse and represent, as a whole, the fair integration between culture and nature.

Due to this complexity and uniqueness, some concerns arise about the foreseeable, and partly in progress, structural and irreversible transformations, which the wide economic opportunities encourage. In order to arrange individual pressures (interests) and collective instances (values) of resilience [1], assessment typically supports the heuristic process of transforming observations into valuations and valuations into decisions [2, 3]. This process needs a robust approach based on a shared recognition and accounting of the landscape units [4], in order to reduce the uncertainty of the

© Springer Nature Switzerland AG 2019
M. Salampasis and T. Bournaris (Eds.): HAICTA 2017, CCIS 953, pp. 35–50, 2019.
https://doi.org/10.1007/978-3-030-12998-9_3

non-structured observations [5, 6] and especially in order to lead back to unity the cultural, physical and perceptive landscape components [7–11].

The planning tools regulating the improvement processes are the Master Plan, the Detailed Ortigia's Masterplan, the Sustainable Development Plan (SDP). Some of the supposed changes of the coastline – the extension of the port area, for the mooring of two cruises at the Sant' Antonio pier, the enlargement and commercial exploitation of the Foro Italico dock, etc. – arise some concerns claiming the definition of the landscape quality in this area. As a consequence, the northern part of the old town, the one located in mainland, is expected to record a significant real estate market as well as Ortigia, due to its uniqueness from the landscape, symbolic and architectural value [12–14]. In the Plemmirio park area no transformation is supposed, except for the accessibility and accommodation.

Referring to the prescriptions of the SDP, we propose a general landscape assessment pattern referring to the identification of "natural structures, technological infrastructures and cultural superstructures" [15].

2   Materials the Landscape Context and the SDP of Syracuse

The peninsula of Maddalena, located South of the city of Syracuse at the closing end of the large area of the "Porto Grande" (big harbour), is a calcareous Miocene plateau of tectonic Horst origin, extending up to 50 m above sea level, and lowering slowly toward the sea as far as the edge cliffs, with a coastline characterised by a various and discontinuous morphologic structures: from Capo Castelluccio to Punta Traversa it is featured by short beach strips, with a shallow and uniform sea bottom in some parts, and very deep in some other parts; from Punta Taverna point to Capo Murro di Porco cape, it is high and bevelled, with important geologic features (caves, cavities, siphons, abrasion pools, deep networks of carsick origin conduits), archaeology features, like the prehistoric site Grotta Pellegrina, and the bronze age Punta della Mola necropolis, anthropologic features such as the six Latomie, linked to the ancient and no longer existing Plemmyrion sub-urban district, or the extensive underground tunnels of Punta Mola, used as anti-aircraft base during the second world war, the network of the dry stone masonry walls of the local agriculture tradition, the "masserie" (old farmyards) and the Barone Beneventano del Bosco villa.

Many archaeological finds have been discovered here, and they are safeguarded in the Paolo Orsi museum in Syracuse. In the area between Punta Castelluccio point and Cala delle Rive Bianche bay some phenomena of erosion and collapsing of the cliff occurred, with rock crops sliding to the sea, and the danger of further subsidence.

The central and southern areas of the peninsula are characterised by an intense holiday homes and farmyards building activity; moreover, it has a footpath and road network on dirt or stone ground, that may be redeveloped for tourism or leisure purpose (Fig. 1). The Communitarian Interest Site (CIS) called "Saline di Siracusa e fiume Ciane" – ITA 090006 is located South of the estuary of the rivers Anapo and Ciane; the one called "Capo Murro di Porco, Penisola della Maddalena e Grotta Pellegrino" – ITA090008 (79/409/CEE e 92/43/CEE directives) is located in the eastern side of the

Maddalena peninsula; here, the Natural Reserve of Plemmirio (1435 ha) was established by Decree of the Ministry of the Environment on 15/09/2004.

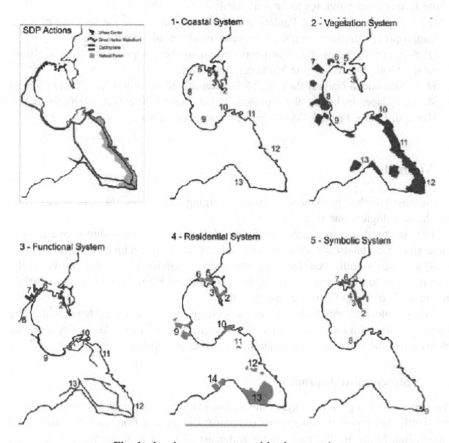

Fig. 1. Landscape systems and landscape units.

The urban and monumental scenario of Ortigia and Maniace Castle – that is the architectural background in front of which the natural contest of Plemmirio increase its landscape value – works as counterpoint to the naturalistic dimension of the Maddalena. A heterogeneous set of landscape units in conflict is located alongside the coastline between them: the Pantanelli industrial area progressive dismantling, extending from the seaplane base to the estuary area of Ciane and Anapo rivers; the Anapo-Ciane Oriented Natural Reserve, comprising the EU interest site of the "Pantani delle Saline" South of the estuary of the two rivers; the southern part of the gulf (via Lido Saraceno – via La Maddalena), dotted by sprawling cottages, extending along the system of promontories and small bays between Punta Faro and Punta Castelluccio, where large hotel is located. The eastern coastline of the peninsula, extending from Punta Mola to Capo Murro di Porco, is preserved free of constructions in an average 350 m width belt.

The Strategic Sustainable Plan (SSP) (2006) includes five Strategic Projects:

SP 4: Urban Center and the Research and Environmental Education Centre within the former Enel buildings to be renovated;

SP 5: improvement of the Pantanelli water front, supposing the removal of some inappropriate buildings, roads, pavements, furniture and street lighting;

SP 6-7: cycling lanes, the first from Ortigia to the Anapo-Ciane Reserve; from Anapo-Ciane Reserve to the Maddalena peninsula.

SP 8: Maddalena Natural Park, a 236 ha area extending from Castelluccio Cape to Milocca Cape, including the Communitarian Interest Site ITA A090008 "Capo Murro di Porco, Penisola Maddalena e Grotta Pellegrino".

3   Methods

The proposed method in founded on two converging approaches: the structuralistic one and the sociological one (Fig. 2).

The structuralistic approach is intended to support the relationship between landscape signs (the landscape units recognisable as standing landmarks and/or featured areas) and their significance (their importance in the landscape as a whole) within the natural and cultural context formed by the Peninsula of Plemmirio, the Islet of Ortigia and the Gulf of Porto Grande connecting them.

The sociological approach aims at recognising the social sub-systems, which, by communicating with each other, contribute to create internal hierarchies influencing the intensity and the extension of the landscape values perception.

3.1   A Structuralist Approach

The structuralist approach analyses the sedimentation of language material (signifier and significance) upon the underlying reference; signs arises from such a consolidated relationship. Signs are the minimum significance units of a statement, and the main players of the life interaction of the upper aggregates, the sematic chains.

Semantic order, connecting significance to signifier, depends on the strength of the vertical linkage – crossing different categories, the linguistic and the real ones – established and kept safe as a result of the "signification agreement"; signification is here assumed as the process by which a significance is conventionally attributed to a signifier. Signifier is the set of characteristics by means of which occurrences (references) are presented within the iterative social communicative interaction, and as such it plays the role of *meaning-bearer*.

Syntactic order, keeping the signs of a semantic chain together all over the time evolution of the related landscape unit, depends on the strength of the horizontal linkage between signs, then on the intentionality degree of the social-communicative interaction, that is the plasticity of the horizontal linkages between signs according to their similarity or complementarity.

The communicative interaction based on the vertical semantic linkage (between signifier and significance) within the sign, occurs at the "extensional" level, that is the

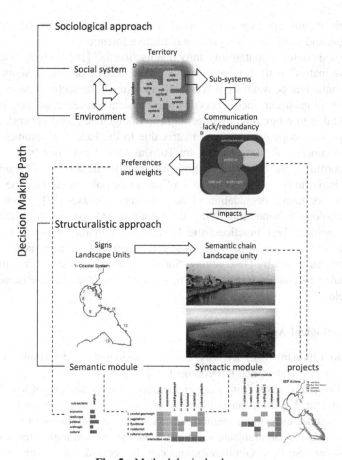

Fig. 2. Methodological scheme.

descriptive or denotative level, the lower creative one typically featuring the unintentional communication, or "*subsistence* communication". The strength of such linkage depends either on how widespread and deep the underlying convention is, or also on the strength of any economic or technological constraints. In the case of the residential urban fabrics, where the buildings work as sings, the semantic chain involves the *life style* (as signifier) of the settlement's and dwells' *shape* (as significance). Such a shape changes when new comforts or building techniques improve performances and symbolic features of dwellings and settlement.

The type of interaction driving the natural evolution of the semantic chains occurs on the "intensional" level, i.e. the level of sense, and therefore of creative communication, and regards the landscape and its evolution also conservative - when it stems a drift of random or weakly caused transformations.

The interaction driving the physiological evolution of the semantic chains occurs at the "intensional" level (the sense level), concerns Landscape and its evolution conservative as well – if it contains accidental or weakly organized transformations.

The semantic chains are exposed to local transformations due to the interactions between signs and need an axiological or collective intentionality.

A landscape context maintains its unity due its "inertia" [16] allowing it to work as a "generative matrix" until: (a) signifier and significance of the single signs separate; (b) the horizontal link between signs is not able to compensate such a separation. When these two conditions occur, inertia gets down to physical resilience, an mere referential characteristic due to orography, hydrogeological arrangement, road network, etc., and the landscape unit stops working as a matrix due to the lack of a common sense of identity. The concept of inertia, meant by Turri as "transformations trap", should be assumed according to the following semiotic meaning: the dissolving of meaning of the signs taken individually – due to the lack of proactive policies causing the abandonment and environmental degradation of the landscape contexts [17] – "releases" the landscape axiological bond, modifying the semantic linkages (such as the cultural habits, the building best practices, the landscape landmarks network knowledge) between the signifiers (some of which lose relevance) and the references, decays to "environment" as meant by [18], getting "inert" in an opposite sense than the Turri's one, i.e. unable to contain transformations within the syntactical consistency of the semantic field.

3.2 A Sociological Approach

According to Luhmann (ib.) territory can be considered as the result of a unity-difference of social system and environment (Fig. 3).

The social system arises from a communication process allowing it to differentiate from environment. Environment is the residual part of the socio-systemic communication, and includes everything (natural, artificial and human environment) which the social system doesn't communicate with: the social system communicates within itself on environment. Such a communication can be considered a sort of external communication.

Landscape, as the shape of territory, is the unitary manifestation of the communicative process by which territory differentiates from environment.

Environment has open boundaries; the social system has closed boundaries that landscape allows us to recognize.

In the ground of landscape accounting and assessment, communicating basically means *sharing*, i.e. including the environmental components potentially affecting the social system, within the public policies for territory enhancement.

Furthermore, the internal communication process gives rise to the progressive break down of the system into several sub-systems, each performing its own code (value system or program), by means of which it selects and includes everything that allows it to increase its self-referential closure, thus strengthening its ability to prevail over the other subsystems it assumes as part of the environment.

Such an increase of the internal communication (between sub-systems) influences the external communication (between social system and environment) as the increase of competition between sub-systems weakens the resilience of the overall social system and as a consequence its ability to cope with the environmental fluctuations (disasters, pollution etc.), potentially affecting the landscape unity.

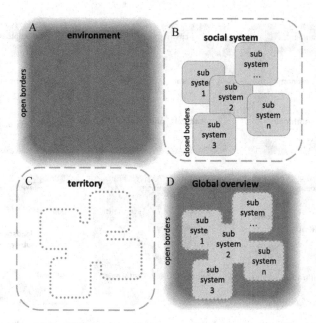

Fig. 3. A. Environment as an entity external to any form of communication. B. The social system as a communicative entity. C. Territory as result of external (social system-environment) and internal (between sub-systems) communication. D. Global overview: unity of environment, social system, and territory.

The progressive breaking-down of social system in many further sub-systems allows some of them to prevail over the weaker ones, as a result of unbalanced internal communication, like in the case of the prevailing of the economic interest over the aesthetic value of the coastal system, the former endorsed by the economic sub-system, the latter by the cultural one. The subsequent new arrangement of the internal power relationships between sub-systems generates an "irritation" of the social system arising as a destruction of the landscape unity, as a part of it decays at the level of environment.

In the proposed case, the economic sub-system actually prevailed, dominating the cultural one to the extent of modifying the coastline in two of the most significant areas, the Foro Italico walk and the Saint Antonio Pier: both has been extended over the sea, the former along its overall water front; the latter prolonged so as to allow two Cruise ships to dock.

Figure 4 conceptually displays the relationships between social system and environment – (A); between sub-systems in normal life, when, for example political, cultural and anthropic sub-systems prevail over the economic one – (B); or vice versa – (C); in (D) political sub-system try to mediate between economic and the other sub-systems unsuccessfully, so that the overall social system decays to the status of environment – (E); in such a case, due to the vacancy of an overarching authority able to balance the internal communication, and as a consequence the external as well, the unity of the landscape context can be safeguarded by a new arising sub-system, which the stakeholders sharing the same landscape code converge to – (F).

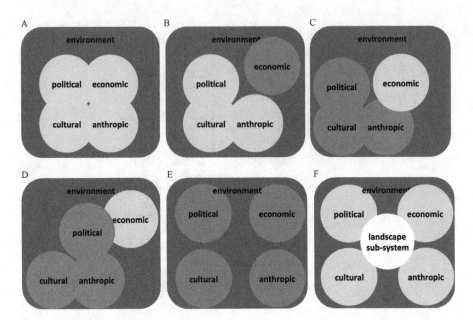

Fig. 4. Synthetic representation of Luhmann's macro-socio-systemic approach, displaying the modification of the relationships between social system and environment, and between sub-systems in the event of an imbalance of communication. Blue fonts and darker background mean environment, grey fonts and lighter background mean social system. (Color figure online)

The lack of coherence between transformations works and landscape values indicates a weakly communicative interaction between sub-systems each of which assumes its own selective code, i.e. the economic one, whose code is money, the political one, whose code is power, the anthropic one, whose code is comfort and security, and the cultural one, whose code is historical/architectural value, each of them in some way conflicting with landscape harmony.

As will be explained later, the valuation pattern is based on a multiple criteria approach in which each criterion needs to be appropriately weighted [19], due to its relative importance than the others [20] according to the different social sub-systems selective code. The prevailing of the weight of some criteria than the others reflects the corresponding prevailing of one or more sub-system than the others.

The valuation module allows us to implement different weight systems each of which corresponding to a different arrangement of the social internal communication.

3.3   The Valuation Pattern Semantic and Syntactic Modules

As a landscape unity, the context of the Ortigia-Plemmirio area works as a semantic chain, i.e. a set of semantic units (signs) interpreting each other, so that the modification in significance of a single item affects the significance of the most similar or close ones.

This textual structure is characterised by tensions due to the typically consonant or dissonant, constructive or destructive, convergent or divergent signs. These tensions can be assessed by referring to many criteria of *structural* (natural), *infrastructural* (technological), *super-structural* (cultural) type [15].

The proposed model establishes:

- semantic relations, defining the internal consistency of signifier (LU) and significance (valuation) based on causal or intentional correspondences;
- syntactic relations, defining the external consistency of LUs, based on motivational and conventional (social, cultural) correspondences.

The pattern works as a set of impact coaxial matrixes composed of the LUs in rows, and some blocks of columns: the syntactic and semantic modules, the set of actions, and the calculations-results one. The semantic module associates a value to each LU according to the well-known method of the value functions [21, 22]. The syntactic module links the signs to each other, individuating the (positive/negative) interactions between the values of the LUs.

The model is composed of the vector of the valuations the 52 LUs: an impact matrix with 15 columns (5 actions × 3 impact types) and 52 rows; an interactive matrix with 52 × 52 elements that quantifies the influences between the LUs (Fig. 5).

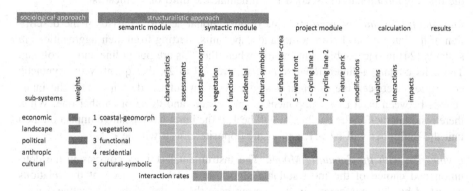

Fig. 5. General valuation pattern scheme

Semantic Module

The semantic module defines the relation between the LUs as described by their characters (indicators) and their values. The module:

- identifies the LUs as potential impact bearers (*extension E, importance* I, *resilience* R) grouped in five systems (Blackstone and Greenb 1991): 1. *Coastal-geomorphologic*, 2. *Vegetation*, 3. *Functional*, 4. *Residential*, 5. *Cultural* [1, 23];
- attributes of a weighing system w, where w_{E_i}, w_{I_i} and w_{R_i} are the weights of $LU_i - th$, for E, I, and R criteria and such that $\sum_k^{E,I,R} w_k = 1$;
- identifies a value for each $LU_i - th$ function of E_{LU_i}, I_{LU_i} and R_{LU_i} in a dimensionless scale ranging from 1 to 5;
- defines "the level of axiological participation" for $LU_i - th$, namely p_i, where $p_i = E_{LU_i} w_{E_i} + I_{LU_i} w_{I_i} + R_{LU_i} w_{R_i}$;

- characterises of LUs in regarding its belonging to the natural structures S_N, to the technological infrastructures I_T and to the cultural superstructures and SS_C;
- identifies of a weighing system t, where $t_{S_{N_i}}$, $t_{I_{T_i}}$ and $t_{SS_{C_i}}$ are the weights of $LU_i - th$, for S_N, I_T and SS_C criteria and such that $\sum_s^{S_N I_T SS_C} t_s = 1$;
- identifies a value for each $u_i - th$ function of S_{N_i}, I_{T_i} and SS_{C_i} in a dimensionless scale ranging from 1 to 5;
- evaluates V_i the value for each LUs by the formula $V_i = \sum_{i=1}^n u_i p_i t_i$, and where n is their number. This value is modified by the actions included in the plan, as explained in paragraph 5.2.

Syntactic Module
The syntactic module formalises the horizontal relations, (communication), binding between themselves several signs, LUs, representing the axiological interactions activated by the foreseen modifications. It is the last passage of the whole valuation, and reanalyses the judgments assigned to the single components, considering their complementarity with all the others; therefore, it provides a different valuation according to the type of connection and the entity assigned to it. It is articulated in three activities, the first organizational, the second instrumental, the third of verification.

Individuation of the Interactions. The organizational activity consists of the description of the interactions between the landscape units, starting from their aggregations in systems [24] in one double entry matrix where the LUs are put in line and in column. The cells contain a-dimensional scores, x_{ij} (from 0 to 2), that quantify the syntactic connections between the different systems by means of the description of the interactions between each LUs component of one system and those of another one. When there is no interaction the coefficient will be 1, if the i unit has a positive impact on the j unit the multiplier will be > 1, and in the opposite case it will be < 1.

Connection with the Semantic Model. The instrumental activity consists in the definition and choice of the most suitable algorithm to take into account the relations described by the coefficients. In the present case the model of the Interactive Matrix proposed by Rizzo [25] was chosen. In this case the connection between the system of the interactions and the values placed on the main diagonal of the matrix, $x_{ij}(i = j)$, called Criteria Action Degree, is provided by $v_j = \prod_j x_{ij}$, where v_j is the "Criterion Total Action Degree", and therefore, in this case, the semantic value of the LU, which is influenced by the interactions with all the other ones.

Analysis of Sensitivity and of Scenario. The verification includes: analyses of sensitivity, concerning the variation of the interactions, performed through a multiplier that modifies them, in order to individuate the LUs that are more influenced by the system effect; scenario analyses, consisting in the implementation of the different "axiological strategies" through the variation of the λ_j weights for each LUs – taking into account the communicative interactions of the social sub-systems – and integrating those calculated in the semantic analysis. The λ_j weights, take part in the calculation of the "Total Assessment Degree", $V = \sum_j v_j \lambda_j$.

4   Implementation and Results

4.1   Semantic Module

The value map given by the semantic analysis highlights a heterogeneous framework of the landscape disunity due to the juxtaposition of excellence and decay. The valuation model highlights the highest quality areas and the criticalities, their absolute or intrinsic value, and the relative or extrinsic value they acquire by the different records of weighing and scoring.

The map represents the prevalence of the cultural features in Ortigia, of the functional and environmental disvalues in the industrial and harbour area, the building parasitism of the zone underlying the salines, the seizure of the highest quality area, the system of inlets between Punta Castelluccio and Punta Mola; the latter closes the large inlet of Porto Grande harbour, and faces Maniac Castle, claiming the function of natural counterweight. Compared to this wound to the potential best combination of the whole unity, the Reserve of Plemmirio, despite being appropriate and even necessary, becomes a mere alibi. The value map partly indicates the forms of axiological non-congruity of the different systems compared, and the conflicts of the different, sometimes divergent development lines as well. A graphical/numerical representation of it (Fig. 6) may be attempted, indicating with a different colour for each of the five systems the value (y axis) of each landscape unit (x axis) [26].

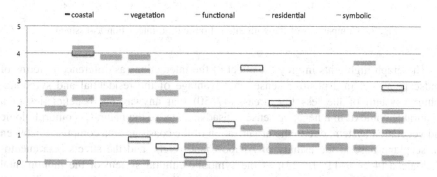

Fig. 6. The value map: graphical/numerical representation.

4.2   Syntactic Module

The results of the interactions' analysis highlight the value system of the landscape complex, and allow us to assess the difference between the valuations of the single elements and those of their combinations in unities [27]. Among the examples of LUs integration, the one between Maniace Castle and Punta Castelluccio-Punta Mola is the most significant: considered separately they assume respectively the residential and symbolic functions, while in the syntactic context of the territorial unity they acquire the maximum landscape tension (geographical, historic and symbolic), at the top of the constructive opposition "nature *vs* culture".

As a consequence the building activity on Punta Castelluccio turns out incongruous, as it attenuates this opposition. In a context in tension even punctual modifications can break the semantic chain compromising the significance of the context [28]. The comparison of the two assessments without project, no-interaction (*Vninp*) and with-interaction (*Vwinp*) is shown in Fig. 7, where all the landscape units are displayed in the *x-axis*, and the valuations in the *y-axis*.

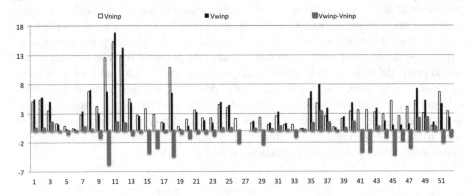

Fig. 7. Comparison of the with-interaction and no-interaction assessments

The graph highlights in grey the effect of the interactions as difference in terms of landscape value: in a positive sense, an advantage of the residential and symbolic-cultural system of the less fine areas, (47–50) that anyway are beneficiaries of a favourable context; in a negative sense a disadvantage: of the natural, geomorphologic and vegetation system, due to the urbanization of the coastline area comprised between the seaplane base at the estuary of Anapo-Ciane rivers, and the streets Sacramento-Maddalena (4–6; 9–11; 18–23); of the symbolic-cultural system of the monumental southern area of Ortigia, as a consequence of the building activity and of the seizure of the naturalistic system comprised between Punta Faro and Punta Castelluccio from public use.

The sensitiveness analyses concern the variation of Total Action Degree (TAD) as effect of the trade off variation of the weights in order to select the most influential criteria, while the analyses of scenario concern the TAD variation regarding the modulation of strategies, that value from time to time the natural structures, the technological infrastructures and the cultural superstructures. The results are reported in Fig. 8.

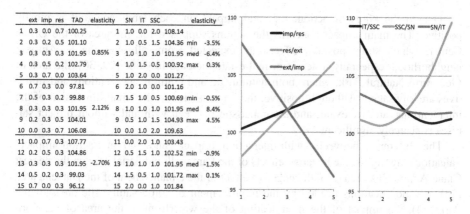

#	ext	imp	res	TAD	elasticity	#	SN	IT	SSC			elasticity
1	0.3	0.0	0.7	100.25		1	1.0	0.0	2.0	108.14		
2	0.3	0.2	0.5	101.10		2	1.0	0.5	1.5	104.36	min	-3.5%
3	0.3	0.3	0.3	101.95	0.85%	3	1.0	1.0	1.0	101.95	med	-6.4%
4	0.3	0.5	0.2	102.79		4	1.0	1.5	0.5	100.92	max	0.3%
5	0.3	0.7	0.0	103.64		5	1.0	2.0	0.0	101.27		
6	0.7	0.3	0.0	97.81		6	2.0	1.0	0.0	101.16		
7	0.5	0.3	0.2	99.88		7	1.5	1.0	0.5	100.69	min	-0.5%
8	0.3	0.3	0.3	101.95	2.12%	8	1.0	1.0	1.0	101.95	med	8.4%
9	0.2	0.3	0.5	104.01		9	0.5	1.0	1.5	104.93	max	4.5%
10	0.0	0.3	0.7	106.08		10	0.0	1.0	2.0	109.63		
11	0.0	0.7	0.3	107.77		11	0.0	2.0	1.0	103.43		
12	0.2	0.5	0.3	104.86		12	0.5	1.5	1.0	102.52	min	-0.9%
13	0.3	0.3	0.3	101.95	-2.70%	13	1.0	1.0	1.0	101.95	med	-1.5%
14	0.5	0.2	0.3	99.03		14	1.5	0.5	1.0	101.72	max	0.1%
15	0.7	0.0	0.3	96.12		15	2.0	0.0	1.0	101.84		

Fig. 8. Syntactic assessment module: results and sensitiveness analysis

5 Application, Results and Discussion

The implementation of the five projects, articulated in the different actions that turn out relevant for the modification of the landscape value, produces the impacts represented in the graph of Fig. 9, that highlights the different characteristics of the 52 landscape unities as above described.

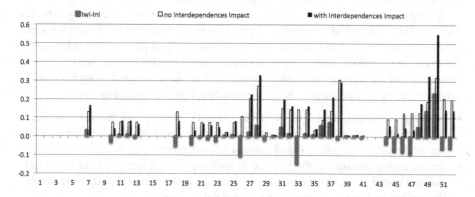

Fig. 9. Impact for each landscape unit, calculated with and without interaction

The modifications of the different actions on the landscape units are represented, in terms of percentage value variation, by three viewpoints, the one of the impact intensity, the one of the impact reversibility (or duration), and the one of the impact ramification (space-time extension of the indirect forecasted or expected effects).

The combination of these assessments gives the value of the impact for each landscape unit, calculated by taking into account the interactions (I_{ni_i}) or not (I_{wi_i}):

$$I_{ni_i} = V_{niwp_i} - V_{ninp_i}; \quad I_{wi_i} = V_{wiwp_i} - V_{winp_i}.$$

Due to the types of action, the total impact on each landscape unit is mostly positive. The main impact concerns the actions supposed for: the area of the Urban Center, which some positive effects are expected from, all over the S. Antonio neighborhood, especially in terms of real estate increase in value [29, 30]; the area of Plemmirio Natural Park, where both naturalistic and cultural interventions and initiatives are envisaged. Although positive, the impacts, due to the small dimension of the interventions, are irrelevant, and a comparison between with and without project statuses is scarcely significant.

The difference between "with-interaction impact" and "no interaction impact" valuations highlights: the negative effects of the Pantanelli industrial area on the nearest Ciane-Anapo CIA area (18), the negative effect of the enhancement of the Darsena area (26); the modifications needed by the improvement of some naturalistic areas of the Park (33); the impact of the modification of the waterfront in the area of the Foro Italico; the effect of an improvement of tourism on some natural areas (45-47). The valuation of these areas is higher if interactions are not considered.

6 Conclusions

The proposed model works as a platform for an analysis finalised to orientate "landscape regeneration strategies", identifying, on the one hand, their most sensitive elements, that are influenced negatively by the interactions, on the other hand the most capable ones, that are influenced positively by the latter.

Basing on the performed valuation, we deduce that the actions envisaged by the planning tools don't deal in depth and extensively as necessary with this territorial complex in its most peculiar aspect, the landscape one, and propose instead punctual and linear interventions with a scarce engaging capacity, considering the inertia of a territory whose invasive human settlements would demand, in some of its large areas, consistent reconversion actions. As a consequence, relevant criticalities persist:

- the large Pantanelli area, apart from the semantic poverty and the syntactic strangeness to the context, arises physical, environmental and functional necrosis due to the weakness of the political and cultural sub-systems;
- the increasing pressure of the large scale harbor activities in the area of S. Antonio pier and Foro Italico, and the building aggression in the part of the coastline suitable for bathing due to the prevailing economic sub-system.

In the articulation of the valuation path, the semantic analysis allowed to start a reflection on landscape in terms of value instead of elements, while the syntactic analysis allowed, in extensive sense, to reason on the landscape in terms of relations, and to consider it, therefore, as form instead of image of the territory.

Despite operating in the folds and shadows of a structural information incompleteness, the model allowed to keep the valuation process in a general level useful to compare heterogeneous territorial aspects, and to perceive the coalescence to an aim: the landscape as substance of the value of the inhabited territory.

Acknowledgments. The paper must be equally attributed to these authors.

References

1. Folke, C.: Resilience: the emergence of a perspective for social-ecological systems analyses. Global Environ. Change **16**, 253–267 (2006)
2. Blanksona, E.J., Greenb, B.H.: Use of landscape classification as an essential prerequisite to landscape evaluation. Landscape Urban Plann. **13**, 149–162 (1991)
3. Giuffrida, S.: The true value. On understanding something. In: Stanghellini, S., Morano, P., Bottero, M., Oppio, A. (eds.) Appraisal: From Theory to Practice. GET, pp. 1–14. Springer, Cham (2017). https://doi.org/10.1007/978-3-319-49676-4_1
4. Tieskens, K.F., et al.: Characterizing European cultural landscapes: accounting for structure, management intensity and value of agricultural and forest landscapes. Land Use Policy **62**, 29–39 (2017). https://doi.org/10.1016/j.landusepol.2016.12.001
5. Dandy, N., Van Der Wal, R.: Shared appreciation of woodland landscapes by land management professionals and lay people: An exploration through fieldbased interactive photo-elicitation. Landscape Urban Plann. **102**, 43–53 (2011). https://doi.org/10.1016/j.landurbplan.2011.03.008
6. Haara, A., Store, R., Leskinen, P.: Analyzing uncertainties and estimating priorities of landscape sensitivity based on expert opinions. Landscape Urban Plann. **163**, 56–66 (2017). https://doi.org/10.1016/j.landurbplan.2017.03.002
7. L. D. 42/2004: Code of Cultural Heritage and Landscape
8. L. 9/2006: European Landscape Convention ratification (Florence 2000)
9. L. D. 157/2006: Corrective and supplementary provisions to Legislative Decree no. 42, in relation to the landscape
10. L. D. 63/2008: Additional Supplementary and Corrective Provisions of L. D. n. 42/2004, in relation to the landscape
11. Zagaria, C., Schulp, C.J.E., Kizos, T., Gounaridi, D., Verburg, P.H.: Cultural landscapes and behavioral transformations: An agent-based model for the simulation and discussion of alternative landscape futures in East Lesvos. Greece, Land Use Policy **65**, 26–44 (2017). https://doi.org/10.1016/j.landusepol.2017.03.022
12. Giuffrida, S., Ferluga, G., Valenti, A.: Clustering analysis in a complex real estate market: the case of ortigia (Italy). In: Murgante, B., et al. (eds.) ICCSA 2014. LNCS, vol. 8581, pp. 106–121. Springer, Cham (2014). https://doi.org/10.1007/978-3-319-09150-1_9
13. Gabrielli, L., Giuffrida, S., Trovato, M.R.: Functions and perspectives of public real estate in the urban policies: the sustainable development plan of syracuse. In: Gervasi, O., et al. (eds.) ICCSA 2016. LNCS, vol. 9789, pp. 13–28. Springer, Cham (2016). https://doi.org/10.1007/978-3-319-42089-9_2
14. Gabrielli, L., Giuffrida, S., Trovato, M.R.: Gaps and overlaps of urban housing sub-market: hard clustering and fuzzy clustering approaches. In: Stanghellini, S., Morano, P., Bottero, M., Oppio, A. (eds.) Appraisal: From Theory to Practice. GET, pp. 203–219. Springer, Cham (2017). https://doi.org/10.1007/978-3-319-49676-4_15
15. Rizzo, F.: Valore e valutazioni. FrancoAngeli, Milano (1999)
16. Turri, E.: La conoscenza del territorio. Metodologia per un'analisi storico-geografica, Marsilio, Venezia (2002)
17. Trovato, M.R., Giuffrida, S.: The monetary neasurement of the flood damage and the valuation of the proactive policies in sicily. Geosciences **8**, 141 (2018). https://doi.org/10.3390/geosciences8040141
18. Luhmann, N.: Sistemi sociali. FrancoAngeli, Milano (1990)

19. Dyer, J.S.: MAUT. In: Figueira, J.R., et al. (eds.) Multiple Criteria Decision Analysis: State of the Art Surveys, pp. 265–295. Springer, New York (2005). https://doi.org/10.1007/0-387-23081-5_7

20. Napoli, G., Schilleci, F.: An application of analytic network process in the planning process: the case of an urban transformation in Palermo (Italy). In: Murgante, B., et al. (eds.) ICCSA 2014. LNCS, vol. 8581, pp. 300–314. Springer, Cham (2014). https://doi.org/10.1007/978-3-319-09150-1_22

21. Ishizaka, A., Nemery, P.: Multi-Criteria Decision Analysis, pp. 81–104. Wiley, Chichester (2013)

22. Ferretti, V., Bottero, M.C., Mondini, G.: Decision making and cultural heritage: an application of the multi-attribute value theory for the reuse of historical buildings. J. Cult. Heritage 15(6) (2014). https://doi.org/10.1016/j.culher.2013.12.007

23. Gunderson, L.H., Allen, G.R., Holling, C.S.: Foundations of Ecological Resilience. Island Press, Washington (2010)

24. Weinstoerffer, J., Girardin, P.: Assessment of the contribution of land use pattern and intensity to landscape quality: use of a landscape indicator. Ecol. Model. 130, 95–109 (2000)

25. Rizzo, F.: Il Capitale Sociale Della Città. FrancoAngeli, Milano (2003)

26. Trovato, M.R., Giuffrida, S.: The choice problem of the urban performances to support the Pachino's redevelopment plan. Int. J. Bus. Intell. Data Min. 9(4), 330–355 (2014). https://doi.org/10.1504/ijbim.2014.068458

27. Giuffrida, S., Napoli, G., Trovato, M.R.: Industrial areas and the city. equalization and compensation in a value-oriented allocation pattern. In: Gervasi, O., et al. (eds.) ICCSA 2016. LNCS, vol. 9789, pp. 79–94. Springer, Cham (2016). https://doi.org/10.1007/978-3-319-42089-9_6

28. Naselli, F., Trovato, M.R., Castello, G.: An evaluation model for the actions in supporting of the environmental and landscaping rehabilitation of the Pasquasia's site mining (EN). In: Murgante, B., et al. (eds.) ICCSA 2014. LNCS, vol. 8581, pp. 26–41. Springer, Cham (2014). https://doi.org/10.1007/978-3-319-09150-1_3

29. Napoli, G., Giuffrida, S., Trovato, M.R., Valenti, A.: Cap rate as the interpretative variable of the urban real estate capital asset: a comparison of different sub-market definitions in Palermo, Italy. Buildings 7(3), 80 (2017). https://doi.org/10.3390/buildings7030080

30. Giuffrida, S., Ventura, V., Trovato, M.R., Napoli, G.: Axiology of the historical city and the cap rate the case of the old town of Ragusa Superiore, Valori e Valutazioni, Issue 18, pp. 41–55 (2017). E-Flow Dei Tipografia del Genio Civile, ISSN: 20362404

A Systematic Review on Collective Awareness Platforms

Thomas Kappas$^{(\boxtimes)}$, Thomas Bournaris, Evangelia Economou,
and Christina Moulogianni

Aristotle University of Thessaloniki, 54124 Thessaloniki, Greece
tkappas@ad.auth.gr

Abstract. In order to improve the agricultural production an important issue is to change farmers' behavior leading them towards sustainability. Altering farmers' behavior is the first step is the first step towards a general societal change. In order to achieve this goal it is vital to involve as many parts of the society as possible. The existing production and consumption model, is not capable to offer such a boost to society. The current financial and social crisis demands on one hand innovative solutions and on the other hand to move beyond the closed Research and Development models to open and collaborative models, such as Collective Awareness Platforms. Collective Awareness Platforms are Information and Communications Technology (ICT) systems leveraging the emerging "network effect" by combining open online social media, distributed knowledge creation and data from real environments, in order to create awareness of problems and possible solutions requesting collective efforts, enabling new forms of social innovation. This paper presents the results of a systematic review that has been based on an analysis of published works on the subject of Collective Awareness Platforms.

Keywords: Sustainability · Collective Awareness Platforms · Collaboration · Social networking · Collective knowledge

1 Introduction

It is truth in our days, there is more and more evidence of crisis in our world, in some areas like finance, environment and society (Sestini 2012). The causes of this crisis are related to the lack of sustainability of the current research and development model that is being used in the developed and developing societies. In other words, the natural resources of our planet are being reduced day by day, in a worried level. Infinite and unsustainable growth, in economy as well as in society, which often has been used to boost the power and the near-term prosperity of nations, is now at the root of the multi-dimension crisis of our "society of knowledge". So the question is, if there is a way to turn this weakness back into an opportunity?

In the agricultural area, which is being related to the environment, the environmental crisis comes from the handling of the environment with an unsustainable way, the huge natural resources and energy consumption, with the ideal of the low cost mass production, to satisfy our consumptive habits. The existing production and consumption

M. Salampasis and T. Bournaris (Eds.): HAICTA 2017, CCIS 953, pp. 51–63, 2019.
https://doi.org/10.1007/978-3-030-12998-9_4

model produces lower quality products and leads to serious problems related to environment (environmental pollution, change of climate, shrinking biodiversity etc.) which disrupt the ecological balance and puts in danger the ecosystems survival and as a result the survival of the human itself (Katzi and Zachariou 2013). At the same time, the environmental crisis is linked with social and economic issues, such as poverty, economic and environmental migrants etc. The reaction to all these issues requires a viable and permanent solution. The Sustainable Development is the kind of development that tries to restore the balance between the three pillars Environment – Economy – Society (Azapagic et al. 2003), by taking them into consideration and seeking to maintain or even improve a long term quality of humans life.

However, the accomplishment of sustainable development, requires a global revolution in the way people think and act, the demolition of the clichés of personal development and profit, and moreover a turn into more collective and cooperative models of action. In addition, it requires the enforcement of respect, of critical thinking, of participation and interest, as well as of the inculcation of moral values in every level of their everyday life. Cooperation and concerted action at international, national and local level, involving both citizens and the state, is therefore needed (Mitoula et al. 2008). In the search of the solution, the role of society and collectivity lies at the heart of research. In other words, the power of the mass and the ability of the citizens - farmers to act and lead to a sustainable production, by actively and responsibly participating in solving these issues, are crucial. The current financial and social crisis demands on one hand innovative solutions and on the other hand to move beyond the closed Research and Development models to open and collaborative models, such as Collective Awareness Platforms.

This paper presents the results of a research analysis concerning the fields and categories of published papers written about Collective Awareness Platforms (CAPS). More specifically, the paper includes a survey that has been based on an analysis of all published works on CAPS from 2001 to 2018, reviewing all documents that are characterized as either conference Papers or articles. The relevant classification of CAPS mentioned in the above papers, is made according to the subject fields of research, the year of publication and the country in which they were published.

2   Collective Awareness Platforms

The Collective Awareness Platforms are ICT systems leveraging the emerging "network effect" by combining open online social media, distributed knowledge creation and data from real environments, in order to create awareness of problems and possible solutions requesting collective efforts, enabling new forms of social innovation (Digital Single Market 2017). Generally we can assume that they are all those applications based on communications (network or mobile) and they use social networking to create communities, offer new services, create innovative knowledge, and harness and promote collective intelligence (Malone and Bernstein 2012). In essence, they are applications that release the enormous potential that stems from the collaboration, interaction, and high connectivity of remote users belonging to a networking community and exchanging knowledge (Bagnoli et al. 2014).

The first of the words used is "collective", which refers to the possibility of people doing things together. Such a concept has been expressed in many ways in the social sciences and in philosophy, talking about groups, publics, spheres, networks, scenes, communities, and so on. Any of these concepts has specific conceptual implications and suggests particular social dynamics. For (Latour and Porter 2009), "collective" is a general term indicating an association of human and non-human entities that can be attributed on the shape of a public or a network. From this perspective, this term points to the fact that it is important to distribute awareness production between human beings and technologies, and that a CAPS initiative should be careful of how this happens. When we refer to the collaboration of human and non-human actors we can think of data being gathered by citizens and sensors, and also about the process of making comprehensible of the information they both provide (Arniani et al. 2014).

In such a distributed meaning of collective life, awareness can be interpreted as an understanding of the activities of others, which provides a context for your own activity (Dourish and Bellotti 1992). To be more understandable, awareness requires access to information and the way in which people acquire information is a crucial topic, for awareness to be leveraged. From this perspective, fostering awareness, one of the keys of CAPS, means questioning the way information is filtered and organized, trying to avoid the consequences of the power and social dynamics of network phenomena like the ones described by Pariser (2011). To be more specific, this filtering now works on the basis of marketing strategies and through invisible technologies, as it segregates internet users into small-scale groups that share professional and leisure interests. The understanding and a kind of transparency of filtering mechanisms is probably the core element of awareness in CAPS initiatives.

Merging these two terms, the picture that surface of collective awareness is a distribution of information on the activities of other participants, human or techno-logical ones that will allow situated emergence of sustainable and socially innovative practices.

Web platforms are the place on which the CAPs projects focus on enabling the dynamics of collective awareness construction. The use of the term "platform" could be reasonably interpreted as a detachment from the closed systems of profit-driven ICT development in favor of more open, participatory-oriented practices. From this point of view a platform becomes an infrastructure for action in the hands of users trying to manage societal challenges. It is a socio-technical solution that is composed of multiple ICT tools, such as websites, forums, social networks, collaborative platforms, delib-erating tools, data visualization, etc. (Arniani et al. 2014).

The first of the societal challenges the European Commission is focusing on with the action of CAPS is sustainability, originally understood as paying attention on the environment as a biological system that is able to endure and remain diverse. The main focus is to maintain a viable environment now and into the future through a wide array of practices that support reduction of well-known ecological problems, like energy and water consumption, land use, etc. However, the concept of sustainability has been extended to include social and economic sustainability as a necessity for assuring future generations a quality of life that is at least comparable to the one available now (Arniani et al. 2014). While the meaning of sustainability is comprehensible, dimensions and versions of this term are so many and interesting, so we are not talking about a simple production technique or methodology, but about a way of life (Lazarides 2000).

The last term included in the CAPS acronym is social innovation, a central topic in these projects.

3 Social Innovation

Searching for the term "social innovation" on Google results there are more than 175 million entries and the popularity graphs on Google Trend see a constant rise in popularity from 2008 onward. The term is particularity popular in Singapore and Canada (Interest for social innovation on Google 2018). It is currently used in different sectors - from the welfare state to urban planning, from local development to social entrepreneurship and, according to different scholars, it has already become a buzzword (Grisoglia and Farragina 2015).

For this reason, defining social innovation is not an easy task but, as a starting point, it is useful to define social innovation using the definition proposed by Murray, as any new products, services or methods that tackle pressing and emerging social issues and, at the same time, transform social interactions promoting new collaboration and relationships (Murray et al. 2010). Social innovation is said to generate a new product/service by simultaneously changing the way in which this product/service is produced. It benefits society "twice", that is, by proposing a solution to a specific problem and by offering new social collaboration opportunities. With reference to the latter of the definition, social innovation is often seen as a way to overcome the classic division between public and private actors pushing for new forms of collaboration among different actors. Social innovation dynamics also mark the emergence of new actors, in some cases including informal organizations such as citizen movements and spontaneous groups that become a point of reference in providing services once offered by the welfare state. The term "social" can also be interpreted as a reference to the engagement of people in the actual resolution of a given social issue so that social innovation is seen as a process that mobilizes citizens in different activities like decision making, planning, sharing of resources and practical, face to face, collaboration. In this sense, social innovation is associated with terms such as participation, engagement, empowerment, co-design, bottom-up, sharing, grassroots initiatives and so forth.

However, social innovation is not synonymous with social change. Social changes occur every day and can be positive or negative, as for example, the growing attention on environmental issues, or, the low birth rate in some European countries, while social innovation only refers to positive innovation that, as in the definition proposed by Philip et al. (2008), is meant to be "more effective, efficient, sustainable, or just than existing solutions". In this sense, social innovation as a term embodies the desire for a more equal, sustainable and fair world. What this does mean, is that in practice it needs to be considered on a case by-case basis. So that social innovation is not a value-free term, as it is by definition, progressive in the sense of being pro-change and also positively seeks to create such change.

4   Benefits and Hurdles of CAPS

Their benefits are many. They aim to "harness the collaborative power of ICT networks to create collective awareness of sustainability threats and enable collective solutions". Under their umbrella, enterprises and civil society deploy collective intelligence platforms to shape the likes of a more open democracy, a collaborative and circular economy, collective environmental action and collaborative consumption for sustainable lifestyles. CAPS engages citizens in initiatives launched by interdisciplinary research teams. These platforms help them to understand, analyze, and perhaps even challenge macro-level official statistics or established data, because their use is easy, straightforward, available online, are not subject to spatial/temporal constraints to communicate with community members, and the subsequent processing and analysis of data collected during their operation can be done easily and quickly with automated way. Its projects spread knowledge, facilitate the internet of value, link to websites that provide valuable information, or even add scale and value to similar initiatives funded nationally and internationally (CORDIS 2016).

However, CAPs mainly rely on the collaboration of people with very different attributes in personality, cognitive strategies, and sensitiveness to social influence. Their behaviors combine in different ratio altruism and rational selfishness and are shaped by real and virtual communities they participate in. Furthermore, many CAPs need to overcome the worries of end users about the privacy of personal data and locations. Additionally CAPs are a new area in the European Research framework with lack of impact assessment methodologies and related assessments of results and can be seen as part of the Digital Social Innovation phenomenon. (Bellini et al. 2016) Finally, CAPs usually represent an example of service provision that strays from familiar rules and prescriptions of market, and may stand competitively against other commercial alternatives. For these reasons, their wide adoption, sustainability, and effectiveness presents major challenges (Bagnoli et al. 2014).

5   Collective Awareness Platforms Foster Sustainable Agriculture

Sustainable agriculture, to be achieved, requires an intensive interaction between scientific knowledge and the knowledge produced by the farmers themselves. The shift towards sustainable agriculture requires the participation and cooperation of farmers, the communication between them, exchange of views, positive examples and practices, in order to finally achieve a massive change of attitude and the adoption of sustainable cultivation. This therefore, entails much more than simple change in cultivation techniques and requires an additional change in attitudes and knowledge that may have been adopted for years. Collective Awareness Platforms (CAPS) are a modern technological means ideal to achieve this goal, that is, this interaction. Teamwork through these platforms of collective consciousness can motivate individual and collective criticism of new practices and methods, as well as experiments on new cultivation processes. Finally, this teamwork can lead to the acceptance of new rules of conduct and new values in the behavior of farmers in agriculture, society and the environment.

Generally in CAPS, providing information is not enough to trigger social innovation. An effective change happens when new ways of perceiving the world and acting are shared and established into a social group. Beyond changing their own behavior, users - farmers must influence others, and social media boosts this process (Fig. 1). The first step before the peer community interaction, however, through Collective Awareness Platforms, is to explore their existing attitude towards sustainable agriculture and to identify the incentives they have to acquire in order to be sensitized and encouraged to adopt practices and behaviors that are in line with the basic principles of sustainable agriculture. Against this background, the cultivation and environmental policies used by farmers, should initially be cost-benefit analyzed and then according to the results that will come, we must step forward to suggest specific practices, attitudes and behaviors that will both strengthen the environmental consciousness of farmers and on the other hand will lead to increasing and sustainable levels of prosperity.

Fig. 1. Loop information ↔ action (Arniani et al. 2014)

6 Examples of CAPS Enhancing Sustainability

The literature review shows that there are many Collective Awareness Platforms developed for different areas. For example, there are CAPS for Sustainability and Social Innovation, for energy efficient smart buildings (Chatzigiannakis et al. 2015), for financial and environmental awareness (Satsiou et al. 2016). On the other hand there are only few researches and CAPS developed for sustainability in agriculture. The CAPSELLA (Collective Awareness PlatformS for Environmentally-sound Land management based on data technoLogies and Agrobiodiversity) project is a great example of CAPs implementation in the general field of agriculture. Among its goals are to raise awareness about existing ICT solutions and the benefits of their adoption, the understanding and collections of farmers and networks needs and requirements in order to develop and deliver tailored made ICT novel solutions, foster understanding and, hopefully, sharing of open data among farmers, which shall lead to build a sustainable technical prototyping platform, a meeting environment for innovation that democratizes access to big data, cloud computing, open data, open software and pilots (Lazzaro et al. 2016).

Another good practice of CAPs is SavingFood. SavingFood offers a novel approach to tackle food waste, by turning this environmental issue into an innovative solution to fight hunger through the redistribution of surplus food to welfare organisations that support people in need. Moving forward from existing food redistribution channels SavingFood seeks to create a social movement for reducing food waste, by engaging all actors of the food waste cycle to become part of the solution (Saving Food Project 2016). The project brings together the food waste community and the technical and scientific community in a mutually beneficial context to provide a complete, sustainable and flexible platform where all participants – food donors, beneficiaries, policy-makers and society at large – can engage, discuss and deliver within a pro-social environment in which everyone's needs are met, information is shared and food is effectively distributed.

In a similar way, our research aims at the creation of a Collective Awareness Platform tailored at a first level to the profile and needs of certain Greek farmer's communities. Through this platform, these networking communities will be able to exchange their practical knowledge on various cultivation issues, communicate and interact with each other. This productive interaction will raise their awareness on many agricultural topics such as sustainable agricultural production, environmentally acceptable cultivation techniques and practices and will lead to the suggestion of innovative solutions. The open data and shared knowledge that will be created, will be open to everyone interested in the domain. In other words, the project will be based and also facilitate a strong community of active farmers by providing them with effective tools supporting coordination of efforts, communication and dissemination, knowledge transfer, collaborative learning, best practices identification and promotion of outcomes for broad impact in society.

7 Methodology

In this paper, we analyze all entries we found on Scopus database (Scopus Preview 2018) concerning CAPs. The purpose of such a systematic review was to identify relevant existing studies based on a prior formulated research question, to evaluate and compose their respective contributions and to report the evidence and the output statistics in a way that clear conclusions with regard to further research and managerial practice can be drawn. We searched the online database using the keyword "Collective Awareness Platform" and we found 97 published papers between the years 2001 and 2018. We have chosen the document type of the search as Conference Paper or Article, to make our search more specific and finally, 73 previous scholarly papers/articles were selected for our review.

The first step was to classify and group the results into subject fields. So based on the online search results we classified the selected papers into thirteen different subject areas including; Computer Science, Social Sciences, Mathematics, Engineering, Management and Accounting, Arts and Humanities, Decision Sciences, Medicine, Psychology, Environmental Science, Earth and Planetary Sciences, Economics, Physics and Astronomy (Table 1). According to the table it is obvious that there are lots of papers that cover more than one subject area. Therefore the total records came to the number of 126.

Table 1. Distribution papers based on subject areas

Subject fields	Number of records	Percentage (%)
Computer Science	46	36.5%
Social Sciences	17	13.5%
Mathematics	15	12%
Engineering	14	11%
Management and Accounting	7	5.7%
Arts and Humanities	6	4.8%
Decision Sciences	4	3.1%
Medicine	4	3.1%
Psychology	4	3.1%
Environmental Science	3	2.4%
Earth and Planetary Sciences	2	1.6%
Economics	2	1.6%
Physics and Astronomy	2	1.6%
Total	126	100%

According to the results shown in the above table, the most popular subject areas were Computer Science and Social Sciences with 46 and 17 published papers respectively, and a total appearance percentage in this review paper of 36.5% and 13.5% each (50% in total).

In the next table you can see the most recently published papers (regarding the years 2018 and 2017), categorized by author, year, application area, study purpose and title (Table 2).

You can see the distribution of articles by year of publication in the next figure (Fig. 2). It is obvious that the research on the use of CAPs (regardless the subject area) met a remarkable growth after the year of 2013 with a steady ascent. In the year of 2016 due to the new call for collaborative projects that has been published from the EU, under the 2016-17 ICT Work Programme, named as ICT-11 (HORIZON 2020 2017): the subject of "Collective Awareness Platforms for Sustainability and Social Innovation", came to a peak and it still continuous to gather a notable research interest.

Table 2. Distribution papers on application areas

Author	Year	Application area	Study purpose	Title
Vilarinho, T., Floch, J., Oliveira, M., Pappas, I.O., Mora, S.	2018	Computer science, Mathematics	Presentation of a social innovation methodology catering citizens without previous social innovation experience and accessible via an ICT platform	Developing a Social Innovation Methodology in the Web 2.0 Era
Veeckman, C., Vanobberghen, W., Kalemaki, E., Madesi, V., Theodoridis, A.	2018	Computer science, Mathematics	Presents SavingFood, a project that involves several grassroots organisations to tackle food waste through digital social innovation	An Engagement-Related Behaviour Change Approach for SavingFood in Greece
Bianchi, L., Liò, P.	2017	Computer science	Discuss the social vulnerability owing to the genome and Internet combined security and privacy weaknesses	Opportunities for community awareness platforms in personal genomics and bioinformatics education
Vlachos, V., Stamatiou, Y.C., Madhja, A., Nikoletseas, S.	2017	Computer science	The project Privacy Flag that has to do with the concepts of crowdsourcing and collective intelligence	Privacy Flag: A crowdsourcing platform for reporting and managing privacy and security risks
Chen, A.T., Carriere, R.M., Kaplan, S.J.	2017	Medicine	To introduce and evaluate the Body Listening Project, to engage the public in the creation of a public resource-to leverage collective wisdom in the health domain	The user knows what to call it: Incorporating patient voice through user-contributed tags on a participatory platform about health management
Roberts, S.	2017	Social Sciences, Arts and Humanities	To explore two exhibitions which provided a platform for children's impressions and experiences of war as seen through their drawings, whilst also raising money and awareness for refugee children's causes	Education, art, and exile: Cultural activists and exhibitions of refugee children's art in the UK during the second world war

(*continued*)

Table 2. (*continued*)

Author	Year	Application area	Study purpose	Title
Kappas, T., Bournaris, T., Oikonomou, E., Moulogianni, C.	2017	Computer science	An initial introduction to the Collective Awareness Platforms for Sustainable Agricultural Production	Collective awareness platforms for sustainable agricultural production
Clarke, S., Arnab, S., Lewis, M., Bogliolo, A., Klopfenstein, L.	2017	Computer science, Social Sciences, Engineering	To explore the approach implemented by the Crowd4Roads project, for providing open data towards boosting traffic conditions in Europe	A gamified approach for facilitating a user-engagement strategy for public-led collective awareness platform for road sensing
Ruiz-Correa, S., Santani, D., Ramírez-Salazar, B., Hasimoto-Beltrán, R., Gatica-Perez, D.	2017	Computer science	To describe SenseCityVity, an approach to engage and support youth in Mexico as they investigate, document, and reflect upon urban problems through mobile crowdsourcing	SenseCityVity: Mobile Crowdsourcing, Urban Awareness, and Collective Action in Mexico
Das, A.N., Doelling, K., Lundberg, C., Sevil, H.E., Lewis, F.	2017	Engineering	To discuss a hybrid swarm autonomy architecture to coordinate a diverse team of robots using an immersive and intuitive interface technology for cooperative control of unmanned platforms	A Mixed reality based hybrid swarm control architecture for manned-unmanned teaming (MUM-T)

Finally, you can see the distribution of papers/articles according to the basic country they were published in (some of them were published in more than one countries). As we can see, United States and United Kingdom are the two main countries that gather the most published papers. Also Europe has a variety of territories with a significant popularity in published CAPS papers. The choice "other" consists of 17 publications in 17 different countries (Table 3).

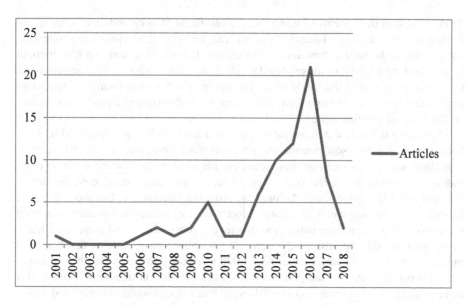

Fig. 2. Distribution papers by year of publication

Table 3. Distribution in countries

Countries	Number of records
United States	13
United Kingdom	12
Greece	7
Italy	5
Netherlands	5
Portugal	5
Austria	2
France	3
Germany	2
Australia	2
Other	17
Total	73

8 Conclusion

Research around CAPS is internationally at an early stage and is an open field for further study. There are already some remarkable studies in the international literature that attempt to present the structure and characteristics of CAPS, categorize them, explore their capabilities and limitations. Efforts have also been made to compare several CAPS together to draw conclusions about the incentives of users involved in them, as well as the benefits of using them. Their future is open and their scope is not limited to specific areas. Instead, their use can be applied to almost any scientific subject. So, in the field of Sustainable Agriculture, the scientific study on how it could be used and the analysis of the expected results is an open challenge. This research will be an important tool in the hands of the farmers involved, giving them the knowledge and the ability to learn through themselves, new ways of agricultural production always on the basis of sustainability.

According to our research on papers published the last 18 years about CAPS, it has been proved that the most popular subject areas were Computer and Social Science. Therefore, we can assume that these areas are the most popular in the research community, nevertheless not the only ones. Other subject areas involve Mathematics, Engineering, Management and Accounting, Arts and Humanities, Decision Sciences, Medicine, Psychology and many others. Moreover, it is noticeable that the research on the use of CAPs met a remarkable growth after the year of 2013, and more specifically in the year of 2016 because of the new call for collaborative projects that has been published from the EU, under the horizon 2020 work programme. It was then (the year of 2016) that the research and simultaneously the publication of papers about CAPS came to a peak with a steady ascent until today, that still continuous to grow and gather a notable research interest amongst the research community. The majority of researchers published their work in United Kingdom and in the United States, leading us to the conclusion that in these countries there is a special interest in the subject of using the power of CAPS in various fields. All of these previously mentioned facts boost the confidence that the subject of Collective Awareness Platforms is an up to date research area and this will be the fact for the years to come.

References

Arniani, M., et al.: Collective Awareness Platforms for Sustainability and Social Innovation: An Introduction (2014)

Azapagic, A., Emsley, A., Hamerton, I.: Polymers: The Environment and Sustainable Development, 1st edn. Wiley, West Sussex (2003)

Bagnoli, F., Guazzini, A., Pacini, G., Stavrakakis, I., Kokolaki, E., Theodorakopoulos, G.: Cognitive structure of collective awareness platforms, pp. 96–101. IEEE (2014)

Bellini, F., Passani, A., Klitsi, M., Vanobberghen, W.: Exploring Impacts of Collective Awareness Platforms for Sustainability and Social Innovation, Roma, p. 23 (2016)

Chatzigiannakis, I., Amaxilatis, D., Livathinos, S.: A collective awareness platform for energy efficient smart buildings. In: Proceedings of the 19th Panhellenic Conference on Informatics, pp. 295–296 (2015)

CORDIS: Digital Social Innovation for Sustainable Societies. Focus Magazine (2016)

Digital Single Market: Collective Awareness Platforms for Sustainability and Social Innovation (2017). https://ec.europa.eu/digital-single-market/en/collective-awareness

Dourish, P., Victoria, B.: Awareness and coordination in shared workspaces. In: ACM Conference on Computer-Supported Cooperative Work (1992)

Grisolia, F., Farragina, E.: Social Innovation on the Rise: yet another buzzword in a time ofausterity? Salute e Società **11**, 169–179 (2015). Roma, Franco Angeli

HORIZON 2020: Horizon 2020 work programme, p. 32 (2017). http://ec.europa.eu/research/participants/data/ref/h2020/wp/2016_2017/main/h2020-wp1617-leit-ict_en.pdf

Interest for social innovation on Google (2018). https://trends.google.com/trends/explore?date=all&q=socialinnovation

Katzi, C., Zachariou, A.: Education for the environment and sustainable development. Frederick Research Centre, pp. 8–9 (2013)

Latour, B., Porter, C.: Politics of Nature: How to Bring the Sciences into Democracy. Harvard University Press, Cambridge (2009)

Lazarides, Ch.: Food technology and sustainability (2000)

Lazzaro, M., Barberi, P., Calabro, G., Toli, E., Ioannidis, Y.: The Horizon 2020 CAPSELLA project: Collective Awareness PlatformS for Environmentally-sound Land management based on data technoLogies and Agrobiodiversity (2016)

Malone, T., Bernstein, M.: Handbook of Collective Intelligence. MIT Press, Cambridge (2012)

Mitoula, R., Astara, O., Kaldis, P.: Sustainable Development, Athens, Rossili (2008)

Murray, R., Caulier-Grice, J., Mulgan, G.: The Open Book of Social Innovation. NESTA, London (2010)

Pariser, E.: The Filter Bubble: What the Internet is Hiding from You (2011)

Philip, A., Deiglmeier, K., Miller, D.: Rediscovering social innovation. Stanf. Soc. Innov. Rev. 6, 34–43 (2008)

Satsiou, A., et al. (eds.): Collective Online Platforms for Financial and Environmental Awareness, 1st edn. Springer, Cham (2016). https://doi.org/10.1007/978-3-319-50237-3

Saving Food Project (2016). https://savingfood.eu

Scopus Preview, (n.d.) (2018). http://www.scopus.com/

Sestini, F.: Collective awareness platforms: engines for sustainability and ethics. IEEE Technol. Soc. Mag. 31(4), 54–62 (2012)

Using Geostatistics and Multicriteria Spatial Analysis to Map Forest Species Biogeophysical Suitability: A Study Case for the Centro Region of Portugal

Luís Quinta-Nova[1,2]([✉]) [ID], Natália Roque[1] [ID], Isabel Navalho[1] [ID],
Cristina Alegria[1,2] [ID], and Teresa Albuquerque[3] [ID]

[1] Instituto Politécnico de Castelo Branco, Escola Superior Agrária,
Quinta da Senhora de Mércules, Apartado 119,
6001-909 Castelo Branco, Portugal
lnova@ipcb.pt
[2] CERNAS - Centro de Estudos de Recursos Naturais, Ambiente e Sociedade,
Instituto Politécnico de Castelo Branco, Escola Superior Agrária,
Castelo Branco, Portugal
[3] Instituto Politécnico de Castelo Branco, Escola Superior de Tecnologia,
Castelo Branco, Portugal

Abstract. There are various methodologies for defining soil uses to promote sustainable utilization of rural land. Many of these methods rely on decision support systems based on multicriteria spatial analysis. In this study, a two-step spatial approach was performed to produce forest species suitability maps. The objectives of the study were: (1) to produce bioclimatic indices maps using a geostatistical approach based on climate data; (2) to produce biogeophysical suitability maps for the main Portuguese forest species by multicriteria spatial analysis using the analytic hierarchy process (AHP) integrating three factors (terrain slope, soil diagnostic features and bioclimatic indices); and (3) to conduct a comparative analysis of the current forest species area distributions to these species biogeophysical suitability areas. With these objectives, the Centro region of Portugal was used as the study area. Our methodological approach allowed us to assess the biogeophysical suitability of Maritime pine, Eucalyptus, Cork oak and Holm oak in the Centro region of Portugal. The findings in this study emphasize the potential that the Centro region of Portugal has for expanding the spread of native oaks as recommended by the National Strategy for Forests to respond to climate changes, improve landscape biodiversity and mitigate fire hazards. The species biogeophysical suitability maps may be important tools for decision support in landscape planning to define species' priority afforestation areas. From an instrumental point of view, the use of this methodology may interest stakeholders and others with roles in planning and land management. Further investigation is needed to integrate the impact of climate change in forest species spatial modeling to assist in supporting future national strategies for forests.

Keywords: Suitability · Forest management · GIS · AHP

M. Salampasis and T. Bournaris (Eds.): HAICTA 2017, CCIS 953, pp. 64–83, 2019.
https://doi.org/10.1007/978-3-030-12998-9_5

1 Introduction

Understanding the spatial relationships between various territorial functions through the establishment of relations of continuity and connectivity between the elements under consideration, together with geographical and alphanumeric information, allows the realization of spatial analysis to determine the degree of functionality of each element in analysis [1].

Multicriteria decision analysis (MCDA) deals essentially with complex decisions that involve a large amount of information, several alternative outcomes and multiple criteria to assess these outcomes. MCDA techniques can be used to identify a single preferred option, to rank options, to short-list a number of options for further investigation, or simply to distinguish acceptable from unacceptable alternatives [2, 3]. Thus, multicriteria evaluation is used to solve spatial decision problems derived from multiple criteria. By integrating the evaluation techniques with GIS, the influential factors are evaluated, and more accurate decisions can be taken [4].

The analytic hierarchy process (AHP) is one of the most widely used methods of multicriteria spatial analysis; it was developed in the 1970s by Saaty [5] and is considered to be relevant to nearly any ecosystem management application that requires the evaluation of multiple participants or involves complex decision-making processes [6, 7]. This process is based on mathematics and psychology and provides a comprehensive and rational framework for structuring a decision problem, allowing the representation and quantification of its elements, to relate these elements with general objectives and evaluate alternative solutions [8].

The AHP has attracted the attention of many researchers mainly because of its precise mathematical properties, and the required input data are comparatively easy to obtain. Basically, it uses informed judgment or expert opinion to determine the relative value or contribution of these attributes and synthesize a solution. According to [9], it is a mathematical tool that allows the comparison of different alternatives or scenarios, based on various criteria, to help decision-makers choose one alternative.

The AHP is based on three main principles, namely, decomposition, comparative judgment and synthesis of priorities. The synthesis principles take the derived ratio scale local priorities at various levels of the hierarchy and construct a composite set of alternatives for the elements at the lowest level of the hierarchy [3].

The AHP decomposes a problem, question or decision, in all the variables that constitute it, in a scheme of criteria and subcriteria and then makes pairwise comparisons between them [10]. The comparison between criteria is made using a scale of 1 to 9, wherein 1 is equally preferred and 9 is highly preferred [8]. The AHP reverts comparisons on numerical values that can be processed and compared to the full extent of the problem. The weight of each factor allows the evaluation of each of the elements within the defined hierarchy. This conversion capability of empirical data in mathematical models distinguish AHP from other decision-making techniques [8].

Determination of criterion weights are crucial in multicriteria analysis. The AHP is a suitable mathematical method for this purpose when analyzing complex decision problems [8]. It derives the weights through pairwise comparisons of the relative importance between every pair of criteria. Through a pairwise comparison matrix, the AHP calculates the weight value for each criterion (w_i) by taking the eigenvector corresponding to the largest eigenvalue of the matrix and then normalizing the sum of the components to a unity. It is necessary to verify the consistency of the matrix after obtaining the weight values.

The consistency is judged based on a consistency ratio CR. The determination of the CR value is critical. The standard CR threshold value of 0.10 has been widely used as a measure of the consistency in a set of judgments of AHP applications in the literature. If CR < 0.10, the pairwise comparison matrix is considered to have acceptable consistency and the weight values calculated are considered valid and can be utilized.

Multicriteria spatial decision analysis has been widely applied in various studies in different fields, many of which are published and have been cited by many authors as processes of relevant decision making. This is the case of Kangas et al. [11] referring to the use of GIS in the decision-making process through the multicriteria analysis in the planning of forest resources conservation actions, allowing actions as directed by the determination of the priority areas.

Quinta-Nova and Roque [12] developed a model based on multicriteria spatial analysis AHP to determine the suitability levels for agroforestry uses of the subregion of Beira Interior Sul. The criteria used were the soil potential, slope and aspect. The authors note that this analysis identified the areas where the use of land should be subject to a conversion and/or a change of management.

In Portugal, as part of its forestry policy, the National Strategy for Forests (NSF) [13, 14] and the Plans of Regional Forest Planning (PRFP) [15] are legal instruments that propose broad guidelines for land cover/use and forest composition and management to promote the sustainable development of forest landscapes by a multifunctional approach. In 2006, the NSF recommended the following goals for forest composition to be attained by 2030: a strong decrease in eucalyptus area (−60%), a slight decrease in maritime pine area (−6%) and a strong increase in cork oak and oak areas (3 and 4 times more the existing area in 2005, respectively) [13]. However, despite the PRFPs identifying the species to be promoted in each of the 21 regions of the country, the NSF goals have not been achieved. In 2015, a new set of goals for forest composition were established in NSF for the next 15 years [14]. After the catastrophic fires in 2017, the imperative need for decreasing the eucalyptus species area and for designing the forest landscape as a mosaic of less inflammable and combustible species such as the native oaks became clear.

In this study, the following research questions were posed. (1) Knowing endogenous variables such as climate data, soil characteristics and terrain elevation, is it possible to determine the suitability of various forest species based on an AHP model to evaluate the different levels of agroforestry suitability? (2) Are the current species distributed in the most suitable areas?

To respond to these research questions, the Centro region of Portugal was adopted as the study area. The objectives of the study were (1) to produce bioclimatic indices maps using a geostatistical approach based on climate data; (2) to produce biogeophysical suitability maps for the main Portuguese forest species by multicriteria spatial analysis using the AHP; and (3) to make a comparative analysis of the current forest species area distribution to these species biogeophysical suitability areas.

2   Materials and Methods

2.1   Study Area

The study area is the Centro region of Portugal that comprises the following six forest management regions (Fig. 1a): Centro Litoral (CL), Douro e Lafões (DL), Pinhal Interior Norte (PIN), Pinhal Interior Sul (PIS), Beira Interior Norte (BIN) and Beira Interior Sul (BIS) [15]. The Centro region forest area (Fig. 1b), according to the National Forest Inventory (IFN), is mainly composed of Maritime pine (*Pinus pinaster* Aiton) (544,585 ha; 51%), Eucalyptus (*Eucalyptus globulus* Labill.) (357,805 ha; 34%), Cork oak (*Quercus suber* L.) (45,221 ha; 4%) and Holm oak (*Quercus rotundifolia* Lam.) (22,408 ha; 2%). The remaining forest area is occupied by other oaks (e.g., *Quercus pyrenaica* Willd., *Quercus faginea* Lam. and *Quercus robur* L.), Stone pine (*Pinus pinea* L.), Chestnut (*Castanea sativa* Mill.), Acacia (*Acacia* sp.), and other broadleaved and other coniferous trees [16].

For each one of the six management regions referred to above, there is a correspondent Plan of Regional Forest Planning (PRFP) [15] proposing forest composition goals for 2010, 2025 and 2045 (Fig. 1c). The National Strategy for Forests (NSF) (DR, 2006) proposes the forest composition goals by forest management region for 2030 (Fig. 1d).

Overall, for the study (Fig. 1e), a substantial decrease in eucalyptus area, a slight decrease in maritime pine area and a substantial increase in oaks areas were recommended.

Regarding the current distribution of forest species in the study area and the forest composition goals for the future, four forest species were selected for further analysis: Maritime pine, Eucalyptus, Cork oak and Holm oak.

The official COS land cover map for 2010 (COS 2010) was used to analyze these species distribution area in the Centro region of Portugal [17, 18]. In 2010, the species distribution areas (Fig. 2) were Maritime pine (*Pinus pinaster* Aiton) (411,499 ha), Eucalyptus (*Eucalyptus globulus* Labill.) (227,559 ha), Cork oak (*Quercus suber* L.) (7,670 ha) and Holm oak (*Quercus rotundifolia* Lam.) (21,463 ha).

Then, the biogeophysical suitability maps were produced for Maritime pine, Eucalyptus, Cork oak and Holm oak using the methodology presented in the following sections. Finally, the species current distribution maps were compared to the species biogeophysical suitability maps obtained in this study.

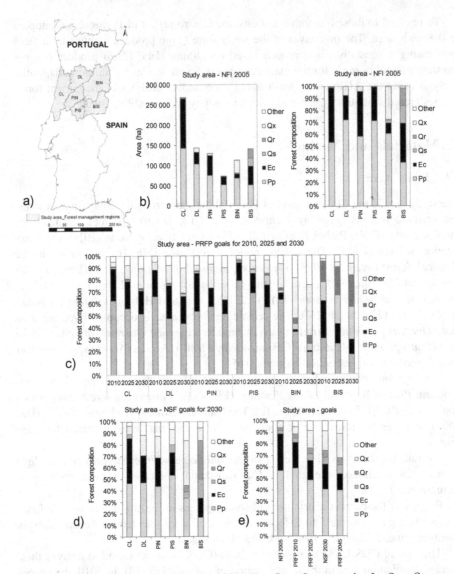

Legend: Pp – *Pinus pinaster* Ait., Ec – *Eucalyptus* sp., Qs – *Quercus suber* L., Qr – *Quercus rotundifolia* Lam.; CL – Centro Litoral; DL – Douro e Lafões; PIN – Pinhal Interior Norte; PIS – Pinhal Interior Sul; BIN – Beira Interior Norte; BIS – Beira Interior Sul; NFI – National Forest Inventory; PRFP – Plans of Regional Forest Planning; NSF – National Strategy for Forests

Fig. 1. Study area: (a) Forest management regions [16] (b) NFI – Forest area (ha) and forest composition (%) by forest management region in 2005 (AFN, 2010); (c) Plans of Regional Forest Planning – forest composition goals 2010, 2025 and 2045; (d) National Strategy for Forests (NSF) – forest composition goals by forest management region for 2030; (e) Forest composition goals for the Centro region [13, 15]

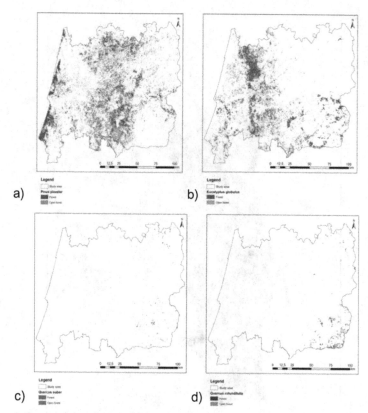

Legend: forest – ground cover higher than 30%; open forest – ground cover between 10–30%.

Fig. 2. Study area forestland cover (COS 2010): (a) Maritime pine – *Pinus pinaster*; (b) Eucalyptus – *Eucalyptus globulus*; (c) Cork oak – *Quercus suber*; (d) Holm oak – *Quercus rotundifolia* (DGT, 2016; DGT, 2017)

2.2 Bioclimatic Analysis

For the development of bioclimatic maps, the following climatic data were used: P_p – precipitation (mm), T_p – Temperature (˚C), T_{max} – average temperature of the warmer month (˚C), T_{min} – average temperature of the coldest month (˚C), T – average medium monthly temperatures (˚C), M – average maximum temperature of the coldest month (˚C) and m – average minimum temperature of the coldest month (˚C). These data were calculated from temporal series corresponding to the climatological normal of the period between 1981 and 2010 referring to 32 stations, located in Portugal and Spain (Fig. 3).

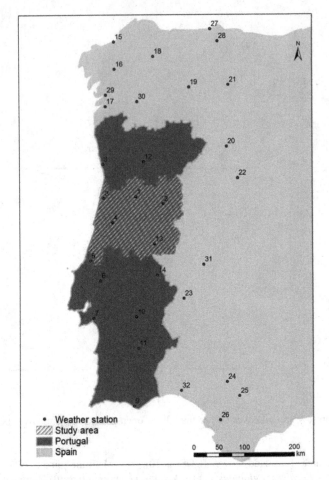

Fig. 3. Location of weather stations used in the preparation of the mapping of bioclimatic indices

The proposed methodology results from the development of maps at the national level, corresponding to each of the attributes to be used in the calculation of bioclimatic indices (Fig. 4).

The structural analysis was performed through the experimental variograms computation since the selected variables can be assumed as regionalized variables [19] and the corresponding models can be assumed to be fitted [20–22]. For computation, SpaceStat V. 4.0-.18. software (https://www.biomedware.com/) was used. Subsequently, ordinary kriging (OK) was used for spatial interpolation aiming to predict the variables' values at any arbitrary spatial location within the study region and thus compute spatial patterns for the considered attributes (P_p, T_p, T_{max}, T_{min}, T, M and me).

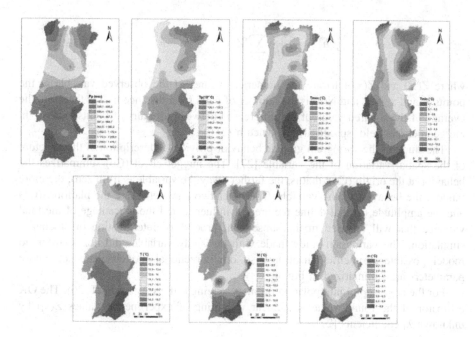

Legend: P_p – precipitation (mm), T_p –Temperature (10*°C), T_{max} – average temperature of the warmer month (°C), T_{min} – average temperature of the coldest month (°C), T – average medium monthly temperatures (°C), M - average maximum temperature of the coldest month (°C) and m – average minimum temperature of the coldest month (°C)

Fig. 4. Representation of cartography at a national level, of the attributes used in the calculation of the bioclimatic indices (P_p, T_p, T_{max}, T_{min}, T, M and m). The omnidirectional variogram is also shown, as are the corresponding adjusted theoretical models in geostatistical modeling by ordinary kriging (Appendix 1)

It is noteworthy that geostatistics is a methodological approach that is valuable for the characterization of spatial patterns, where the data available is typically scarce. Ordinary kriging (OK) accounts for local fluctuations of the mean by limiting the stationary field of the mean to the local neighborhood [23]. For the computation, the Space-Stat Software V. 4.0.18, Biomedware was used [24].

The experimental variograms γ(h) were computed and then fitted by a theoretical model, $γ^{\wedge}$(h) [25]. The adjusted parameters for the seven attributes allow us to see that the obtained models are fairly fit. Indeed, all the attributes have a nugget effect below 60% of the total variance for all the properties. The error associated with the interpolation procedure, ordinary kriging (OK), is therefore minimized.

The variogram is a vector function, applicable to regionalized variables [19], whose argument is the distance vector h, which quantifies the variance of the increments of the first order function [26]. Experimental estimation function from the set of experimental data was performed by applying the formula:

$$\gamma(h) = \frac{1}{2N(h)} \sum_{i=1}^{N(h)} [Z(x_i) - Z(x_i + h)]^2 \tag{1}$$

where $Z(x_i)$ and $Z(x_i + h)$ are the numerical values of the observed variable at the points x_i and $x_i + h$, and $N(h)$ is the number of pairs for a distance h. It is therefore the average of the squared value of the differences between all pairs of points existing in the geometrical field, spaced at a distance h [21].

The study of the variogram graphic behavior provides a description of the structure of the spatial variation of the variable [27]. The nugget effect (Co) summarizes the behavior at the origin (Co); that is, the farther away the variable is from zero, the more random the behavior of the variable. The other two parameters are the platform (C1) and the amplitude (a) that define the area of influence and the percentage of the total variance that will be used in the subsequent process of interpolation or stochastic simulation. The variogram study made with the study variables did not allow us to model possible geometric anisotropy, so omnidirectional models were set whose parameters are summarized in Fig. 4.

For the next step of interpolation ordinary kriging (OK) was used [21, 26]. The OK estimator of the found value is a linear weighting of experimental values $Z(x_i)$ by unknown λ_i coefficients [27]:

$$Z_{KO}(x) = \sum_{i=l}^{n} \lambda_i Z(x_i) \tag{2}$$

Then, the following indices were calculated using map algebra: continentality index ($I_c = T_{max-Tmin}$); thermicity index ($I_t = 10 * (T + M + m)$) and ombrothermic index ($I_o = P_p/T_p$). The SpaceStat 4.0.14 software (Biomedware) and ArcMap 10 (ESRI) were used in the calculation process. The bioclimatic map was obtained by the combination of three indices (I_c, I_t and I_o) in a geographical analysis function, which groups the different ranges of each climatic domain in a new entry that groups in different combinations.

2.3   Soil Diagnostic Features for the Forest Species

Based on the methodology developed by [28], the soil units present in the study area were classified in "diagnostic features" according to the soil conditions for the development and growth for the forest species (Table 1): Maritime pine, Eucalyptus, Cork oak and Holm oak. To each soil family was assigned the correspondent diagnostic feature according to the limitation for the forest species development and growth.

Table 1. Soil diagnosis characteristics [29, 30]

Species	Superior (3)	Reference (2)	Inferior (1)
Pinus pinaster Ait.	Expandable depth	Textural discontinuity	Rocky outcrops Unproductive areas
Eucalyptus globulus Labill.	Expandable depth Textural discontinuity	–	Rocky outcrops Unproductive areas
Quercus suber L.	Expandable depth	Textural discontinuity	Rocky outcrops Unproductive areas
Quercus rotundifolia Lam.	Expandable depth Textural discontinuity	–	Rocky outcrops Unproductive areas

The production of the soil diagnostic features map for each species relied on the definition of three suitability classes, considering a reference class. In the case of soil, the reference class is characterized by no constraints to the development and growth of the forest species. The classes that are higher and lower than the reference classes have fewer and more restrictions, respectively, for the survival, growth and development of the forest species [30]. Thus, the soil diagnostic features maps for each forest species are classified into three classes: higher than the reference class (3), the reference class (2), and lower than the reference class (1) (Table 2).

2.4 Multicriteria Spatial Analysis Using AHP

The interpretative model of the methodological procedures (Fig. 5) followed three working lines: (i) interpolation and geoprocessing for determining slope; (ii) spatial analysis to determine the soil diagnostic features for the forest species; and (iii) stochastic modeling using OK to calculate the bioclimatic indices (I_c – continentality index; I_o – ombrothermic index and I_t – thermicity index).

Then, the bioclimatic indices (I_c, I_t and I_o) were classified for each species into three classes: higher than the reference (3); reference (2); lower than the reference (1) (Appendix 2). For each species a final bioclimatic index was obtained by combining the three bioclimatic indices maps (I_c, I_t and I_o) and reclassifying into the three classes assigning the most limiting classification (Table 2).

The slope map was produced by interpolation of the terrain elevation (altimetry) and classified into three classes according to its limitation for forest species afforestation (Table 2).

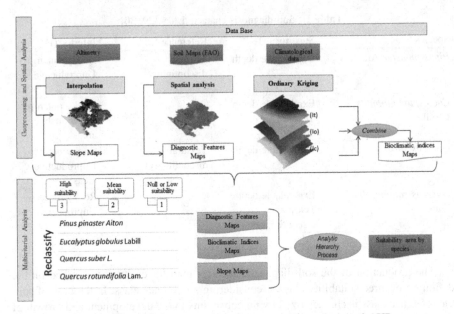

Fig. 5. Methodological procedures for geographic analysis and AHP

Table 2. Criteria for the factors

Criteria	Description	Classification
Slope (d)	$0 < d < 8\%$	3
	$8 < d < 15\%$	2
	$15 < d < 30\%$	2
	$d > 30\%$	1
Soil diagnostic features: Maritime pine, Eucalyptus, Cork oak and Holm oak	Higher than reference	3
	Reference	2
	Lower than reference	1
Bioclimatic indices: Maritime pine, Eucalyptus, Cork oak and Holm oak	Higher than reference	3
	Reference	2
	Lower than reference	1

Legend: 1 – Low and/or null suitability, 2 – Medium suitability and 3 – High suitability

The AHP was performed using the weights through pairwise comparisons of the relative importance between each pair of criteria (Table 3). After obtaining the weight values, the consistency of the matrix was verified based on the consistency ratio (CR) using a threshold value of 0.10. Thus, if CR < 0.10, it is deemed that the pairwise comparison matrix has acceptable consistency and the weight values calculated are valid and can be utilized.

Table 3. Comparison matrix for the factors

Criteria	Bioclimatic indices	Soil diagnostic features	Slope
Slope	1/7	1/5	1
Bioclimatic indices	1	3	7
Soil diagnostic features	1/3	1	5

3 Results

3.1 Bioclimatic Indices Maps

The analysis of the maps of the bioclimatic indices (I_c – continentality index; I_o – ombrothermic index and I_t – thermicity index; Fig. 6) showed a consistent zoning with the Portuguese Centro region.

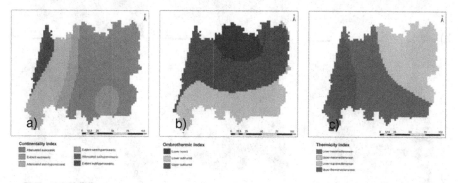

Fig. 6. Modeling (climatic normals 1981–2010): (a) I_c – continentality index; (b) I_o – ombrothermic index; (c) I_t – thermicity index

The contribution of the terrain elevation in calculating the indices proved unpromising since the correlation coefficients (r) were not very significant (Fig. 7). The continentality index shows a value of r of −58%. Therefore, in future works, methods of stochastic simulation using altitude as auxiliary variable will be used, to characterize the associated spatial uncertainty.

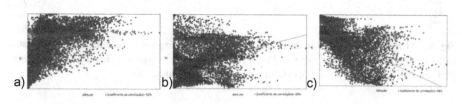

Fig. 7. Correlation coefficients: (a) I_c – continentality index; (b) I_o – ombrothermic index; (c) I_t – thermicity index

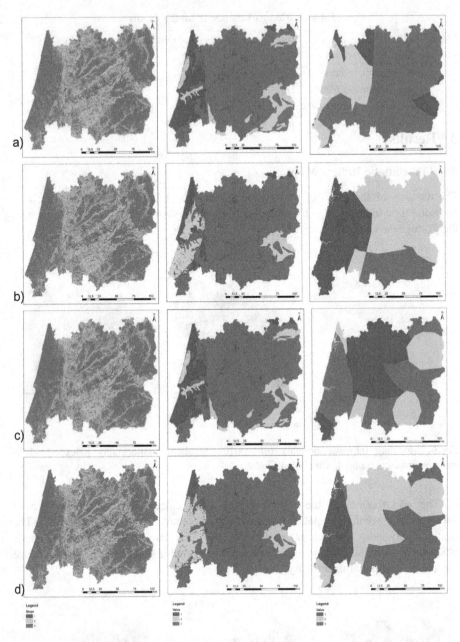

Fig. 8. AHP – input maps for each species (slope, soil diagnostic features and bioclimatic indices maps): (a) Maritime pine – *Pinus pinaster*; (b) Eucalyptus – *Eucalyptus globulus*; (c) Cork oak – *Quercus suber*; (d) Holm oak – *Quercus rotundifolia*

3.2   Species Biogeophysical Suitability Maps Using AHP

The AHP analysis in the studied species indicates that the bioclimatic influence is determinant in the development of these species, since its weight in the AHP analysis was 64.9%, followed by the soil diagnostic features (27.9%) (Table 3). The input maps for each species used to perform the AHP are shown in Fig. 8. The analysis of the consistency ratio (CR) of the AHP showed that there was consistency in the pairwise comparison matrix (Table 4), and thus, the weight values calculated (Table 3) could be considered valid.

Table 4. Criteria weights for the factors

Criteria	Eigenvector	Higher eigenvector	Weight (%)
Slope	−0.0325	0.1013	7.2
Soil diagnostic features	−0.0325	0.3928	27.9
Bioclimatic indices	3.065	0.914	64.9
Consistency ratio (RC) = 0.0625 < 0.1			

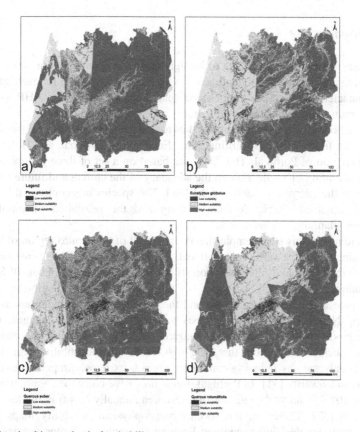

Fig. 9. Species biogeophysical suitability maps: (a) Maritime pine – *Pinus pinaster*; (b) Eucalyptus – *Eucalyptus globulus*; (c) Cork oak – *Quercus suber*; (d) Holm oak – *Quercus rotundifolia*

Table 5. Current species area (COS2010) by suitability class (%)

Species	Suitability class		
	1	2	3
Pinus pinaster Ait.	0.7%	23.7%	75.6%
Eucalyptus globulus Labill.		61.9%	38.1%
Quercus suber L.		6.1%	93.9%
Quercus rotundifolia Lam.		7.9%	92.1%

The species biogeophysical suitability maps produced by the AHP allowed us to verify (Fig. 9) that the current native oaks distributions (Table 5) were mainly in high suitability class for two species (Cork oak – 93.9%; Holm oak – 92.1%) followed by Maritime pine (75.6%). Conversely, the current eucalyptus distribution is mainly in medium suitability class (61.9%) (Table 5).

Moreover, when comparing these species biogeophysical suitability maps (Fig. 9) to the COS forest cover maps (Fig. 2), the potential that the Centro region of Portugal has for expanding the spread of native oaks can be seen.

4   Discussion

In this study, spatial modeling, due to its significance in spatial patterns forecast, was performed in a two-step spatial approach: 1. Ordinary kriging (OK) for each attribute's spatial characterization and 2. multicriteria spatial analysis using the AHP with three factors (terrain slope, soil diagnostic features and bioclimatic indices).

This methodological approach allowed us to assess the biogeophysical suitability of the four main forest species (Maritime pine, Eucalyptus, Cork oak and Holm oak) in the Centro region of Portugal. The AHP was based on a set of three factors and three criteria contributing to a reflection on the adequacy of the current and future forestland cover due to the carrying capacity of the land. The species biogeophysical suitability maps thus obtained enable decision making and the resolution of problems in afforestation planning.

The findings in this study emphasize the potential of the Centro region of Portugal for expanding the native oaks (e.g., Cork oak and Holm oak), which is consistent to the goals set in the National Strategy for Forests (NSF) [13, 14] and the Plans of Regional Forest Planning (PRFP) [15]. In fact, is key to reduce the current distribution areas of Maritime pine and Eucalyptus and expand the areas of native broadleaves as recommended by National Strategy for Forests to respond to climate changes, improve landscape biodiversity and mitigate fire hazards. Moreover, changing the current pattern of the species' distributions that have high levels of combustibility (e.g., Maritime pine and Eucalyptus) by reducing continuous areas is extremely important to decrease fire spread and severity [31]. In Portugal, forest fires have consumed approximately an average of 108,951 ha yr^{-1} (e.g., 3% of forest area annually burnt) in the last decades (1980–2010) [32]. Therefore, the species biogeophysical suitability maps may be important tools for decision support in landscape planning to define species priority afforestation areas. However, for regional and local applications, the input data spatial resolution must be improved to be valuable.

From the instrumental point of view, the use of this methodology may be of interest to stakeholders and other persons with roles in planning and land management. However, further investigation is needed to integrate the impact of climate change in forest species spatial modeling to assist in supporting future national strategies for forests.

Appendix 1

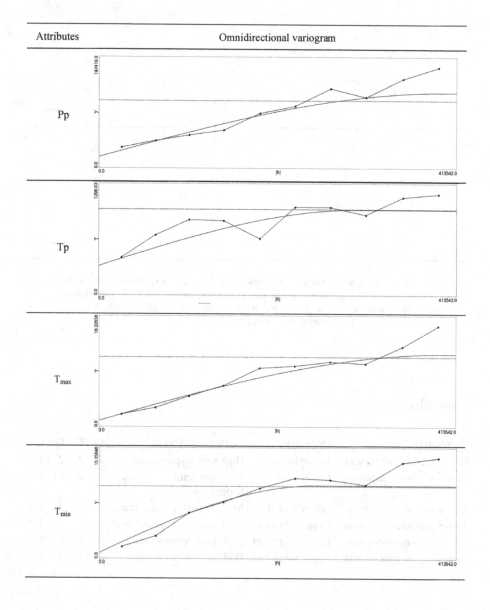

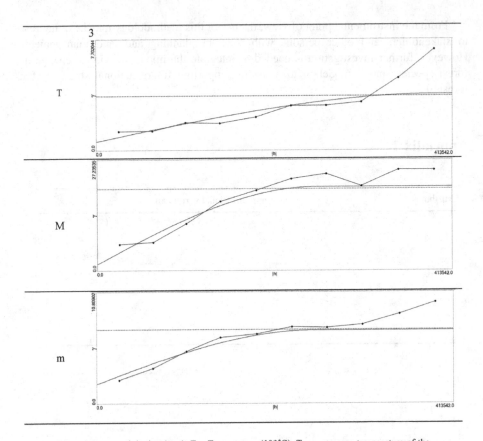

Legend: P_p – precipitation (mm), T_p –Temperature (10*°C), T_{max} – average temperature of the warmer month (°C), T_{min} – average temperature of the coldest month (°C), T – average medium monthly temperatures (°C), M - average maximum temperature of the coldest month (°C) and m – average minimum temperature of the coldest month (°C)

Appendix 2

Thermotype	Ombrotype	Continentality index	Pb	Ec	Qr	Qr
Lower mesomediterranean	Lower humid	High semi-hyperoceanic	1	2	2	1
Lower mesomediterranean	Lower humid	Moderate semi-hyperoceanic	1	2	2	1
Lower mesomediterranean	Lower humid	Moderate sub-hyperoceanic	1	2	2	2
Lower mesomediterranean	Upper subhumid	Moderate sub-hyperoceanic	1	1	3	2
Lower mesomediterranean	Upper subhumid	High semi-hyperoceanic	2	1	2	1
Lower mesomediterranean	Upper subhumid	High semi-hyperoceanic	2	1	2	1

(continued)

(*continued*)

Thermotype	Ombrotype	Continentality index	Pb	Ec	Qr	Qr
Lower mesomediterranean	Upper subhumid	Moderate semi-hyperoceanic	2	1	2	1
Lower mesomediterranean	Lower humid	High euoceanic	3	2	2	1
Lower mesomediterranean	Lower subhumid	High euoceanic	3	3	3	3
Lower mesomediterranean	Lower subhumid	Moderate euoceanic	3	3	3	2
Lower mesomediterranean	Lower subhumid	Moderate semi-hyperoceanic	3	2	2	2
Lower mesomediterranean	Upper subhumid	High euoceanic	3	2	2	1
Lower mesomediterranean	Upper subhumid	Moderate euoceanic	3	2	3	2
Upper mesomediterranean	Lower humid	Moderate semi-hyperoceanic	1	2	2	1
Upper mesomediterranean	Lower subhumid	Moderate euoceanic	1	2	3	3
Upper mesomediterranean	Lower humid	High euoceanic	3	2	2	1
Upper mesomediterranean	Lower subhumid	Moderate euoceanic	3	3	3	2
Upper mesomediterranean	Upper subhumid	High euoceanic	3	2	3	3
Upper mesomediterranean	Upper subhumid	Moderate euoceanic	3	3	3	2
Lower supramediterranean	Lower humid	High euoceanic	3	2	2	2
Lower supramediterranean	Upper subhumid	High euoceanic	3	2	2	2
Upper thermomediterranean	Upper subhumid	High sub-hyperoceanic	1	1	1	3
Upper thermomediterranean	Lower subhumid	High euoceanic	2	2	2	2
Upper thermomediterranean	Upper subhumid	High semi-hyperoceanic	2	1	1	3
Upper thermomediterranean	Upper subhumid	Moderate sub-hyperoceanic	2	1	1	3
Upper thermomediterranean	Lower subhumid	High semi-hyperoceanic	3	1	1	3
Upper thermomediterranean	Lower subhumid	Moderate semi-hyperoceanic	3	2	2	2

Legend: Pb – Maritime pine; Ec – Eucalyptus; Qs – Cork oak; Qr – Holm oak.

References

1. Guiomar, N., Fernandes, J.P., Neves, N.: Modelo de Análise Espacial para Avaliação do carácter Multifuncional do Espaço. In: Atas do III Congresso de Estudos Rurais (III CER), Faro, Universidade do Algarve, 1–3 November 2007, SPER. Évora (2007)
2. Collins, M.G., Steiner, F.R., Rushman, M.J.: Land-use suitability analysis in the United States: historical development and promising technological achievements. Environ. Manage. **28**(5), 611–621 (2001)
3. Malczewski, J.: GIS-based land-use suitability analysis: a critical overview. Prog. Plann. **62** (1), 3–65 (2004)

4. Parimala, M., Lopez, D.: Decision making in agriculture based on land suitability – spatial data analysis approach. J. Theor. Appl. Inf. Technol. **46**(1), 17–23 (2012)
5. Steiguer, J.E., Liberti, L., Schuler, A., Hansen, B.: Multi-Criteria Decision Models for Forestry and Natural. USDA Forest Service, Northeastern Research Station, pp. 8; 16–23 (2003)
6. Schmoldt, D.L., Mendosa, G.A., Kangas, J.: Past developments and future directions for the AHP in natural resources. In: Schmoldt, D.L., Kangas, J., Mendoza, G.A., Pesonen, M. (eds.) The Analytic Hierarchy Process in Natural Resource and Environmental Decision Making, pp. 289–305. Kluwer Academic Publications, Dordrecht (2001)
7. Reynolds, K.M., Hessburg, P.F.: Decision support for integrated landscape evaluation and restoration planning. For. Ecol. Manage. **207**, 263–278 (2005)
8. Saaty, T.L.: The Analytical Hierarchy Process: Planning, Priority Setting, Resource Allocation, 1st edn. McGraw-Hill, New York (1980)
9. Roy, B.: Multicriteria Methodology for Decision Aiding. Kluwer Academic, Dordrecht (1996)
10. Antunes, O.E.D.: Análise Multicritério em SIG para Determinação de um Índice Espacializado de Pressão Antrópica Litoral. Casos de Espinho, Caparica e Faro. Dissertação de Mestrado em Gestão do Território. Área de Especialização em Deteção Remota e Sistemas de Informação Geográfica. Universidade Nova de Lisboa. Faculdade de Ciências Sociais e Humanas, Lisboa (2012)
11. Kangas, J., Store, R.L., Leskinen, P., Mehtatalo, L.: Improving the quality of landscape ecological forest planning by utilizing advanced decision-support tools. For. Ecol. Manage. **132**, 157–171 (2000)
12. Quinta-Nova, L.C., Roque, N.: Agroflorestal suitability evaluation of a subregional area in Portugal using multicritéria spacial analysis. In: Internacional Congress of Landscape Ecology – Understanding Mediterranean Landscapes Human vs. Nature, 23–25 October, Antalaya, Turkey (2014)
13. DR: Resolução de Conselho de Ministros no. 114/2006. Estratégia Nacional para as Florestas. Diário da República, I Série, no. 179 de 15 de setembro (2006). https://dre.pt/application/file/539887. Accessed 9 Mar 2018
14. DR: Resolução de Conselho de Ministros no. 6-B/2015. Estratégia Nacional para as Florestas. Diário da República, I Série, no. 24 de 4 de fevereiro 2015 (2015). https://dre.pt/application/file/66432612. Accessed 9 Mar 2018
15. ICNF: Planos regionais de ordenamento florestal (2018). http://www2.icnf.pt/portal/florestas/profs. Accessed 9 Mar 2018
16. AFN: Inventário Florestal Nacional Portugal Continental. 5º Inventário Florestal Nacional 2005–2006. Relatório Final. Autoridade Florestal Nacional (2010). http://www.icnf.pt/portal/florestas/ifn/ifn5/relatorio-final-ifn5-florestat-1. Accessed May 2015
17. DGT: Especificações técnicas da Carta de Uso e Ocupação do Solo de Portugal Continental para 1995, 2007 e 2010. Relatório Técnico. Lisboa, Direção-Geral do Território (2016). http://www.dgterritorio.pt/cartografia_e_geodesia/cartografia/cartografia_tematica/cartografia_de_uso_e_ocupacao_do_solo__cos_clc_e_copernicus_/. Accessed 27 July 2017
18. DGT: Catálogo de serviços de dados geográficos. Lisboa, Direção Geral do Território (2017). http://mapas.dgterritorio.pt/geoportal/catalogo.html. Accessed 27 July 2017
19. Matheron, G.: La théorie des variables régionalisées, et ses applications. Centre Géostatistique et Morphologie Mathématique. Ecole Nationale Supérieure des Mines de Paris, Paris (1970)
20. Matheron, G.: The theory of regionalized variables and its applications. Les Cahiers du Centre de Morphologie Mathématique, no. 5, Ecole des Mines de Paris, 211 p. (1971)
21. Journel, A.G., Huijbregts, C.J.: Mining Geostatistics. Academic Press, London (1978)

22. Journel, A.G., Huijbregts, C.J.: Mining Geostatistics (1978). Gringarten and Deutsch
23. Goovaerts, P.: Geostatistics for Natural Resources Evaluation. University Press, New York, Oxford (1997)
24. Albuquerque, M.T.D., Antunes, I.M.H.R., Seco, M.F.M., Oliveira, S.F., Lobón, G.S.: Sequential gaussian simulation of uranium spatial distribution - a transboundary watershed case study. Procedia Earth and Planet. Sci. (2014). ISSN 1878-5220. https://doi.org/10.1016/j.proeps.2014.05.002
25. Isaaks, E.H., Srivastava, R.M.: An Introduction to Applied Geostatistics, p. 413. Oxford University Press, New York (1989)
26. Soares, A.: Geoestatística para as ciencias da terra e do ambiente, 206 pp. Editorial Press (2000)
27. Chica, M.: La Geoestadística como herramienta de análisis espacial de datos de inventario forestal. In: Actas de la I reunión de inventario y teledetección forestal. Cuad. Soc. Esp. Cienc. For., vol. 19, pp. 47–55 (2005)
28. Ferreira, A.G., et al.: Plano Específico de Ordenamento Florestal para o Alentejo. Universidade de Évora, Évora (2001)
29. Correia, A.V., Oliveira, A.V.: Principal Espécies Florestais com Interesse para Portugal – Zonas de influência atlântica. Estudos e Informação no. 322. Direção Geral de Florestas, Lisboa (2003)
30. Dias, S.S., Ferreira, A.G., Gonçalves, A.C.: Definição de zonas de aptidão para espécies florestais com base em características edafo-climáticas. Silva Lusit. **16**, 17–35 (2008)
31. Fernandes, P.M., Luz, A., Loureiro, C.: Changes in wildfire severity from maritime pine woodland to contiguous forest types in the mountains of northwestern Portugal. For. Ecol. Manage. **260**, 883–892 (2010). https://doi.org/10.1016/j.foreco.2010.06.008
32. ICNF: IFN6 – Áreas dos usos do solo e das espécies florestais de Portugal continental. Resultados preliminares. Instituto da Conservação da Natureza e das Florestas, Lisboa (2013). http://www.icnf.pt/portal/florestas/ifn/ifn6#dad. Accessed 29 July 2018

CAP 2020 Regionalization Design:
A Decision Support System

Dimitris Kremmydas[1]([⊠]), Michael Malliapis[1], Leyteris Nellas[1],
Apostolos Polymeros[3], Stelios Rozakis[2], and Kostas Tsiboukas[1]

[1] Department of Agricultural Economics & Rural Development,
Agricultural University of Athens, Iera Odos 75, 11855 Athens, Greece
{kremmydas, michael, enellas, tsiboukas}@aua.gr
[2] Department of Environmental Engineering, Technical University of Crete,
Chania, Greece
srozakis@isc.tuc.gr
[3] Directorate of Agricultural Extension, Greek Ministry of Agriculture,
Athens, Greece
apolymeros@minagric.gr

Abstract. The latest Common Agricultural Policy reform provides national authorities with several implementation options for fine tuning individual goals. Among other, member states can opt for regionalization, i.e. vary the basic payment unit value between national agronomic or administrative regions that have been defined at the beginning of the programming period. We present a Decision support System that support national authorities to implement regionalization in a transparent way facilitating collaboration with different shareholders.

Keywords: Common Agricultural Policy · Decision Support System · Basic Payment Scheme

1 Introduction

Common Agricultural Policy (CAP) is the agricultural policy of the European Union (EU), introduced in 1962 and fully implemented in 1968. It is considered to be the first real EU common policy replacing all relevant national agricultural policies while since then numerous reforms have been applied (Table 1). For the last 20 years, CAP is absorbing more or less about 0,5%–0,6%[1] of the EU GDP and 50%–60%[2] of the EU budget annualy. Therefore CAP evaluation is a persisting issue in the Agricultural Economics field.

---

[1] "CAP expenditure and CAP reform path", accessed from http://ec.europa.eu/agriculture/cap-post-2013/graphs/graph2_en.pdf.

[2] "CAP expenditure in the total EU expenditure", accessed from http://ec.europa.eu/agriculture/cap-post-2013/graphs/graph1_en.pdf.

© Springer Nature Switzerland AG 2019
M. Salampasis and T. Bournaris (Eds.): HAICTA 2017, CCIS 953, pp. 84–96, 2019.
https://doi.org/10.1007/978-3-030-12998-9_6

Table 1. EU-CAP reform milestones

Year	Short description
1979	Overproduction problems. Measures are put in place to align production with market needs. Introduction of market quotas and expenditure ceiling
1992	"McSharry reform". The CAP shifts from market support to producer support. Introduction of direct aid payments, "set-aside" payments, measures to encourage retirement
1999	"Agenda 2000". Introduction of two Pillars, production support and rural development. Agri-environment schemes became compulsory
2003	"Midterm CAP reform". The link between subsidies and production is cut. Introduction of "Decoupled payments" and "Cross-compliance". "Multifunctionality of agriculture" notion
2006	Sugar regime reform
2008	"Health Check". Enforcement of the 2003 reform
2013	"2014–2020 CAP reform". Introduction of "national envelopes" for members states, i.e. flexibility in the budgeting and implementation of first pillar measurements. Introduction of "Basic Payment Scheme", "Green Payment", "Young Farmers Scheme" and "Redistributive Payment". Gradual abolition of "Historical model"

Compiled from:
a. "The Common Agricultural Policy: A story to be continued", European Commission, accessed from http://ec.europa.eu/agriculture/50-years-of-cap/files/history/history_book_lr_en.pdf
b. Pezaros (2000)
c. "Overview of CAP Reform 2014–2020", European Commission, accessed from http://ec.europa.eu/agriculture/policy-perspectives/policy-briefs/05_en.pdf

The new CAP design, acknowledging the wide diversity of agronomic production potential and climatic, environmental as well as socio-economic conditions and needs across the EU, offers implementation flexibility to member states. Indicatively, member states may: differentiate the basic payment per hectare according to administrative or agronomic criteria; choose from different options for internal convergence for payments per hectare until 2019; opt in for the right to use a redistributive payment for the first hectares; enable the "small farm scheme", where small farms receive an annual subsidy of 500€–1250€ with minimal administrative burden; preserve a limited amount for coupled payments; grant an additional payment for areas with natural constraints (as defined under Rural Development rules)[3].

The latest Common Agricultural Policy reform (CAP2020) provides national authorities with several implementation options for fine tuning individual goals. 30% of the national CAP funding is connected to the farmers' compliance to a predefined set of pro-environmental practices. Up to 5% can be devoted to farms of areas with natural constraints, up to 13% to coupled payments, up to 10% to small farmers' scheme, up to 2% to new farmers' scheme and up to 3% to the national rights stock. The rest, called

---

[3] Compiled from European Commission MEMO, "CAP Reform – an explanation of the main elements", accessed from http://europa.eu/rapid/press-release_MEMO-13-621_en.htm

basic payment scheme (BPS) is the main layer of income support (over 50% of the national budget), based on payment entitlements activated on eligible land and decoupled from production.

Within this scheme, among other options, Member States (MS) can opt to apply BPS in finer scale than the national level, termed hereafter as *regionalization*.

In the Direct Payments regulation (1307/2013), Article 23(1) notes

> *Member States may decide, by 1 August 2014, to apply the basic payment scheme at regional level. In such cases, they shall define the regions in accordance with objective and non-discriminatory criteria such as their agronomic and socio-economic characteristics, their regional agricultural potential, or their institutional or administrative structure.*

Thus, MS can differentiate the unit value of the basic payment (BP) on the basis of national, agronomic or administrative regions that have been defined at the beginning of the programming period. Policy assigned regionalization regions (RR) can coincide with administrative or geographic regions but can also be not related to them, such as the case of agronomic criteria where a region is defined on the basis of specific crop areas (e.g. arable or permanent crops). Hence, regionalization regions may represent a broader category than administrative or geographic regions and shall not be confused with them.

The only regulation guideline regarding regionalization is that it should be in accordance with objective and non-discriminatory criteria. Practically MS are totally free to draw the regions and allocate the BPS budget.

This flexibility provides to policy makers numerous different alternatives on how to form regions and allocate the budget. Additionally the fact that different stakeholders are affected in a distinct way, call for a transparent design process. Towards this end we propose a Decision support System (DSS) that will support national authorities to implement regionalization in a transparent way facilitating collaboration with different shareholders. In this paper we present its design overview and give a proof-of-concept implementation.

In Sect. 2, we provide details on the mathematical representation of modeling regionalization; in Sect. 3 we give a small review of the use of decision support systems in agricultural policy evaluation; in Sects. 4 and 5 we present the design and the implementation of the employed regionalization DSS.

2   Modeling CAP2020 Regionalization

There are three regionalization types, based on how regionalization regions (RR) are defined.

- RRs are administrative-based partitions (e.g. prefecture-based) or socio-economic related partitions (e.g. mountainous vs. non-mountainous areas). The distinctive feature in this case is that each farm is related with only one RR. The farm's basic payment unit value (BPUV) equals to the RR basic payment unit value that the farm belongs to (Eq. 1).

- RRs are agronomic based partitions (e.g. Arable vs. Tree crops). In this case farms can be related to more than one RR, e.g. half of farm area is connected to arable RR and the other half to tree RR. The farm's BPUV equals the average of each agronomic region (agronomic = crop) basic payment unit value weighted by the share of each crop area to total farm area in a reference year, as in Eq. 2.
- RR definition is a hybrid case of the previous two cases. For example when the RRs are mountainous vs. non-mountainous arable crops vs. non-mountainous permanent crops. Then the farm's BPUV is like the second case but the agronomic basic payment unit value can differ from one farm to another, as in Eq. 3.

Administrative-based regionalization

$$BP_f^F = BP_{r(f)}^R \quad \forall f \quad BP_r^R = BP_r^{BUDGET} / \sum_{f(r)} TL_f^E \tag{1}$$

Agronomic-based regionalization

$$BP_f^F = \frac{\sum_g \sum_{c(g)} \left(BP_g^R \cdot X_{f,c} \right)}{TL_f^E} \quad BP_g^R = BP_g^{BUDGET} / \sum_{c(g)} \sum_f X_{f,c} \tag{2}$$

Combined regionalization

$$BP_f^F = \frac{\sum_g \sum_{c(g)} \left(BP_{g,r}^R \cdot X_{f,c} \right)}{TL_f^E} \quad BP_{g,r}^R = BP_{g,r}^{BUDGET} / \sum_{c(g)} \sum_{f(r)} X_{f,c} \tag{3}$$

where

BP_f^F: Basic payment unit value applicable to farm-f (euro/ha)

BP_r^R: Basic payment unit value applicable to administrative region-r, where $r(f)$ is the region of farm-f) (euro/ha)

BP_r^{BUDGET}: The Basic Payment budget for region-r, where $f(r)$ is the set of farms that belong to region-r (euro)

$BP_{g,r}^R$: Basic payment unit value applicable to agronomic region-g under administrative region-g, where $c(g)$ is the crop-set related to g (euro/ha)

$BP_{g,r}^{BUDGET}$: The Basic Payment budget for agronomic region-g under administrative region-g, (euro)

TL_f^E: Total eligible land for farm-f (ha)

$X_{f,c}^B$: Area of crop-c in farm-f in the reference period (ha).

For an illustrative example regarding those three regionalization types, see Kremmydas et al. (2018).

Therefore the policy-makers options regarding regionalization can be decomposed to the following sequential decisions:

(a) the regionalization type, i.e. administrative, agronomic or hybrid
(b) the allocation of farms and/or crops to the corresponding RRs (defining $f(r)$ and $c(g)$ sets)
(c) the allocation of the total budget to the defined RRs (defining BP_r^{BUDGET}, BP_g^{BUDGET}, $BP_{g,r}^{BUDGET}$).

The DSS addresses those three phases, as described in Sect. 4.

3   Decision Support Systems and Agricultural Policy Evaluation

Decision Support System (DSS) is any kind of a computer program facilitating decision making process. It is an umbrella term that covers any computerized system that supports decision making in an organization. DSS enhances the capability of decision makers to take more accurate and on-time decisions. It has been acknowledged that decisions utilizing DSS can be made more quickly and accurately than unaided decisions (Djamasbi and Loiacono 2008; Todd and Benbasat 2000; Chan et al. 2017).

A properly designed DSS is an interactive software-based system intended to help decision makers compile useful information from a combination of raw data, documents, and personal knowledge, or business models to identify and solve problems and make decisions (Sprague 1980).

According to Power and Sharda (2007), there are five categories of DSS which can be recognized by identifying the dominant architectural component that provides the functionality for supporting decision-making (Power 2002). The five categories include model-driven DSS, as well as communications-driven, data-driven, document driven and knowledge-driven DSS. The architecture is most often comprised of three fundamental components: the database or knowledge base, the model (i.e., the decision context and user criteria) and the user interface. The database or knowledge base holds the data used by the model to derive its conclusions. The user interface is the way through which the user interacts with the DSS to provide the necessary inputs and pick the results.

Agricultural policy needs strategic decisions and requires DSS to evaluate and understand the outcome of each alternative for optimal decision-making. So, the domain is a privileged area for the technology of DSS. There are a lot of DSS covering several aspects of this area and some distinguished papers are mentioned below.

Manos et al. (2010) present a DSS for sustainable development and environmental protection of agricultural regions. The system aims at the optimization of the production plan of an agricultural region taking in account the available resources, the environmental parameters, and the vulnerability map of the region. In their paper, Borges et al. (2010) demonstrate the use of a model base approach to anticipate the impacts of changes in CAP and/or in prices on land use in rural areas (including forest land). In Louhichi et al. (2010) is presented a bio-economic farm model for different bio-physical and socio-economic contexts, facilitating the linking of micro and macro analysis. Model use is illustrated with an analysis of the impacts of the CAP reform of 2003 for arable and livestock farms in a context of market liberalization. Bournaris and Papathanasiou (2012), present a DSS for the planning of agricultural production in agricultural holdings or in agricultural areas. The system simulates different scenarios and policies and proposes alternative production plans. Finally, a paper of Rovaia et al. (2016) presents a comprehensive model for the governance of rural landscape and a first simplified application to a cultural landscape.

4   The CAP2020 Regionalization Decision Support System

National authorities have a great flexibility on how to draw regionalization regions and allocate budget. Consequently they can potentially pursue a wide range of objectives. This means that the required data in order to evaluate the objectives can only approximately be determined during the development of the DSS and very probably new data will be requested during the consultation with other stakeholders.

The DSS knowledge base currently contains data from the Greek Payments Authority on previous CAP regime; the current direct payment allocation per farm size and prefecture. However the database can easily be extended to contain other socio-economic data like the income indicators per farm size and farm activity from the national FADN database; the regional GDP per sector from the national statistical authorities; etc.

The DSS models the effects of the policy makers decisions regarding the three regionalization options (type, region definition, budget allocation) to the Single Farm Payment value for each farm, as described in Sect. 2. Output is provided in the basis of farm grouping of farm economic size and type of farming. Spatial output is also present, providing a visual representation of the effects n each prefecture. In any case the model can be extended to provide output for other measures that represent individual policy goals.

Overall, given an established strategic goal, the DSS provides a clear picture of how that goal is affected for any selected scenarios. The DSS usage is expected to be in an iterative mode: policy makers and stakeholders draw regions, try some budget allocations and observe the effects and then restart the process to fine tune policy results.

We distinguish two DSS use cases that correspond to the regionalization design decisions that are described in Sect. 2 and another one that extends the DSS with collaboration features.

4.1   Select Regionalization Type and Define Regions

Policy makers form a regionalization scenario, i.e. select regionalization type and define regions, by means of exploratory analysis. The definition of regions is based on some partition variables, e.g. the NUTS nomenclature, the altitude or some crop classification like arable vs. permanent crops. Thus the user selects the partition variables which identify the different regions. The user very probably will further consolidate those regions to more homogeneous ones. In order to do so, he will examine certain regions' property variables, e.g. the prevailed crop pattern, the importance of agriculture, the current single payment unit value, etc. He can thus refine initial region creation either manually or through a clustering tool that will suggest him the regions that are as homogeneous as possible. The activity diagram of this use case is provided in Fig. 1.

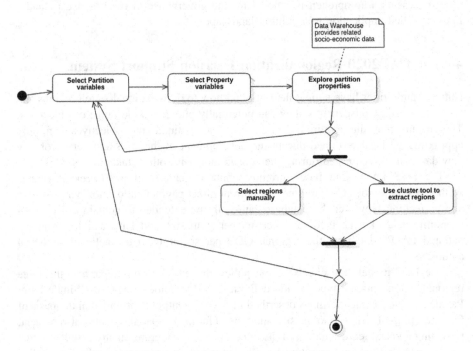

Fig. 1. Activity Diagram for exploratory extraction of regions

4.2 Budget Allocation Across Regionalization Regions

When the user has concluded to a region formation scenario he is ready to set budget allocation. This is expected to be a trial and error exercise where policy makers investigate the effects across different stakeholders for different allocations. Users can manually set the budget share or can use tools of predefined allocations, e.g. budget share proportional to the number of entitlements or to the gross value of direct payments in each region. Then the DSS engine will calculate the indicators and present them to the user. Based on the results the user can save the regionalization scenario and restart the process. The indicators of the scenario effect will span to different stakeholder classes, e.g. farms per NUTS administrative level or per type of farming or per farm income class. The activity diagram of this use case is provided in Fig. 2.

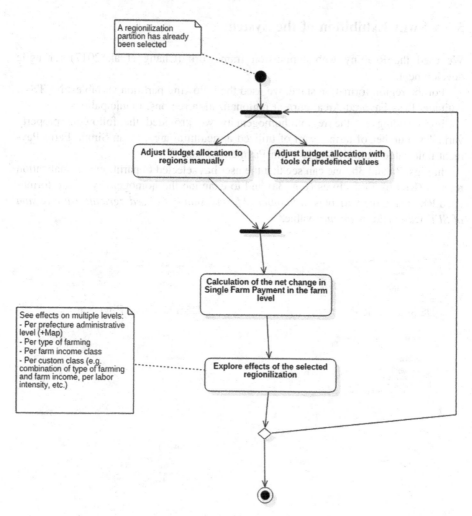

Fig. 2. Activity Diagram for exploring the effects of various budget allocations between regions

4.3   Dissemination and Collaboration

Dissemination and collaboration use case: Due to the different interests of stake-holders, collaboration is a very important aspect of the regionalization decision process and thus is incorporated into the DSS. When a user is satisfied with a scenario (re-gionalization region definition + budget allocation) he can save it and choose to share it, either with other users of the system or in public. A discussion channel, e.g. a forum thread, will be automatically created so that other users can comment and discuss scenarios. Users will also be able to load the scenarios of other users in order to adjust them to their point of view.

5   A Swift Exhibition of the System

We used the R-Shiny web application framework (Chang et al. 2017) for agile development.

For the region formation stage, we used the following partition variables: NUTS-3, Altitude, Less-Favored-Area, current regionalization regions, municipalities.

For deciding on the region homogeneity we provided the following property variables: number of farms, sum of utilized agricultural area, mean Single Farm Payment unit value, sum of Single Farm Payment value.

In Figs. 3a and 3b, one can see that the user has selected to partition regionalization regions (RR) by Prefectures (Fig. 3a) and to examine the homogeneity of the formulated RRs using the variables of *number of farms, sum of utilized agricultural rea, sum of SFP value* and *mean unit* value.

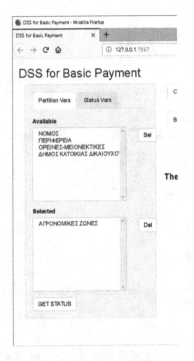
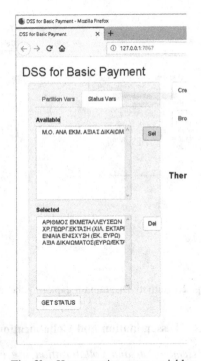

Fig. 3a. Partition variables   **Fig. 3b.** Homogeneity status variables

In Fig. 4a we show the status of the DSS when the user has clicked the STATUS button. The values of the status variables are shown grouped by the partition variables. The user can sort prefectures based on status variables and/or filter values. Furthermore on the clusters tab the user can perform a hierarchical or a k-means clustering in order effectively see the homogeneous RRs. In Fig. 4b, the user has selected to perform k-means cluster, eliciting 3 regions based on the number of farms contained in an RR and the mean SFP unit value. The DSS outputs the mean values of the clusters and also adds to CI.G column the number of the cluster that each RR belongs to (see Fig. 4c).

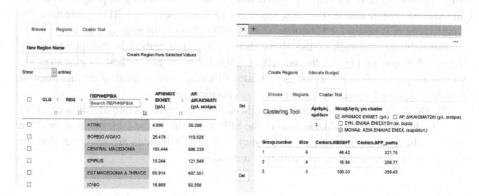

Fig. 4a. Values of status variables grouped by partition variables (STATUS button)

Fig. 4b. Clustering tool

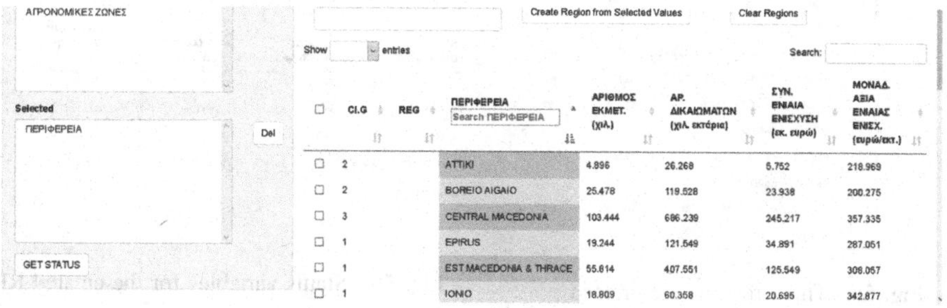

Fig. 4c. Transfer of cluster analysis results

After the user has a clear picture of the homogeneity of the potential RRs, he can further proceed on creating the real RRs. In Fig. 5a, the user has created three regions (Region 1, 2 and 3) after sorting by the CI.G column (the cluster number the region belongs to). Those RRs are a further grouping of the potential RRs. For instance Region 1 is composed of *NOTIO AGAIO, VOREIO AGAIO, ATTIKI, WESTERN MACEDONIA, EPIRUS*. The user can explore many further groupings since the DSS provides instantly their properties regarding the status variables. This is shown in Fig. 5b.

When the user has concluded to a certain RR formation he proceeds to the Budget allocation phase, as shown in Fig. 5c. There, apart from defining the total SFP budget (in this case 1159 mil. Euro), he allocates it to the different regions. It will be also be possible to define Convergence and Redistributive Payment scheme parameters; however this is still under development.

When the user click the *See Effects* button the DSS model is run and all relevant results are given back. They are given grouped by NUTS-3, by Prefecture, by economic size and by type of farming, so that the user can explore the effects on several dimensions (Fig. 6). Also there is a *Complete* option that provides a detailed grouping of all above dimensions. For instance, the user can explore the effects on KRITI prefecture for Arable type of farming for economic size of *2000–8000* economic size group.

Furthermore, for each of the above dimensions, information is also presented by means of maps. In Fig. 7a the net effect (mil. Euro) of the current Regionalization scenario for each NUTS-3 region is presented in a map. Users can also see this map for a certain type of farming or for a certain economic size.

Finally the distribution of the SFP unit value is given in a table and in a chart. In Fig. 7b, the user sees the distribution of the SFP unit value in the current situation (blue line) vs. the user created scenario (red line). Those distributions are also provided for the economic size and type of farming dimensions.

	□	Cl.G	REG	ΠΕΡΙΦΕΡΕΙΑ Search ΠΕΡΙΦΕΡΕΙΑ	ΑΡΙΘΜΟΣ ΕΚΜΕΤ. (χιλ.)	ΑΡ. ΔIF (χι.
Del						
	□	2	Region 1	NOTIO AIGAIO	16.938	73.4
	□	2	Region 1	BOREIO AIGAIO	25.478	119.
	□	2	Region 1	ATTIKI	4.896	26.2
	□	2	Region 1	WESTERN MACEDONIA	21.461	235.
	□	1	Region 1	EPIRUS	19.244	121.
	□	1	Region 2	EST MACEDONIA & THRACE	55.814	407.
	□	1	Region 2	WESTERN GREECE	68.7	366.
	□	1	Region 2	STEREA ELLADA	51.079	293.
	□	1	Region 2	THESSALIA	64.651	513.
	□	3	Region 3	PELOPONESE	89.54	320.
	□	1	Region 3	IONIO	18.809	60.3
	□	3	Region 2	CENTRAL MACEDONIA	103.444	686.
	□	3	Region 3	KRITI	108.011	436.

Fig. 5a. Three regions are created

Create Regions   Allocate Budget

Browse   Regions   Cluster Tool

Show 25 ⌄ entries   Search:

ΠΕΡΙΦΕΡΕΙΑ ΒΑΣΙΚΗΣ ΕΝΙΣΧ.	ΑΡΙΘΜΟΣ ΕΚΜΕΤ. (χιλ.)	ΑΡ. ΔΙΚΑΙΩΜΑΤΩΝ (χιλ. εκτάρια)	ΣΥΝ. ΕΝΙΑΙΑ ΕΝΙΣΧΥΣΗ (εκ. ευρώ)	ΜΟΝΑΔ. ΕΝΙΣΧ. (
Region 1	87.017	576.3428	130.8351	227.0091
Region 2	343.868	2266.5583	759.0724	334.3009
Region 3	216.360	818.2015	294.9938	360.5393
ΠΕΡΙΦΕΡΕΙΑ ΒΑΣΙΚΗ	ΑΡΙΘΜΟΣ ΕΚΜΕΤ	ΑΡ. ΔΙΚΑΙΩΜΑΤΩΝ (χιλ.	ΣΥΝ. ΕΝΙΑΙΑ ΕΝΙΣΧΥΣ	ΜΟΝΑΔ

Showing 1 to 3 of 3 entries   Previous

Fig. 5b. Status variables for the created RRs

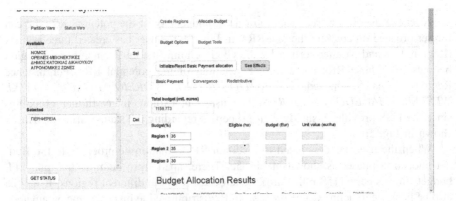

Fig. 5c. Budget allocation panel

NOMOS	#EKM.	ΠΑΛΙΑ ΣΥΝ. ΕΝΙΑΙΑ ΕΝΙΣΧΥΣΗ (εκ. ευρώ)	ΝΕΑ ΣΥΝ. ΕΝΙΑΙΑ ΕΝΙΣΧΥΣΗ (εκ. ευρώ)	ΔΙΑΦΟΡΑ ΝΕΑΣ - ΠΑΛΙΑΣ (εκ. ευρώ)	ΔΙΑΦΟΡΑ ΝΕΑΣ - ΠΑΛΙΑΣ (%)
AITNIA	27659	61.607800	29.7427785	-31.86502153	-0.517223817
ACHAIA	17131	27.829906	16.2958875	-11.53402026	-0.414446946
HLEIA	23916	30.822798	19.5840548	-11.23874277	-0.364624358
IMATHIA	12413	23.076123	9.8083265	-13.26779656	-0.574967783
THESSALON	18268	49.920239	26.2747482	-23.64549038	-0.473665413
PELLA	17086	33.525315	15.1370477	-18.38826717	-0.548489022
SERRES	22953	61.373779	28.8470720	-32.52670680	-0.529977254
XALKIDIK	11106	20.855646	13.9335766	-6.92206903	-0.331903847
PIERIA	10599	23.997346	9.4827406	-14.51460545	-0.604842112
KILKIS	11087	32.468705	19.4158882	-13.05281714	-0.402012245

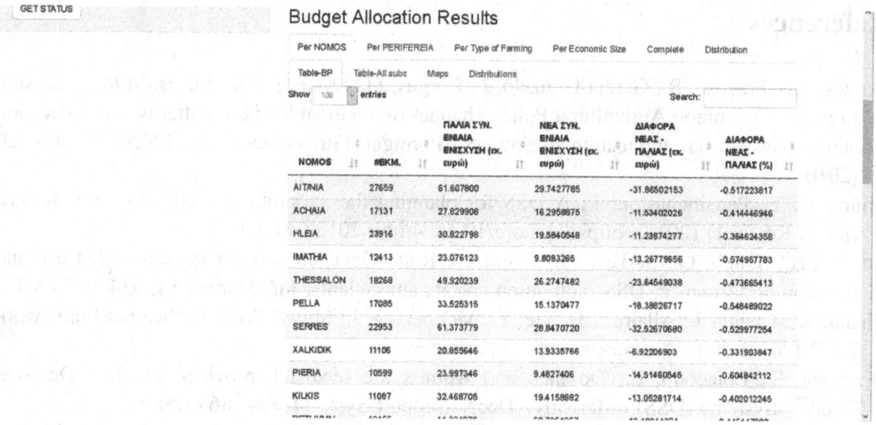

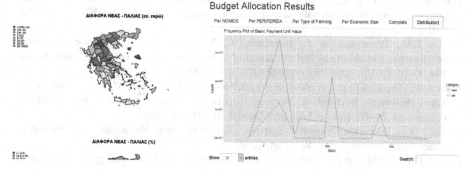

Fig. 6. Budget allocation results

Fig. 7a. Three regions are created

Fig. 7b. Status variables for the created RRs (Color figure online)

6 Conclusions

The latest Common Agricultural Policy reform (CAP2020) provides national authorities with several implementation options for fine tuning individual goals. This creates the need for a transparent policy design process. Towards this end we presented a DSS that support regionalization design in a transparent way facilitating collaboration with different shareholders, in three distinct steps: selection of regionalization type and definition of regions; budget allocation across regionalization regions; dissemination and collaboration between stakeholders.

In the future we plan to extend the DSS database with socio-economic data. Furthermore a mathematical programming farm model will be incorporated so that the adaptation of farms to selected policy scenarios can be evaluated. Finally a pilot implementation with selected stakeholders is also planned.

References

Borges, P.J., Fragoso, R., Garcia-Gonzalo, J., Borges, J.G., Marques, S., Lucas, M.R.: Assessing impacts of Common Agricultural Policy changes on regional land use patterns with a decision support system: an application in Southern Portugal. For. Policy Econ. **12**(2010), 111–120 (2010)

Bournaris, T., Papathanasiou, J.: A DSS for planning the agricultural production. Int. J. Bus. Innov. Res. **6**(1) (2012). https://doi.org/10.1504/ijbir.2012.044259

Chan, S.H., Songb, Q., Sarkerc, S., Plumleed, R.D.: Decision support system (DSS) use and decision performance: DSS motivation and its antecedents. Inf. Manag. **54**, 934–947 (2017)

Chang, W., Cheng, J., Allaire, J.J., Xie, Y., McPherson, J.: Shiny: Web Application Framework for R (2017). https://cran.r-project.org/package=shin

Djamasbi, S., Loiacono, E.: Do men and women use feedback provided by their Decision Support Systems (DSS) differently? Decis. Support Syst. **44**, 854–869 (2008)

Kremmydas, D., Kampas, A., Rozakis, S., Tsiboukas, K., Vlahos, G.: CAP regionalization scheme in Greece: a rapid policy assessment method. In: 162nd EAAE Seminar, 26–27 April 2018, Budapest, Hungary (2018)

Louhichi, K., et al.: FSSIM, a bio-economic farm model for simulating the response of EU farming systems to agricultural and environmental policies. Agric. Syst. **103**(2010), 585–597 (2010)

Manos, B.D., Papathanasiou, J., Bournaris, T., Voudouris, K.: A DSS for sustainable development and environmental protection of agricultural regions. Environ. Monit. Assess. **164**, 43–52 (2010). https://doi.org/10.1007/s10661-009-0873-1

Pezaros, P.: The C.A.P. in the pliers of the multilateral trading system: origins, evolution and future challenges. In: Bilal, S., Pezaros, P. (eds.) Negotiating the Future of Agricultural Policies, pp. 51–80. Kluwer Law International, The Hague (2000)

Power, D.J.: Decision Support Systems: Concepts and Resources for Managers. Greenwood/Quorum Books, Westport (2002)

Power, D.J., Sharda, R.: Model-driven decision support systems: concepts and research directions. Decis. Support Syst. **43**, 1044–1061 (2007)

Rovaia, M., Andreolia, M., Gorellib, S., Jussila, H.: A DSS model for the governance of sustainable rural landscape: a first application to the cultural landscape of Orcia Valley (Tuscany, Italy). Land Use Policy **56**, 217–237 (2016)

Sprague, R.: A framework for the development of decision support systems. MIS Q. **4**(4), 1–25 (1980)

Todd, P., Benbasat, I.: The impact of information technology on decision making: a cognitive perspective. In: Framing the Domains of IT Management, pp. 1–14 (2000)

Strategic Decision Making and Information Management in the Agrifood Sector

Maria Kamariotou[⊠], Fotis Kitsios, Michael Madas, Vicky Manthou, and Maro Vlachopoulou

Department of Applied Informatics, University of Macedonia, Thessaloniki, Greece
mkamariotou@uom.edu.gr,
{kitsios,mmadas,manthou,mavla}@uom.gr

Abstract. In recent years, many economic, technological and societal changes have transformed the agrifood sector. Such transformations significantly influence the entire food processing chain which includes agricultural production, food processing and distribution of food to customers. As Supply Chain Management (SCM) emphasizes on seeing the whole supply chain as one system, Decision Support Systems (DSSs) are Information Systems that help managers in logistics to identify the most effective processes with the highest strategic impact on the logistics that have to be implemented. Managers try to deal with the current complex environment using the Strategic Information Systems Planning (SISP) process. The purpose of this chapter is to propose a strategic DSS model based on the strategic management process and the SISP process to provide a holistic approach to effective decision making in logistics in the agrifood sector. The proposed model is based on the strategic process of DSSs and it involves the phases which are based on the formulation of business and IT strategy.

Keywords: Strategic information systems planning · Strategic management · Logistics · Decision support systems · Business strategy · Agrifood

1 Introduction

During the last decade or so, scholars and practitioners have focused on the strategic role of logistics. The importance of logistics function is conceived in businesses that place special emphasis on customer service as the core value of their business model [21].

An effective and timely decision-making process is required because the business environment is getting more and more turbulent. The improvement of efficiency and the reduction of complexity are achieved using decision support technology. Many studies have focused on the efficiency of Decision Support Systems (DSSs) [2]. DSSs are Information Systems that help managers in logistics to identify the most effective processes that have to be implemented because of the objectives and business strategies with the highest either positive or negative impact on the logistics [21].

Findings from previous studies in this area examined the impact of Information Technology (IT) on the effectiveness of decision making. Especially, findings have

M. Salampasis and T. Bournaris (Eds.): HAICTA 2017, CCIS 953, pp. 97–109, 2019.
https://doi.org/10.1007/978-3-030-12998-9_7

presented the benefits of using computer-based systems to support decision makers in logistics, especially in transportation and warehousing [1, 27].

In recent years, many economic, technological and societal changes have transformed the agrifood sector. Such transformations significantly influence the entire food processing chain which includes agricultural production, food processing and distribution of food to customers. Innovation processes are significant for businesses in this sector and play a crucial role in increasing and sustaining their competitive advantage [4].

The development of technology and the use of computer networks have transformed the production processes, access, transformation and use of information in the agrifood distribution sector. The spreading of communication technologies provide easier access to knowledge, as well as, more effective sharing of information [34].

Although the fact that Small and Medium Enterprises (SMEs) are essential providers of economic growth of contemporary economies and have a key role to play particularly in rural economies, few studies have examined the innovation practices of SMEs in the agrifood sector [4]. The agrifood sector contributes significantly in the EU economy. Furthermore, the agrifood sector contributes to both economic output and employment [4, 11]. As the theory of Supply Chain Management (SCM) considers to seeing the whole supply chain as one system, previous researchers have focused mostly on how to increase the value of supply chains in the agrifood sector in developing countries [11]. Furthermore, theoretical studies examined the specific challenges of smallholder farmers in accessing global chains due to market constraints, deficient infrastructures and lack of resources [11].

The purpose of this chapter is to propose a strategic DSS model based on the strategic management process and the Strategic Information Systems Planning (SISP) process to provide a holistic approach to effective decision making in logistics in the agrifood sector.

The structure of this chapter is the following: A conceptual framework based on the literature review about strategic planning and DSS, as well as, strategy and DSS models in logistics are initially analysed in Sect. 2. In Sect. 3, the steps for a model linking the DSS and SISP process related to logistics in the agrifood sector are discussed, whereas the final section summarises the concluding remarks of the paper.

2 Strategic Management in Supply Chain

Academics and practitioners have recently payed attention on the strategic role of logistics. Businesses that are interested in customer service as the value core of their business focus on the strategic role of logistics. Logistics is an integrated approach which combines the management of material and information flows and it is a significant function to satisfy customers' demand. As the logistics strategy identifies the selection of products, services and markets and sets the goals of the logistics system of the company, it should be aligned with business strategy [21]. The achievement of Sustainable Supply Chain Management is significant because it allows businesses to increase the effectiveness of supply chains and achieve their goals [32].

In strategic planning, the first step is the definition of the key goals for the company in order to compete in a turbulent environment. Therefore, in logistics strategic planning process, managers conduct a situational analysis which includes important strategic issues, such as the formulation of the vision for the supply chain, strategic goals and objectives for the improvement of the supply chain, as well as strategies and action plans for logistics operation. The purpose of this analysis is to identify the strengths, weaknesses, threats and opportunities by analysing both the logistic system and the business environment. Furthermore, this analysis helps in the definition of significant elements of logistics process, such as Information Systems (IS) used in supply chain, logistical structure and logistical costs, the implementation of logistics functions such as inventory management, materials handling and transportation and the organizational structure. The scanning of both the environment and business resources are necessary to identify the long-term direction for the logistics function [21].

Specifically, the vision is an important strategic element because it describes a desired future situation for the logistics organization. Furthermore, it presents the direction of the implementation of strategic objectives and the logistics activities. Therefore, it should be aligned with business vision. Logistics vision can be translated in specific performance measures and operating models such as inventory management, transportation, warehousing, order processing, customer service, IS and organization with the support of goals and strategies. These goals and strategies that regard the implementation of logistics function are aligned with other business functions, such as marketing and production, to increase business competitive advantage. Additionally, a detailed description of the operational and short-term activities that are defined in strategy formulation is taken into consideration during the development of action plans [21].

Strategic management execution supports organizations to scan the environment, which significantly influences the logistics function. Three phases are involved in the logistics strategic management process: (i) the analysis of the trends and the assessment of their impact and urgency, (ii) the evaluation of priorities and (iii) the implementation of the strategic plan [21].

The process of logistics strategic planning can form strategic decision outcomes or environmental forces. Changes in the logistics vision, goals and objectives of supply chain and strategies or action plans of logistics operation are possibly required. Therefore, strategic issues management process supports the periodic planning process. The process of strategic management combines the benefits of strategic planning and the flexibility of continuous strategic management. Additionally, it aligns the business's logistics processes with the capability to be strategically oriented and to react efficiently to the external and internal challenges [21].

The influence of innovation on business success in the agrifood sector seems to be very much comparable to that in other industries. Few decades ago, agrifood businesses tended to pay attention on cutting down production costs rather than increasing benefits to the final customers. Recently, due to globalization, pressures such as, nutritional quality and customers' demand for convenience, the need to ensure food safety, new opportunities offered by the biotechnology revolution, as well as variety and quality have changed attitudes. Consequently, the agrifood sector is increasingly oriented to develop products that meet customers' demand [9].

3 Decision Making Models in Logistics

Strategic decisions imply the design of a distribution/logistics network is complex because it involves significant commitments in resources over several years. Strategic logistics planning, including required customer service levels, aims to minimize the inventory-related costs which are combined with producing and storing products from manufacturers to customers [27]. Therefore, the logistics strategy is required for achieving long-term competitive advantages in business, especially in a logistics distribution network which is a significant factor in transportation and inventory cost. Furthermore, it is important for achieving customer satisfaction regarding logistics response [17].

Previous surveys in this area examined the significance of IT to support decision makers to achieve more efficient decisions and to increase their effectiveness. Specifically, existing studies presented the benefits of using computer-based systems to support logistics management, especially in transportation and warehousing [17, 30, 33]. Limited surveys have been conducted in the areas of inventory and product forecasting [1, 27].

A DSS is defined as *"an interactive, flexible and adaptable Computer Based Information System which uses decision rules, models and model base as well as a database and the decision makers apply decisions in solving problems which would not be willing to manage visualization models per se"* [36].

Another definition is based on the view that a DSS is *"an interactive and adaptable Computer Based Information System which helps non-organized management problems"* [3, 26].

Table 1 summarizes different DSS and their functionalities in logistics. Then, the similarities among them are discussed in the next paragraphs. These findings are a basis for the suggested DSS model.

The first step in the strategic management process comprises the scanning of the external and internal environment. The second step involves the estimation of the effect and urgency of the issues, the evaluation of priorities for the previous problems and the identification of the type of response for these issues. Finally, the last step contains the planning of the required responses for the strategic issues. DSSs are used to define the impact of strategic decisions on the logistics and to identify the most effective processes to be performed in coordination with the goals and strategic plan with the highest either positive or negative effect on logistics [21].

Some basic features have to be considered for the development of the systems. DSS involve many basic components as follows. Firstly, the data component usually contains a Database Management System (DBMS). The DBMS involves modeling tools and general programming languages. Data used can either be internal or external, either cross-sectional data or time series. Organization's internal functions provide internal data as an input in the DBMS that concern resource allocation data, products and services prices, data related to costs such as payroll cost or cost per product and financial data. External data regard on competition market share, government arrangements and anything that comes from external sources such as market research, government agencies, the web. The data stored in the DSS database are used as input to

Table 1. DSS in logistics.

DSS	DSS Functionalities	Reference
DSS for operational and tactical decisions in logistics	Data used is related with products and services prices, resource and budget allocation, payroll cost, cost per product Simulation events such as demands, departures and arrivals of means of transportation at terminals and acquisitions and releases of resources by vehicles Identification of the performances of the systems Evaluation of the selected parameters which can improve the performance indices	[8]
DSS model for vehicle routing	Demand analysis Analysis of data (number of drivers, strength of vehicle, mileage per vehicle) Decision analysis for the transportation personnel requirements, vehicle demands, path choosing optimization and resource transportation information	[33]
Logistics distribution network	Preliminary analysis (information such as GMS locations, transportation costs of listed distribution centers and customers) Evaluation of the alternatives for the logistics distribution network Estimation of the delivery time, quality, unexpected demand Calculation of the transportation cost The implementation and feedback	[17]

the optimization processes associated with models. The DSS information is provided by other data files, which could be business' internal or external files. The next module is the model component, which includes a simulation model, a mathematical model as well as optimization algorithms to support the analysis of the impact of the selections on the system performances [8, 37]. Cyberphysical systems and service-oriented technology can be also used for data visualization in the logistics sector. These systems are useful because they provide real-time and multisource data [39, 42]. Precisely, several methods, models, theories, and algorithms are implemented to develop and analyze the alternative decisions in DSS. Examples of these techniques are the intelligent analysis of data, the simulated and fuzzy modeling, the use of genetic algorithms and neural networks, the decision-making theory and fuzzy theory [20]. As logistics are characterized by a high level of automatization, interdisciplinarity and the need of flexible processes, companies have to integrate the heterogeneous systems and technologies in order to reach competitive production. This can be achieved with the use of smart technologies that integrate information level, material level and organization level with databases [40, 41].

A significant area of DSS in Logistics has been applied to perform an evaluation of supply chain. Current changes in global production had intensified supply chain complication and increased the argument that logistics strategies are significant aspects of business strategy. Recent business environment highlights the need for supplier relationship development to improve businesses sustainable management. The purpose of the supplier selection and assessment process is to limit risk and increase overall value to the customer. As supplier selection is considered to be a multiple criteria decision-making process, this process signifies an even more complicated problem. The decision-maker needs to analyze a large amount of data considering multiple factors to apply a more effective evaluation. Businesses have to pay attention to each factor to reduce the costs and to increase their profit, because of the increased globalization of trade and the expansion of competition. Businesses formulate strategies concerning the supplier selection process paying attention to the sustainability and environmental responsibility requirements, to deal with the higher level of competition. Several researchers argue that sustainability is a significant aspect which has to be considered by managers in supplier selection and performance evaluation [16].

Thus, the criteria taken into consideration for the supplier selection and assessment can be categorized as follows. The first category concerns quality, the second one is the price, the next category is related to the capability of supply/delivery, and the fourth type involves factors about the service. Another category sought by decision makers take into consideration for the supplier selection and assessment is the Environment Protection. In conclusion, management system, corporate social responsibility, and performance are the last categories [16].

4 Strategic DSS Model for Logistics in the Agrifood Sector

More specifically, Yoo and Digman (1987) [37] proposed a strategic DSS which includes four subsystems. In the first subsystem, named "Environmental Analysis Subsystem", decision makers gather information related with raw materials, inventory, economic conditions, production, industry, human resources, R & D, culture, marketing, technology, financial resources, market and government. This information is useful to forecast and analyze both the external and internal business environment. The staff, customers, managers, consultants as well as reports are the main sources of this information. In the second subsystem, named "Goal-setting Subsystem" a model base which generates alternatives models is included. One or more of them are selected according to identified goals and objectives as well as business's mission and purpose. The Goal-setting subsystem produces results that should be used as an input as well as in the strategy operating subsystem. Additionally, the strategy operating subsystem uses the results of each phase of the strategic management process as an input for reparative actions and future effectiveness. The third subsystem named Decision Support Subsystem includes a DSS model base, application programs and a DSS database which maintain the flow of information within the system. This subsystem uses files on various transactions and files of historical, managerial and environmental data as an input for the DSS database. The DSS model base includes models which are useful for the solution of strategic problems. In the fourth subsystem named "Strategy

Operating Subsystem", the decision maker identifies, evaluates and selects alternative strategies. Then, the selected strategy is implemented and evaluated based on information provided by the Decision Support Subsystem. This subsystem maintains each phase of strategic management process as it has been previously presented. Table 2 summarizes the functionalities of each subsystem.

Table 2. DSS model for strategic management

Subsystems	Functionalities
Environmental Analysis Subsystem	Gathering information related to raw materials, inventory, economic conditions, production, industry, human resources, R & D, culture, marketing, technology, financial resources, market and government. This information is useful to forecast and analyze both the external and internal business environment
Goal-setting Subsystem	Generating alternative models Assessment of alternatives
Decision Support Subsystem	DSS model base, application programs and a DSS database
Strategy Operating Subsystem	Strategy execution

Adapted from: Yoo and Digman (1987) [37]

The suggested model that is based on the previous ones includes four categories of subsystems, named; Situation Analysis Subsystem, Strategic Awareness Subsystem, Decision Support Subsystem and SISP Subsystem (Fig. 1).

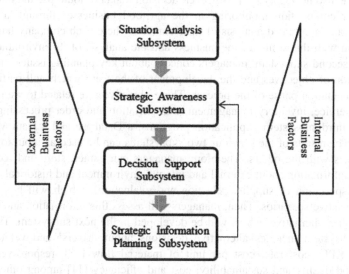

Fig. 1. Strategic DSS Framework for Logistics in the Agrifood Sector

As the agrifood sector can rely on the principles of innovation management, developed in high-tech sectors [9], the proposed framework (Fig. 1) is based on previous SDSS and combines the phases of SISP process in order to suggest a completed model for decision makers in logistics in the agrifood sector.

The first subsystem includes the identification of the problem, for the business to make the appropriate decisions. A situation analysis is conducted in order to analyze the existing business environment. Moreover, decision makers analyze the current external IT and business environment to determine new trends in IT. Regarding the internal environment, managers analyze strengths and weaknesses concerning economic conditions, logistical structure and logistical costs, inventory management, transportation, warehousing, IS and materials handling.

The determination of threats and opportunities in the business environment is important for the sustainable competitiveness and performance of every organization. It becomes even more important in the agrifood sector because companies are highly interdependent. The awareness of developments in competitors, markets, business partners and products is considered a significant factor in firm performance success for businesses. The analysis of the information needs requires a systematic scanning and a linkage with the needs of network companies [10]. In the agrifood sector, innovation increases organisational success, firm performance and the sustainable competitive advantage of companies. It is often driven by pressure from the external environment, and especially from resource scarcity, competition, customer demand, deregulation and isomorphism [4].

Information about distribution channels, economic situation of suppliers, relation demands to product characteristics, market segments where competitors are active and buying power, and quality of suppliers are required [10, 23]. Additionally, data such as food production, rural economy, healthy eating and consumer values and the environment are also necessary [35]. However, decision makers should use the information sources for competition monitoring in the agrifood businesses through a focused, systematic and automated analysis of their content, where each company has to offer information with the results of the business and the analysis of its environment [10].

In the second subsystem, managers concern about key planning issues such as the identification of objectives and the development of the team which will participate in the implementation phase of the process. These objectives are related to warehousing, customer service, inventory management, transportation and order processing.

In the third subsystem, Application programs, a Database and a Data Model are included. The results of the previous two subsystems can be used as input to the DSS that interacts with the others. Therefore, managers can gather, store and reclaim the necessary information about external and internal environment and historical data (e.g. about transportation or supplier selection and evaluation), which will help them to create alternative scenarios. Then, managers will assess this information and they will select the best alternative, which will be developed in the next subsystem. The output of this subsystem includes alternative decisions about drivers' and vehicle transportation, KPIs, cost rate, cost per unit of material flow [38], responsiveness and agility, food quality and sustainability, cost and efficiency [11] among other factors. Data can be stored for further working out and sensitivity analysis. The user interface helps decision maker with this process by providing a set of menus and question/

answer dialogues [38]. Alternative solutions are developed through mathematical models according to the problem that has been determined. Furthermore, the models are created to analyse the alternatives. Next, the selection of the most suitable alternative follows. The analysis of alternative decisions in DSS is based on several methods, models, theories and algorithms. Examples of these techniques are the intelligent analysis of data and the fuzzy theory.

In the last subsystem, the identification of important IT goals and objectives for implementation are applied. Also, this subsystem includes the evaluation of goals and the execution of the technological strategy. Then, the definition of new IT architectures, processes, projects and the priorities over them are developed. Finally, activities concerning changes in management process, such as the implementation of the opportunities, the goals, the plans and the new processes, the action plan, its evaluation and control are implemented [5–7, 12–19, 22, 24, 25, 28, 29]. Results from this subsystem should give feedback into the Strategic Awareness Subsystem as well as each phase in the Strategy Information Planning Subsystem for corrective action and future effectiveness [37]. Table 3 summarizes the functionalities of each subsystem of the suggested model.

Table 3. SDSS functionalities for Logistics in the agrifood sector

Subsystems	Functionalities
Situation Analysis Subsystem	Identification of the problem
	Analysis of Information Systems (IS) used in supply chain, logistical structure and logistical costs, the implementation of logistics functions such as inventory management, materials handling and transportation and the organizational structure
	Analysis of distribution channels, economic situation of suppliers, relation demands to product characteristics, market segments where competitors are active and buying power, and quality of suppliers, food production, rural economy, healthy eating and consumer values and the environment
Strategic Awareness Subsystem	Identification of objectives related to customer service, transportation, order processing, inventory management and warehousing
Decision Support Subsystem	DSS model base, application programs and DSS database
	Alternative decisions about drivers' and vehicle transportation, KPIs, cost rate, cost per unit of material flow, responsiveness and agility, cost and efficiency, food quality and sustainability
SISP Subsystem	Definition of new IT architectures, processes, projects and priorities
	Strategy execution
	Strategy evaluation

The proposed model has few advantages in comparison with the previous ones which have been presented in Table 1. Those models have been implemented for specific logistics functions such as distribution, vehicle routing and tactical decisions. The proposed framework (Fig. 1) is based on the strategic process of DSSs and it involves the phases which are based on the formulation of business and IT strategy, which are excluded from the previous models. The identification of objectives, the analysis of business and IT environment, the organization of planning team, the evaluation of opportunities, the improvement of business processes and the assessment of the process, are significant phases when managers formulate IT strategy. So, the proposed framework can be implemented by decision makers in each function of logistics in agrifood distribution sector.

The proposed model gives some benefits to managers in the agrifood sector. First, various strategic decision variables and steps can be considered comprehensively. Second, it can be considered as an effective strategic management system which makes easier the decision making process. Next, the system provides updated information to managers as they can scan the business and IT environment. So, the environmental uncertainty is minimized and company risk under dynamic change. Another benefit is that the evaluation process is implemented in order to examine whether the strategy is being implemented and whether the goals are being achieved. If not, corrective action may be necessary to change the implementation activities or even to change the strategy itself. Finally, the system includes various levels of managers, so their participation enhances the increased use of the system and the effectiveness in decision making.

5 Conclusions

The integration of strategic planning with DSS is an emerging research area. This contribution can significantly enhance the strategic decision making effectiveness. Careful planning is an important element to achieve the benefits of SDSS. Future studies in DSS research field and IS will urge new stimulations for successful SDSS developments [26].

The planning of DSSs depends on the needs for information of the existing organisational functions. In the future, DSSs will include tools based on environmental changes and business information needs, which will support decision makers so as to adapt their working practice for future demands [31].

The suggested model integrates SISP process and DSSs in logistics. The suggested framework contributes to the agrifood sector and increases the communication among producers and consumers, supporting a redistribution of value for primary producers. Moreover, if producers in the agrifood sector use the DSS, the latter can give customers insight into sourcing and production methods enable producers to evaluate their customer base and increase the competitive advantage by achieving supply chain visibility and transparency [35].

The contribution of this paper is twofold. Firstly, it helps academics as it bridges the gap in the literature regarding the integration between strategic planning processes and DSS. Second, it helps practitioners because it suggests a new model for decision makers with general applicability to various industries, including the agrifood sector.

Implications for future research are suggested based on the identification of the phases that support managers' decision making. Academics and practitioners in the logistics industry, such as decision makers should expand, optimize and test this model, to assess the efficiency of SISP phases in the process of decision making. As the model has not been tested yet, the results of an exploratory study will be summed up in an expanded conceptual model for future research.

References

1. Accorsi, R., Manzini, R., Maranesi, F.: A decision-support system for the design and management of warehousing systems. Comput. Ind. **65**(1), 175–186 (2014). https://doi.org/10.1016/j.compind.2013.08.007
2. Alalwan, J.A.: A taxonomy for decision support capabilities of enterprise content management systems. J. High Technol. Manag. Res. **24**(1), 10–17 (2013). https://doi.org/10.1016/j.hitech.2013.02.001
3. Alyoubi, B.A.: Decision support system and knowledge-based strategic management. Procedia Comput. Sci. **65**, 278–284 (2015). https://doi.org/10.1016/j.procs.2015.09.079
4. Baregheh, A., Rowley, J., Sambrook, S., Davies, D.: Innovation in food sector SMEs. J. Small Bus. Enterp. Dev. **19**(2), 300–321 (2012). https://doi.org/10.1108/14626001211223919
5. Brown, I.: Strategic information systems planning: comparing espoused beliefs with practice. In: Proceedings of 18th European Conference on Information Systems, pp. 1–12 (2010)
6. Brown, I.T.J.: Testing and extending theory in strategic information systems planning through literature analysis. Inf. Res. Manag. J. **17**(4), 20–48 (2004). https://doi.org/10.4018/irmj.2004100102
7. Dooley, L., O'Sullivan, D.: Decision support system for the management of systems change. Technovation **19**(8), 483–493 (1999). https://doi.org/10.1016/S0166-4972(99)00023-1
8. Fanti, M.P., Iacobellis, G., Ukovich, W., Boschian, V., Georgoulas, G., Stylios, C.: A simulation based Decision Support System for logistics management. J. Comput. Sci. **10**, 86–96 (2015). https://doi.org/10.1016/j.jocs.2014.10.003
9. Fortuin, F.T., Omta, S.W.F.: Innovation drivers and barriers in food processing. Br. Food J. **111**(8), 839–851 (2009). https://doi.org/10.1108/00070700910980955
10. Fritz, M.: Modeling external information needs of food business networks. In: Pardalos, P.M., Papajorgji, P.J. (eds.) Advances in Modeling Agricultural Systems, pp. 149–166. Springer, Boston (2009). https://doi.org/10.1007/978-0-387-75181-8_8
11. Gold, S., Kunz, N., Reiner, G.: Sustainable global agrifood supply chains: exploring the barriers. J. Ind. Ecol. **21**(2), 249–260 (2017). https://doi.org/10.1111/jiec.12440
12. Kamariotou, M., Kitsios, F.: Strategic information systems planning: SMEs performance outcomes. In: Proceedings of the 5th International Symposium and 27th National Conference on Operational Research, pp. 153–157 (2016)
13. Kamariotou, M., Kitsios, F.: Information systems phases and firm performance: a conceptual framework. In: Kavoura, A., Sakas, D.P., Tomaras, P. (eds.) Strategic Innovative Marketing. SPBE, pp. 553–560. Springer, Cham (2017). https://doi.org/10.1007/978-3-319-33865-1_67
14. Kamariotou, M., Kitsios, F., Madas, M., Manthou, V., Vlachopoulou, M.: Strategic decision support systems for logistics in the agrifood industry. In: Proceedings of the 8th International Conference on Information and Communication Technologies in Agriculture, Food and Environment, pp. 781–794 (2017)
15. Kamariotou, M., Kitsios, F.: Strategic information systems planning. In: Khosrow-Pour, M. (ed.) Encyclopedia of Information Science and Technology, 4th edn, pp. 912–922. IGI Global Publishing, Florida (2018). https://doi.org/10.4018/978-1-5225-2255-3.ch078

16. Karthik, B., Raut, R.D., Kamble, S.S., Kharat, M.G., Kamble, S.J.: Decision support system framework for performance based evaluation and ranking system of carry and forward agents. Strateg. Outsourcing Int. J. **8**(1), 23–52 (2015). https://doi.org/10.1108/SO-02-2015-0008

17. Kengpol, A.: Design of a decision support system to evaluate logistics distribution network in Greater Mekong Subregion Countries. Int. J. Prod. Econ. **115**(2), 388–399 (2008). https://doi.org/10.1016/j.ijpe.2007.10.025

18. Kitsios, F., Kamariotou, M.: Decision support systems and business strategy: a conceptual framework for strategic information systems planning. In: Proceedings of the 6th International Conference on IT Convergence and Security, pp. 149–153. IEEE (2016). https://doi.org/10.1109/icitcs.2016.7740323

19. Kitsios, F., Kamariotou, M.: Decision support systems and strategic information systems planning for strategy implementation. In: Kavoura, A., Sakas, D.P., Tomaras, P. (eds.) Strategic Innovative Marketing. SPBE, pp. 327–332. Springer, Cham (2017). https://doi.org/10.1007/978-3-319-56288-9_43

20. Kondratenko, Y.P., Klymenko, L.P., Sidenko, I.V.: Comparative analysis of evaluation algorithms for decision-making in transport logistics. In: Jamshidi, M., Kreinovich, V., Kacprzyk, J. (eds.) Advance Trends in Soft Computing. SFSC, vol. 312, pp. 203–217. Springer, Cham (2014). https://doi.org/10.1007/978-3-319-03674-8_20

21. Korpela, J., Tuominen, M.: A decision support system for strategic issues management of logistics. Int. J. Prod. Econ. **46**, 605–620 (1996). https://doi.org/10.1016/0925-5273(95)00178-6

22. Maharaj, S., Brown, I.: The impact of shared domain knowledge on strategic information systems planning and alignment: original research. S. Afr. J. Inf. Manag. **17**(1), 1–12 (2015). https://doi.org/10.4102/sajim.v17i1.608

23. Manthou, V., Vlachopoulou, M., Folinas, D.: Virtual e-Chain (VeC) model for supply chain collaboration. Int. J. Produ. Econ. **87**(3), 241–250 (2004). https://doi.org/10.1016/S0925-5273(03)00218-4

24. Mentzas, G.: Implementing an IS strategy- a team approach. Long Range Plan. **30**(1), 84–95 (1997). https://doi.org/10.1016/S0024-6301(96)00099-4

25. Mirchandani, D.A., Lederer, A.L.: "Less is More:" information systems planning in an uncertain environment. Inf. Syst. Manag. **29**(1), 13–25 (2014). https://doi.org/10.1080/10580530.2012.634293

26. Moormann, J., Lochte-Holtgreven, M.: An approach for an integrated DSS for strategic planning. Decis. Support Syst. **10**(4), 401–411 (1993). https://doi.org/10.1016/0167-9236(93)90070-J

27. Moynihan, G.P., Raj, P.S., Sterling, J.U., Nichols, W.G.: Decision support system for strategic logistics planning. Comput. Ind. **26**(1), 75–84 (1995). https://doi.org/10.1016/0166-3615(95)80007-7

28. Newkirk, H.E., Lederer, A.L.: The effectiveness of strategic information systems planning under environmental uncertainty. Inf. Manag. **43**(4), 481–501 (2006). https://doi.org/10.1016/j.im.2005.12.001

29. Newkirk, H.E., Lederer, A.L., Johnson, A.M.: Rapid business and IT change: drivers for strategic information systems planning? Eur. J. Inf. Syst. **17**(3), 198–218 (2008). https://doi.org/10.1057/ejis.2008.16

30. Salam, M.A., Khan, S.A.: Simulation based decision support system for optimization: a case of Thai logistics service provider. Ind. Manag. Data Syst. **116**(2), 236–254 (2016). https://doi.org/10.1108/IMDS-05-2015-0192

31. Salmela, H., Ruohonen, M.: Aligning DSS development with organization development. Eur. J. Oper. Res. **61**(1–2), 57–71 (1992). https://doi.org/10.1016/0377-2217(92)90268-E
32. Shi, P., Yan, B., Shi, S., Ke, C.: A decision support system to select suppliers for a sustainable supply chain based on a systematic DEA approach. Inf. Technol. Manag. **16**(1), 39–49 (2015). https://doi.org/10.1007/s10799-014-0193-1
33. Songbai, H., Yajun, W., Dianxiang, Y., Yaqing, A., Ke, Z.: The design and realization of vehicle transportation support DSS under contingency logistics. In: Proceedings of the 2nd International Conference on Advanced Computer Control, pp. 463–466 (2010). https://doi.org/10.1109/icacc.2010.5487100
34. Sturiale, L., Scuderi, A.: Information and Communication Technology (ICT) and adjustment of the marketing strategy. In: Proceedings of the Agrifood System HAICTA 2011, pp. 77–87 (2011)
35. Volpentesta, A.P., Della Gala, M.: Analyzing mobile services in alternative agrifood networks. In: Camarinha-Matos, L.M., Scherer, R.J. (eds.) PRO-VE 2013. IAICT, vol. 408, pp. 314–323. Springer, Heidelberg (2013). https://doi.org/10.1007/978-3-642-40543-3_34
36. Waxlax, J.: An object-oriented DSS for strategic management. Comput. Ind. Eng. **25**(1–4), 573–576 (1993). https://doi.org/10.1016/0360-8352(93)90347-Z
37. Yoo, S., Digman, L.A.: Decision support system: a new tool for strategic management. Long Range Plan. **20**(2), 114–124 (1987). https://doi.org/10.1016/0024-6301(87)90013-6
38. Zviran, M.: ISSPSS: a decision support system for information systems strategic planning. Inf. Manag. **19**(5), 345–359 (1990). https://doi.org/10.1016/0378-7206(90)90048-M
39. Zhang, Y., Guo, Z., Lv, J., Liu, Y.: A framework for smart production-logistics systems based on CPS and industrial IoT. IEEE Trans. Ind. Inf. **14**(9), 4019–4032 (2018). https://doi.org/10.1109/TII.2018.2845683
40. Forkel, E., Schumann, C.A.: Smart interoperable logistic environment innovation driver for modern technologies. In: Proceedings of the IEEE 2017 International Conference on Engineering, Technology and Innovation (ICE/ITMC), pp. 1162–1165 (2017)
41. Tu, M.K., Lim, M., Yang, M.F.: IoT-based production logistics and supply chain system– Part 2: IoT-based cyber-physical system: a framework and evaluation. Ind. Manag. Data Syst. **118**(1), 96–125 (2018). https://doi.org/10.1108/IMDS-11-2016-0504
42. Illés, B., Varga, A.K., Czap, L.: Logistics and Digitization. In: Jármai, K., Bolló, B. (eds.) VAE 2018. LNME, pp. 220–225. Springer, Cham (2018). https://doi.org/10.1007/978-3-319-75677-6_18

Water Data Sharing in Italy with SIGRIAN WebGIS Platform

Raffaella Zucaro[✉], Gianfranco Giannerini, Antonio Gerardo Pepe,
Fabrizio Luigi Tascone, and Marco Martello

CREA Council for Agricultural Research and Economics,
Research Centre for Agricultural Policies and Bioeconomy, Rome, Italy
sigrian@crea.gov.it

Abstract. SIGRIAN (National Information System for Agriculture Water Management) is a web GIS platform developed and managed by the Council for Agricultural Research and Economics, Centre for Politics and Bio economics (CREA-PB). This GEOdatabase is operating since 1998 and recently it has been established by the Italian Ministry of Agriculture (MIPAAF) as the reference repository for the irrigation data collection at national scale. SIGRIAN collects both geographical information concerning the hydraulic network schemes of the national water boards (Consortia and Water Associations) and information technically and economically related to the management of water resources in agriculture. SIGRIAN will be used as database for economic evaluations to address policy related to water resources in agriculture and to support the assessment of optimal water resource allocation.

Keywords: Irrigation · Water policy · Water Framework Directive (WFD) · Rural Development Program (RDP) · Web GIS · Geodatabase

1 Introduction

"We commit to approaches that improve sustainability of water use in food and agricultural production while ensuring food security and nutrition in accordance with our multilateral trade commitments". This obligation is taken from G20Agriculture Ministers' Action Plan 2017 entitled *Towards food and water security: fostering sustainability, advancing innovation* [1] and it shows the pressure on water Governance and water-related policies ensuring the sustainable use and management of water. The total irrigable area in EU-28 is circa 18.7 million ha, with 10.2 million ha actually irrigated and the amount of water used for irrigation estimated around 40 billion cubic meters. The highest volume of water used for irrigation in absolute terms was in Spain, where 16.7 billion m^3 is used, followed by Italy with 11.6 billion m^3 (Eurostat[1]). In these two Mediterranean countries the economic sustainability of farms is strongly dependent on irrigation, due to the scarce rainfalls and its uneven distribution across the year [2]. Water is critical for economy, food security, environment, and well-being of

---

[1] Eurostat 2016 http://ec.europa.eu/eurostat/statistics-explained/index.php/Agri-environmental_indicator_-_irrigation.

© Springer Nature Switzerland AG 2019
M. Salampasis and T. Bournaris (Eds.): HAICTA 2017, CCIS 953, pp. 110–117, 2019.
https://doi.org/10.1007/978-3-030-12998-9_8

citizens. At the same time, water scarcity, pollution of fresh water sources, and the effects of more frequent and intense floods and droughts can have severe societal and economic impacts.

The European Environment Agency (EEA) report on water clearly states the balance between water demand and availability has reached a critical level in many areas of Europe, the result of over-abstraction and prolonged periods of low rainfall or drought [12]. Overexploitation is not sustainable.

To prevent these risks, investment and innovative solutions are essential. In this context IT solutions play a crucial role in providing support for the optimal water allocation and water saving; they can also drive the water policies providing the rulers with the impact assessment. The assessment of policy options provides the water authorities with socio-economic and environmental analysis impacts for all options.

The 2000 Water Framework Directive (WFD) [3] and other water-related directives have contributed to improving water protection in the EU. WFD is widely accepted as the most substantial and ambitious piece of European environmental legislation to date. The purpose of the Directive was to establish a framework for the protection of European waters in order for Member States to reach "good status" objectives for water bodies throughout the EU. Pollution from urban, industrial and agricultural sources is subject to regulation. The implementation of WFD relies on Member States taking a range of cost-effective measures (PoMs) in a transparent and participatory way: the identification of management action (the distance between current and desired water body state) and the process used to monitor the effectiveness of PoMs (measures applied to reduce this distance) require a large amount of information.

Concerning the European Agricultural Fund for Rural Development (EAFRD) some ex-ante conditionalities (EACs) are set out in the Fund specific rules and reflect existing commitments or obligations that should be fulfilled as a general rule by programme adoption. In case applicable ex-ante conditionalities are not fulfilled (either completely or partially not-fulfilled), Member States need to indicate in their Programmes and Partnership Agreement the actions to be taken, the responsible bodies and a timetable to ensure their fulfillment. If the Commission concludes that the applicable EACs have not been fulfilled, then EACs dependent payments may be suspended. Compliance with EAC 5.2, on water pricing and cost recovery in the agriculture sector (implementation of WFD article 9) applies to investments in irrigation under Priority area 5 A (water efficiency).

In the context outlined above a robust monitoring infrastructure is crucial to manage the requirements and commitments set up by the EU water policies. SIGRIAN is at the heart of this data network.

The effective management of water is becoming more and more important as the world supply of clean, fresh water is steadily decreasing. United Nations [4] and European Commission [5] recognize ICT as an important enabler to improve the management of the valuable natural resource.

2 SIGRIAN Information Content

SIGRIAN (Fig. 1) is the reference database for the irrigation sector identified by the Italian Ministry of Agriculture. It is a Geographic Information System managed by the Council for Agricultural Research and Economics, Research Centre for Agricultural Policies and Bioeconomy (CREA-PB) and realized in collaboration with the National Water Boards and the Regions. It contains geographic and alphanumeric spatial data concerning irrigation features in collective irrigation areas (Irrigation and Land Reclamation Consortia, Consortia for land improvement, Irrigation associations etc.), such as:

- Administrative boundaries
- Irrigated and irrigable areas
- Irrigation supply
- Irrigation networks
- Hydrographic network
- Crop type
- Climatic characteristics

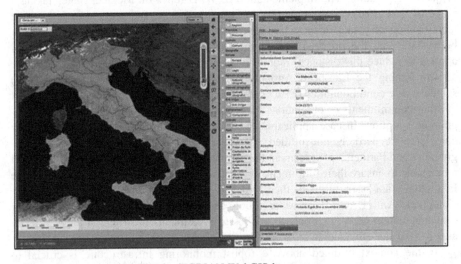

Fig. 1. SIGRIAN WebGIS home page

SIGRIAN is a repository and a catalogue which ensures integrity of data and information acquired and produced by the Italian irrigation sector. It allows the data exchange and sharing with appropriate users, including download of data reports and information for different user groups. It provides facts and figures about the Irrigation infrastructure compiled from a variety of authoritative sources, it provides information, diagrams and other pertinent information on hydraulic networks, irrigation schemes, reservoirs and gauges.

Environmental Information Systems (EIS), are understood as an organized set of resources (staff, data, procedures, hardware, software,...) for collecting, storing, processing data and for delivering information, knowledge, and digital products. In the context of water resources management, these information systems are sometimes also called hydrological information systems (HIS) [6–8]. Within this category SIGRIAN is a water information system (WIS) which integrates many sources of information related with irrigation water resources:

- Irrigation projects funded by the National Irrigation Infrastructure Plan
- Meteorological data from the National Agrometeorological Network (RAN)
- Data on natural disasters and related damage of municipal and provincial details coming from official acts of the Italian Ministry of Agriculture (MIPAAF)
- Crops and related irrigation volumes calculated with hydrological models such as Irriframe developed by ANBI [9]
- Estimated irrigation needs in areas covered by the FATIMA-SIRIUS[2] model based on satellite information [10]
- Irrigation volume withdrawn, used and returned both for collective irrigation and for self-provided irrigation (i.e. wells)
- Agronomic information from CAP payments applications (crops, fields size, irrigation etc.)

Many WIS are available in European countries and all over the world. The Water Information System for Europe called WISE[3] collects information on European water issues and it comprises a wide range of data and information gathered by EU institutions to serve several stakeholders. The WISE-WFD database contains data from River Basin Management Plans reported by EU Members States according to article 13 of the Water Framework Directive. WISE also provides guidelines and datasets for the water quantity and quality reporting from countries as part of implementation of EU directives. SIGRIAN is compliant with the EU WISE datasets.

AQUASTAT is FAO's global water information system, developed by the Land and Water Division[4]. It is the most quoted source on global water statistics. It collects, analyze and disseminate data and information by country on water resources, water uses, agricultural water management.

The California Irrigation Management Information System (CIMIS)[5], developed in 1982 by DWR and the University of California, manages a network of over 145 automated weather stations in California and was designed to assist irrigators in managing their water resources more efficiently.

Orange–Senqu water information System (wiS)[6] [11] promotes the equitable and sustainable development of the resources of the Orange-Senqu River (Botswana,

---

[2] FATIMA project: http://fatima-h2020.eu/.

[3] WISE: https://www.eea.europa.eu/data-and-maps/data/wise_wfd.

[4] ACQUASTAT FAO: http://www.fao.org/nr/water/aquastat/main/index.stm.

[5] CMIS: http://www.cimis.water.ca.gov/.

[6] wiS: http://wis.orasecom.org/.

Lesotho, Namibia and South Africa) and supports data and information sharing between the ORASECOM riparian States.

In comparison with other platforms SIGRIAN has its strong point in managing both strategic information about the irrigation networks (like WISE or ACQUASTAT) and operational seasonal data concerning water volumes, flows and water usage (like wiS or CIMIS). In this way SIGRIAN acts as a government data hub for shared data and collaborative monitoring work for source water protection and planning of the national irrigation infrastructure. The spatial and financial information collected about the publicly financed irrigation and drainage investment projects over the last 10 years support and assist practitioners to plan irrigation investment projects and programmes that will realize and sustain their full potential and the financing institutions involved in planning or appraising such projects.

The current SIGRIAN platform is the culmination of the experiences of studies and research carried out in the period 1994–1999 for the Italian regions of the south and starting from 2003 also in those of the North. These databases initially separated between the north and south of the country were merged in 2007 into a single platform that took the name of SIGRIAN.

3 Users and Platform Usage

SIGRIAN is fully web-based and the different stakeholders are able to edit and update the information operating online. It has been developed using open source software: PHP as programming language, PostgreSQL as GeoDB and Map Server as cartographic engine and it is hosted on a Windows server.

SIGRIAN is not a platform open to the public because most of the information has a strategic significance and includes financial aspects. The registered users are about 350 which are part of the decision makers and planners of the national irrigation sector:

- Ministry of agriculture MIPAAF
- Ministry of environment MATTM
- Ministry of Infrastructures and Transport MIT
- Regional administration
- Water management boards: Consortia and Irrigation associations
- River basin authorities

In the user group both the final users of the water resource like the water management boards of the agricultural sector and the authorities in charge of ruling and planning the resource allocation at regional and basin level together with the policies makers (Ministries) are represented. Data elaborations are provided on demand to other public bodies, universities and research centers.

In 2016 the number of logins per month was around 300 and the number of data report requests was ten per month. The DB size is currently around 700 Mb.

4 Details on the Information Content

SIGRIAN contains data concerning irrigation features in collective irrigation areas that are gathered by Water Management Boards (Consortia and Irrigation associations), with the support of National Association for Land Reclamation and Irrigation (ANBI), and Regions. Anyhow data integrated in SIGRIAN are validated by Regions and are available for all Italian institutions with administrative competence on water management.

Data collected are about administrative boundaries, personnel and concerned areas, irrigation supply, irrigation network characteristics, hydrographic network, crops. Data on private irrigation volumes at municipal and water body basis scale will be available by 2018. The ever-changing system allows the integration of other information useful for administrative and technical water management and for analysis, such as: financial and structural data on projects funded at National and Regional level, types of crops and irrigation water volumes used on collective irrigation areas (measured or estimated) by decision support models for irrigation water management applied by Consortia (mainly Irriframe-ANBI platform), irrigation water abstraction volumes (measured or estimated) and quantitative and qualitative status of water bodies (Ministry of the Environment).

Through this GEOdatabase, all stakeholders can easily access to a large amount of information, both technically and economically related to the water resource management in agriculture (Figs. 2 and 3). It will be used as a DSS (Decision Support System) platform for economic evaluations to address policy related to water resources in agriculture.

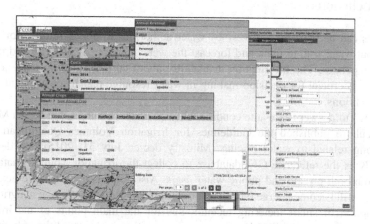

Fig. 2. Sample of financial information on collective irrigation in SIGRIAN

SIGRIAN is useful to assess the optimal allocation of water resources and is providing also support to the National Observatories of Water Uses (OWU). During 2016 the Italian Government identified measures to prevent and monitor the negative consequences of drought. According to Water Framework Directive (WFD), the OWUs

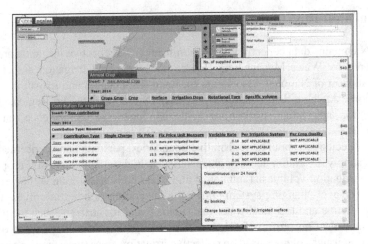

Fig. 3. Sample of district crops and related information on irrigation fees

were established. The OWUs were included among the measures provided in the River Basin Management Plans for each Italian River Basin District. Members of the OWU are the public water authorities.

SIGRIAN is also a key tool for data sharing to lead water-saving actions and economic evaluation of externalities (negative or positive) related to drainage and irrigation.

5   Conclusions

ICT tools can be used innovatively by water authorities to obtain information in real time about water use, to track and forecast the water resource availability and to drive the water polices. The information availability about current situation on a near real time basis is crucial for decision making in water resource management mainly under crisis conditions.

In 2015 to answer to ex-ante conditionality on water resources, the Italian Ministry of Agriculture published the Guidelines for Irrigation Volumes Quantification and Monitoring related to water pricing (Ministry decree July 31, 2015) that designate SIGRIAN as the reference GEOdatabase to collect the irrigation volumes data originated from both private and public water users. Also for this reason in the next years SIGRIAN will become a large repository of seasonal data on water usage in agriculture. The adoption of smart metering technologies for the main points of the irrigation network will provide SIGRIAN users with information in near real-time about water use, thus monitoring water wastefulness and having better control over the national water demand for irrigation.

Concerning the future development of the platform a new adaptive user interface will be released in the next year together with a group of REST calls for the system integration.

References

1. G20 Agriculture Ministers' Action Plan (2017) Towards food and water security: Fostering sustainability, advancing innovation in Berlin, 22 January 2017
2. Berbel Vecino, J., Gutiérrez Martín, C.: Sustainability of European irrigated agriculture under Water Framework Directive and Agenda 2000. WADI, European Commission, Luxembourg (2004)
3. Directive 2000/60/EC of the European Parliament and of the Council of 23 October 2000 establishing a framework for Community action in the field of water policy, OJ L 327, 22 December 2000
4. ITU-T Technology Watch: ICT as an Enabler for Smart Water Management. Report (2010)
5. EC DG Connect: ICT for water management roadmap. Report (2015)
6. Badjana, H., Zander, F., Kralisch, S., Helmschrot, J., Flügel, W.: An information system for integrated land and water resources management in the Kara river basin (Togo and Benin). Int. J. Database Manage. Syst. **7**(1), 15–27 (2015). https://doi.org/10.5121/ijdms.2015.7102
7. Briquet, J.-P.: Hydrological information systems and database management issues. In: 10th WHYCOS International Advisory Group, WMO, Geneva, Switzerland, 10–11 October 2013
8. Haklay, M.: From Environmental Information Systems to Environmental Informatics - Evolution and Meaning (CASA Working Paper 7). Centre for Advanced Spatial Analysis, University College London, London (1999)
9. Giannerini, G., Genovesi, R.: The water saving with Irriframe platform for thousands of Italian farms. J. Agric. Inform. **6**(4), 49–55 (2015). (ISSN 2061-862X)
10. Altobelli, F., et al.: Applications for precision agriculture: the Italian experience of SIRIUS project. In: Proceedings of 11th International Conference on Precision Agriculture, pp. 1–4 (2012)
11. The Orange–Senqu River Basin Infrastructure Catalogue ORASECOM report (2013) 001/2013
12. EEA Report No 2/2009: Water resources across Europe - confronting water scarcity and drought ISBN 978-92-9167-989-8, p. 5 (2009)

Towards the Commercialization of a Lab-on-a-Chip Device for Soil Nutrient Measurement

Georgios Kokkinis[1,2(✉)], Guenther Kriechhammer[1], Daniel Scheidl[1], Bianca Wilfling[1], and Martin Smolka[3]

[1] Pessl Instruments, Werksweg 107, 8160 Weiz, Austria
georgios.kokkinis@metos.at
[2] TU Wien, Gusshausstrasse 27-29, 1040 Vienna, Austria
[3] Joanneum Research FmbH, Franz-Pichler-Straße 30, 8160 Weiz, Austria

Abstract. In this paper, we present a soil nutrient sensor based on the capillary electrophoresis chip technology. As a product intended for commercial use in soil nutrient analysis, we focused on the analysis of $-NO_3$ and $-SO_4$. The sensing core of the device is the microfluidic chip. The design of chip, adapted to the needs of a portable handheld device, hinders the flow of sample in the detection area - due to non-planarity of instalment or pressure differences - via a narrow injection channel. A known issue, is the injection discrepancies caused by chip-to-chip variances and overall ion strength, thus turning quantitative analysis into a challenge. We overcame this by adopting bromide as an internal standard. In order to discriminate bromide from ubiquitous chloride in soil samples we used polyvinylpyrrolidone (PVP) as a separation additive in our background electrolyte. An in-house algorithm was developed for the identification of the measurement peaks, consisting of a baseline smoothing and subtraction along with an optimized quantification of the area under the peaks and thus the ion concentration. For the detection of the ion concentration on-chip electrodes were utilized for a capacitively coupled conductivity measurement. Tests were performed with soil sample extractions from different regions and the results were cross-referenced with an ion chromatographer. The sensor's response had to be corrected for different ions and it exhibited a second order polynomial response with an average absolute error of 5%.

Keywords: Lab-on-a-chip · Capillary electrophoresis · Microfluidics · Precision agriculture · Soil analysis · Nitrate sensor

1 Introduction

Fertilizers containing nitrate, phosphate and potassium are indispensable for modern agriculture and necessary to nourish the current world population. The calculated fertilizer demand for the year 2015 alone is around 186.6 million tons. This number combines the single amounts of N, P_2O_5 and K_2O and the annual demand is expected to grow beyond 199 million tons by 2019 [1].

© Springer Nature Switzerland AG 2019
M. Salampasis and T. Bournaris (Eds.): HAICTA 2017, CCIS 953, pp. 118–130, 2019.
https://doi.org/10.1007/978-3-030-12998-9_9

Although there is an undeniable need for fertilizers in industrial agriculture, their production as well as utilization has an enormous ecological and social impact. The use of fertilizers leads to eutrophication with all its known negative effects on affected ecosystems, such as reduction in biodiversity, habitat loss and acceleration of global warming via release of ammonia. Furthermore phosphate and potassium in fertilizers originate mainly from fossil deposits with an expected peak phosphorus estimated around 2030 [2]. To aggravate the ecological problems fertilizers are often overused, i.e. applied in quantities that don't increase yield any further while indeed increasing the negative impacts. According to recent EU estimates about 60% of applied fertilizers are in fact overuse and would therefore be dispensable. Farmers have a genuine interest to be as resource efficient as possible and would reduce the use of fertilizers on their own if only they had access to information about the nutrient concentration in their soil. This access suffers from often poor availability, high costs and long delays of established soil laboratories in most parts of the world [3–5].

Microfluidics originated in the junction of semiconductor manufacturing, life sciences, chemistry and nanotechnology in the late 80s of the last century. It has long gone beyond pure academia and found practical applications in ever more fields in medicine, industry and now finally agriculture. Sophisticated manufacturing has shrunk prices for lab-on-a-chip applications tremendously allowing for ever more applications in previously unthinkable areas [6, 7].

Capillary electrophoresis (CE) was developed in the 70s of the last century and has long been seen as a complementary method to ordinary chromatography and thus mainly used for niche applications in academia. The main reason for this neglect was due to the difficult method development, the low sensitivity and therefore poor reproducibility in its early days which rendered CE effectively a 2nd choice method for academic laboratories [8]. The implementation of electrochemical detection via contactless capacitively coupled conductivity detectors (C4D) [9], ever better optical sensors and the adoption of meaningful internal standards (ISTD) gradually overcame these limitations and first applications were seen in pharmaceutical industry mainly as a means of quality control [10]. With the advent of microfluidics CE finally moved into focus as it allows for easy automation and had its breakthrough with CE being massively implemented in DNA sequencers. For the same ease of automation CE has become popular in modern lab-on-a-chip (LOC) applications, which rely heavily on its robustness and relative low cost integration. As LOC is spread in ever more daily use scenarios so is CE and has thus finally reached everyday life [11].

The method itself is based on the fact that different ion species of a sample migrate with different velocities, at the presence of an electric field, when suspended in a background electrolyte. CE is performed as follows; the sample is, with different methods, introduced into a BGE filled capillary or microfluidic channel. Then high voltage (HV) is applied, through electrodes, at the ends of the channel so that an strong electric field is exerted on the different ion species of the sample. Cations and anions start to migrate towards the respective electric pole. During this migration and due to their different mobilities, the ion species start to separate. At the end of the channel a detector registers the separated ions which appear as peaks at the detector's output electric signal. The ion concentration is directly proportional to the area defined by the peak.

In this paper we present a novel lab-on-a-chip device which allows for fast and easy measurement of soil nutrients and does not require any advanced laboratory skills by the user. A highly streamlined procedure leaves taking samples and in-house extraction as only remaining requirement. The sample is subsequently inserted into the device and measured in an automated manner.

2   Materials and Methods

2.1   Chip Fabrication

The sensing core of the soil nutrient analysis device is the chip. It consists of the microfluidic part and the electrical part. The former has two branching channels. The separation and the injection channel. The separation channel has a rectangular cross-section of 300×50 µm and 81 mm length while the injection channel has a triangular cross-section with 50 µm depth and 10 µm width of its base. A pair of detection electrodes is used for implementing the capacitively coupled conductivity measurement (C4D) and interfacing the chip to the analog electronics of the device. The dimensions of the electrodes are 500×100 µm and are fabricated on the outer side of the channel. That way and by not being in contact with the buffer the electrodes are protected against corrosion [12].

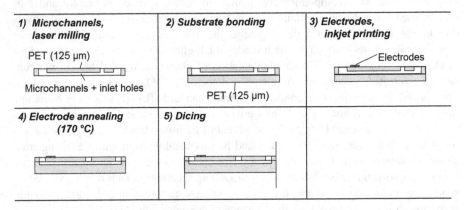

Fig. 1. The chip fabrication steps; (1) laser milling of a 125 µm thick PET foil, (2) thermo-compressive bonding, (3) inkjet printing of the electrodes on the outer part of the milled foil, for proximity to the liquid, (4) annealing of the electrodes, (5) final cutting of the chips out of the wafer with laser dicing.

For the fabrication of the chip two PET foils (Fig. 1), each 125 µm thick, are used due to the versatility and low cost of the polymer. Channels were carved out by laser milling resulting in a 50 µm depth with 10% surface roughness. The open side channel would theoretically allow for hydrostatic sample leakage. Due to the highly viscous nature of our buffer and the small cross-section of the channel, this did practically not occur.

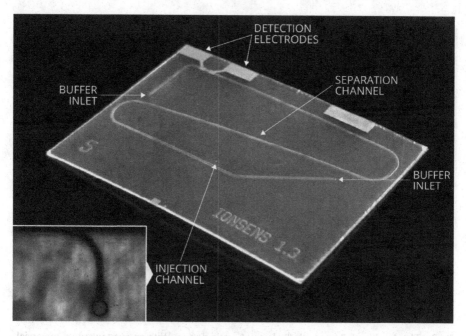

Fig. 2. The fabricated chip. In sight are the detection electrodes, the buffer inlet/outlet holes, the separation channel and the injection channel.

The structured and the non-processed PET foil were then thermocompressively bonded under vacuum. The electrodes were inkjet printed, on the outer side of the channel, after bonding. A fabricated chip is seen in Fig. 2. The chip was introduced in an interchangeable manner in the device containing the fluidic and electronic interfaces.

2.2 Device Production

The device (Fig. 3), intended for mass production consists of the following modules:

Electrical Interface. Coaxial probes were used for picking up the signal from the electrodes and transmitting it to the signal processing circuit. That way stray capacitances, capacitive coupling and electromagnetic interferences were diminished.

Fluidic Interface. The fluidic interface between the chip and the buffer and sample reservoirs, was crucial to the stability of the device as bubbles, nucleated at different points of the fluidic path and due to different reasons, were compromising the operation of the measurement setup (Fig. 4). The problem was adequately resolved by making the connections as short as possible like in Fig. 4.

Electronic Printed Circuit Board (PCB). There are two separate PCBs. One for analogue signal processing, USB interfacing and automation signals and one for providing the high voltage (HV) for the injection and separation of the ions. The signal processing circuit is described by [1].

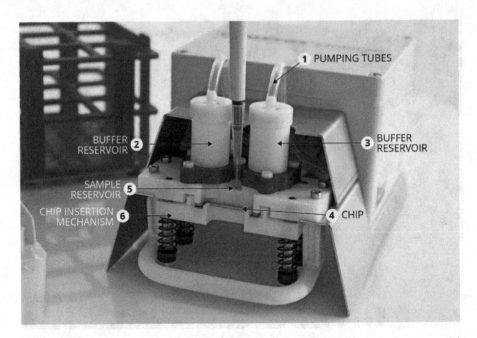

Fig. 3. The developed chip capillary electrophoresis device. With an eye towards commercialization, the design efforts have been focused on producibility and usability. In the photo can be seen: (1) the pumping tubes connected with a vacuum pump, (2), (3) Buffer reservoirs for the background electrolyte, (4) the microfluidic chip, (5) the sample reservoir where the soil extracted sample is pipetted, (6) the chip insertion mechanism; based on springs a force is exerted on the chip for keeping a firm contact with the fluidic and electric interface.

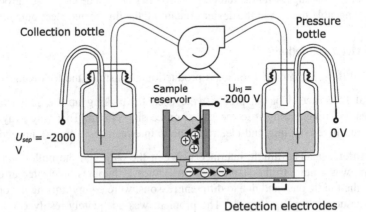

Fig. 4. Schematic of the measurement set up during the sample injection: a high potential difference U_{inj} is applied between pressure bottle and sample reservoir. This causes sample ions to pass the injection channel and to enter the separation channel. In the case depicted, the voltage pattern is suited for anion injection.

Fluidic Module. In order to design a device that allows for serial and automated measurements, it is important to provide the possibility of changing the BGE in the separation channel. This is done by pumping BGE between the two buffer reservoirs via pressure driven flow. The functionality of equalizing the pressure-between the reservoirs- after pumping and interchanging the flow direction is provided by two three-way valves.

2.3 Measurement Procedure

The measurement setup is seen in Fig. 4. The procedure follows the typical steps of a capillary electrophoresis measurement [13].

Injection. In CE attention must be given to the development of the appropriate injection strategy. In the proposed device we have developed a reproducible injection routine. Considerable designing effort has been put to the injection channel; a narrow cross-section poses high hydrodynamic flow resistance, such that there is no involuntary, pressure driven sample injection into the separation channel. Thus for the injection high voltage (HV) pulses were employed. The pulses were of 1500 V in amplitude, 1 s in duration with a 15% duty cycle. After optimizing between lower limit of detection (LOD) and separation ions (no overlapping peaks), 16 such pulses were employed for a reproducible and high resolution detection.

Separation. Once the sample was injected in the separation channel DC HV, 2000 V in amplitude was applied in electrodes in the inlet and outlet buffer reservoirs (Fig. 4). Both the length of the channel and the amplitude of the HV along with the BGE viscosity and the coordination effect of the PVP contribute to the adequate separation of the ions.

Detection. As already mentioned the detection cell comprises of two electrodes (one for the excitation and one for the detection) for the conductivity detection (C4D). The excitation was a 50 V_{pp}, 4 MHz sinusoidal signal and the detection signal was amplified by a transimpedance amplifier, then rectified by a full bridge precision rectifier and with a final amplification and smoothing step before the analogue to digital converter (ADC) [14].

2.4 Chemistry

Extraction. As the device is meant to be used for soil sample analysis an ion extraction protocol from the sample had to be employed. First a soil sample had to be acquired from the ground, from 0.5 m depth. Then it has to be sieved, all stones, root or any other material removed. Then sieved through a 2 mm mesh sieve. After sieving manually the soil had to be well mixed. 10 g of the sieved soil was mixed with 30 ml of extraction solution (5 mM Calciumlactate (Cacium L-lactate hydrate 1,0911 g/L)). A shaker was used for agitating the samples and allow for the best possible extraction within 30 min. The solution then is left to sediment for 15 min. 1 ml of the supernatant was the extracted sample.

Internal Standard. Due to the peculiarities of the electrokinetic injection, often is not possible to inject reproducible concentration of ions in the separation channel [15]. For that reason and for improving the overall accuracy of the system we resolved to the utilization of an internal standard. Internal standard is a substance of known concentration dissolved into the sample. This substance, an ion, will be present as a peak on the electropherogram. By relating an ion concentration to the area under a peak, we can directly relate each area to a concentration. That way the relative error was drastically diminished. The internal standard was utilized by suspending 1 ml of solution (300 µM Chloride + 500 µM Bromide (Potasiumchloride solid -2,924 g/L for a 40 mM Stocksolution- 7,5 µL in the Eppendorf vial + Bromide (basically Sodiumbromide) with the concentration of 12,52 mM Bromide) in an Eppendorf tube and heating it up to evaporate the water. The extracted sample was then pipetted into the same tube with the crystalized ISTD.

Background Electrolyte (BGE). As already mentioned, the ion separation takes place in a buffer solution, the background electrolyte. The synthesis of the BGE is the following: 100 mM MES & His + 15% PVP (19,520 g/L 2-(N-Morpholino) ethansulficacid; 15,516 g/L L-Histidin; 150 g/L Polyvinylpyrrolidone K15). PVP was added in order to increase the separation of the ions and the viscosity of the sample so that unintended sample leakage was inhibited. On the other hand, too viscous BGE is hard to pump and it decreases the conductivity. Low conductivity decreases the so called effect of Field Amplified Sample Stacking [15] and the concentration of the injected ions. Thus the concentration of PVP had to be optimized at 10%.

2.5 Data Processing

The data collected from the sensor are processed using an in-house developed algorithm, written in Python 3.6. It comprises several data preprocessing steps, peak detection, peak integration, calculation of component concentrations and calibration.

Preprocessing. Since the raw data are not regularly spaced, the first step is an interpolation to regular time steps of 0.1 s. Next, the baseline is fitted using the *asymmetric least square smoothing* algorithm (ALS) [16]. The baseline corrected data is then interpolated to timesteps of 0.02 s.

The last preprocessing step is a discrete wavelet transform smoothing as described by [17]. It was implemented using the python module *pywt*. The Symmlet 4 wavelet with a 4 level decomposition and the soft thresholding method yielded the best results.

Peak Detection. The peak detection uses the peak detection routine *peak_indexes* from the python module *peakutils* [18]. The routine detects peaks based on the first order difference and returns the positions of the peak maxima. The result can be tuned by specifying a minimum distance between two peaks and a minimum height of a peak relative to the largest peak.

The first peak of the signal is assumed to be chloride in anion measurement and rubidium in cation measurement. It is detected by applying the *peak_indexes* routine to the signal and removing all returned peak maxima smaller than a certain threshold. The first of the remaining peaks is accepted as chloride/rubidium peak.

The arrival time of the first peak is then used to define time windows for all other expected peaks. For each expected peak, *peak_indexes* is applied to the respective time window and the largest of the returned peaks is accepted as the expected peak.

Peak Integration. Since ill-defined peak fronts/tails and imperfect baseline fits introduce uncertainty about the peak boundaries, the peak boundaries are defined as the position before and after the peak maximum where the signal falls below 20% of the peak maximum height. The height to width ratios of the peaks are checked to exclude artefacts of bad baseline fits. The peak areas under curve (AUC) are then integrated using the Simpson's rule method [19].

3 Experimental Results

Experiments were carried out with soil samples taken from different areas of Austria and Germany. The user was guided by in house developed software through the steps of the measurement procedure. The process produces graphs like the one depicted on Fig. 5a. After the subtraction of the fitted baseline the electropherogram is reduced to the graph of Fig. 5b.

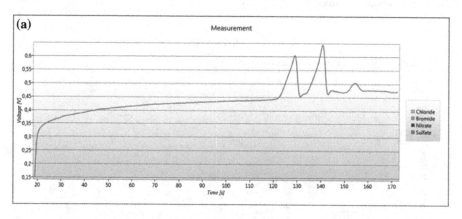

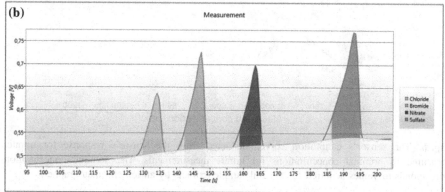

Fig. 5. Electropherograms (a) values of the sensor voltage output over time registered and plotted at the time of the measurement (b) the sensor's voltage output over time after the fitted baseline is subtracted (the graphs do not demonstrate the same measurement).

3.1   Calculation of Component Concentrations and Calibration

The concentration of each component is calculated as follows:

$$c_i = c_s \times \frac{A_i}{A_s} \tag{1}$$

where c_i is the molar concentration of component i, c_s is *the* molar concentration of internal standard, A_i is the AUC of component i and A_s is the AUC of the internal standard.

The calculated concentrations showed a polynomial response, which is corrected by:

$$c_{i,cal.} = ac_i^2 + bc_i + c \tag{2}$$

with a, b and c being the calibration coefficients.

The last version of the data processing module including the calibration was tested on a series of 359 measurements, comprising nominal concentrations of nitrate and sulfate from about 30 µmol to 1200 µmol.

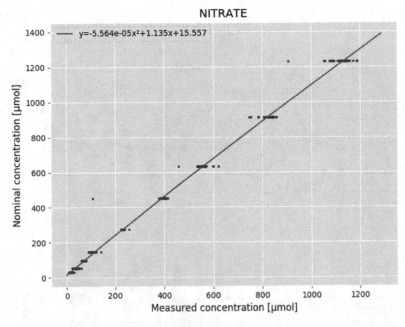

Fig. 6. The sensor's calibration curves deducted from the sensor's response for nitrate; measured vs nominal concentrations for nitrate measurements. The nominal concentration corresponds to values acquired for the soil sample extracts by an ion chromatographer.

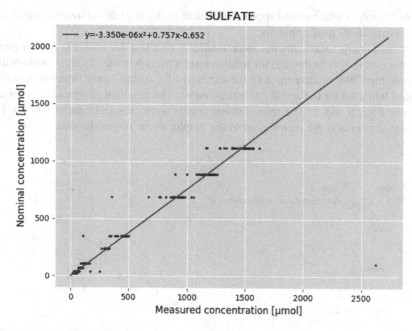

Fig. 7. The sensor's calibration curves deducted from the sensor's response for nitrate; measured vs nominal concentrations for sulfate measurements. The nominal concentration corresponds to values acquired for the soil sample extracts by an ion chromatographer.

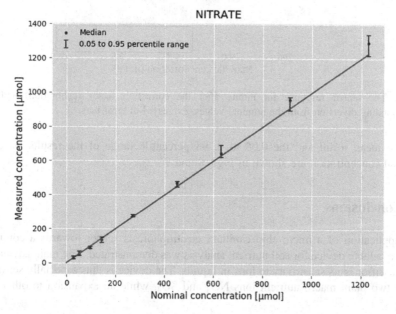

Fig. 8. The sensor response for nitrate after the correction factor (calibration) and the corresponding diversion from the nominal values, expressed in error bars

The algorithm failed to find appropriate nitrate peaks in 23 of the measurements and sulfate peaks in 98 measurements.

The remaining measurements were manually checked for outliers. A first guess calibration curve was fit through the median results of each nominal value. Outliers that had more than 50% relative error (3 for nitrate, 14 for sulfate) were then preliminarily excluded while fitting the actual calibration curve. The resulting calibration curves are shown in Figs. 6 and 7. The measurement results were cross-referenced with an ion chromatographer and are represented to the graphs as the nominal value.

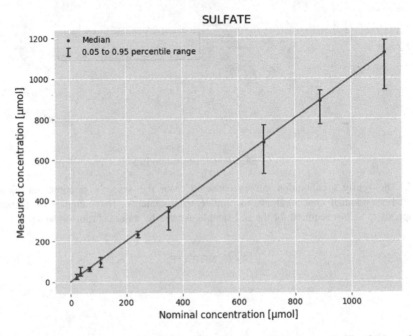

Fig. 9. The sensor response for nitrate after the correction factor (calibration) and the corresponding diversion from the nominal values, expressed in error bars.

The mean result and the 0.05 to 0. 95 percentile range of the results for each nominal concentration are shown in Figs. 8 and 9.

4   Conclusions

The application of a micro-chip capillary electrophoresis sensor towards a commercially available device for soil nutrient analysis was demonstrated. The main advantage of this sensor is its sensitivity to ions in liquids. The device is thus especially sensitive to the two plant macro-nutrient ions NO_3 and SO_4, while an expansion to other soil nutrients is also possible with minor adjustments. The sensor response exhibited a second order polynomial response with high accuracy and low relative error (of the order of 5% for the majority of the measurements). This renders this cost effective hand-held sensor equivalent to much more costly and bulky benchtop laboratory equipment.

Near field nutrient measurements with simplified extraction methods strongly simplify the fertilizer need determination (no need for cooled transport) and reduce analysis costs in comparison to standard laboratory analysis. Thus, the presented device becomes a valuable mobile sensor for plant macro-nutrients availability measurements.

References

1. FAO: "World Fertilizer Trends and Outlook to 2018." Food and Agriculture Organization of United Nations, 66 pages (2015)
2. Cordell, D., Drangert, J.-O., White, S.: The story of phosphorus: global food security and food for thought. Glob. Environ. Change **19**, 292–305 (2009)
3. Lawlor, D.W., Mengel, K., Kirkby, E.A.: Principles of plant nutrition. Ann Bot. **93**(4), 479–480 (2004)
4. Ceccotti, S.P.: Plant nutrient sulphur-a review of nutrient balance, environmental impact and fertilizers. In: Rodriguez-Barrueco, C. (ed.) Fertilizers and Environment, vol. 66, pp. 185–193. Springer, Dordrecht (1996). https://doi.org/10.1007/978-94-009-1586-2_30
5. http://ec.europa.eu/eurostat/statistics-explained/index.php/Agri-environmental_indicator_-_mineral_fertiliser_consumption
6. Sackmann, E.K., Fulton, A.L., Beebe, D.J.: The present and future role of microfluidics in biomedical research. Nature **507**, 181 (2014)
7. Whitesides, G.M.: The origins and the future of microfluidics. Nature **442**, 368 (2006)
8. Grossman, P.D., Colburn, J.C.: Capillary Electrophoresis: Theory and Practice. Academic Press, San Diego (2012)
9. Zemann, A.J.: Capacitively coupled contactless conductivity detection in capillary electrophoresis. Electrophoresis **24**, 2125–2137 (2003)
10. Huang, X., Luckey, J.A., Gordon, M.J., Zare, R.N.: Quantitative determination of low molecular weight carboxylic acids by capillary zone electrophoresis/conductivity detection. Anal. Chem. **61**, 766–770 (1989)
11. Rossier, J., Reymond, F., Michel, P.E.: Polymer microfluidic chips for electrochemical and biochemical analyses. Electrophoresis **23**, 858–867 (2002)
12. Zemann, A.J., Schnell, E., Volgger, D., Bonn, G.K.: Contactless conductivity detection for capillary electrophoresis. Anal. Chem. **70**, 563–567 (1998)
13. Smolka, M., Puchberger-Enengl, D., Bipoun, M., et al.: A mobile lab-on-a-chip device for on-site soil nutrient analysis. Precis. Agric. **18**, 152–168 (2017). https://doi.org/10.1007/s11119-016-9452-y
14. Brito-Neto, J.G.A., Fracassi da Silva, J.A., Blanes, L., do Lago, C.L.: Understanding capacitively coupled contactless conductivity detection in capillary and microchip electrophoresis. Part 2. Peak shape, stray capacitance, noise, and actual electronics. Electroanalysis **17**, 1207–1214 (2005)

15. Breadmore, M.C.: Electrokinetic and hydrodynamic injection: making the right choice for capillary electrophoresis. Bioanalysis **1**, 889–894 (2009)
16. Eilers, P.H.C., Boelens, H.F.M.: Baseline correction with asymmetric least squares smoothing. Leiden University Medical Centre report. Leiden Univ Leiden, NL (2005)
17. Cao, W., Chen, X., Yang, X., Wang, E.: Discrete wavelets transform for signal denoising in capillary electrophoresis with electrochemiluminescence detection. Electrophoresis **24**, 3124–3130 (2003)
18. https://pypi.python.org/pypi/PeakUtils
19. McKeeman, W.M.: Algorithm 145: adaptive numerical integration by Simpson's rule. Commun. ACM **5**, 604 (1962)

SheepIT, an IoT-Based Weed Control System

Luís Nóbrega[1(✉)], Paulo Pedreiras[1(✉)], and Pedro Gonçalves[2(✉)]

[1] DETI/IT, University of Aveiro, Aveiro, Portugal
{lnobrega,pbrp}@ua.pt
[2] ESTGA/IT, University of Aveiro, Aveiro, Portugal
pasg@ua.pt

Abstract. The SheepIT project aims at developing a solution for monitoring and controlling grazing sheep in vineyards and similar cultures. The system should operate autonomously and guarantee that sheep only feed from infestant weeds, leaving untouched the vines and their fruits. Moreover, the system should also collect data about sheep activity for logging and analysis purposes. This paper presents the overall system's architecture and its rationale, with focus on the posture monitoring and control subsystem. It includes practical results, obtained from a use case. These results are encouraging, showing that the developed system is able to estimate the sheep's posture with a high accuracy, that the stimuli are applied efficiently and that sheep have sufficient cognitive capacity to learn quickly which behaviours they should avoid. Despite being preliminary, these results provide good indications regarding the practicableness of the system.

Keywords: Autonomous herd management · IoT · Sensing · Posture control

1 Introduction

The continuous growth of the world population and their demands are triggering important changes in the primary sector. The quantity of goods required to satisfy the current needs is getting increasingly higher, reaching a point where the humanity is consuming more resources than the planet has to offer. Regarding specifically human nutrition, there was a wide adoption of intensive and non-sustainable farming solutions that have important negative impact in the environment. Albeit being utopic to think, at least in the short term, about solutions capable of satisfying the world population nutrition needs without harmful environment effects, it is of utmost importance to develop ways to minimize them.

Information and Communication Technologies (ICT) are being adopted to increase the efficiency in the production of goods and to reduce cost, environmental impact and human labour [1], both in the food and livestock sectors. Hence, precision agriculture, e-agriculture and intelligent farming systems arose, supported by tools such as Ubiquitous Computing, Cloud Computing, Satellite Monitoring, Remote Sensing, Context-Aware Computing and Internet of Things (IoT) [2].

The viticulture sector represents a paradigmatic example, where the application of these technologies may play an important role, especially in Portugal. As the business

M. Salampasis and T. Bournaris (Eds.): HAICTA 2017, CCIS 953, pp. 131–147, 2019.
https://doi.org/10.1007/978-3-030-12998-9_10

expansion is strictly limited to the availability of suitable terrains (namely in the Douro Region), producers are seeking for high quality products instead of high quantities. To reach this goal, production control and process enhancements are vital.

The constant growth of unwanted and undesirable weeds is one of the major problems felt by wine producers. These infestant weeds compete with the vines for soil nutrients and water, forcing producers to repeatedly remove them through the use of mechanical and chemical methods [3]. These methods include the use of machinery, such as plows and brushcutters, to remove weeds between plant rows, and herbicides on the line between plant feet, to kill or prevent the growth of weeds. Nonetheless, such methods are considered aggressive and harmful to vines and even to the public health. On the one hand, mechanical mechanisms may damage the leaves and grapes, contribute to soil erosion and use fossil fuel, thus being a source of greenhouse gases. On the other hand, the application of herbicides may injure the grapes, due to drift and may contaminate groundwaters and the fruits [4]. Moreover, such processes must be repeated over the year, entailing a significant economic impact. Particularly, in the case of vineyards, eliminating infesting weeds represents 20 to 35% of total manpower, with costs per hectare ranging from 80 €/ha up to 380 €/ha [5].

The use of animals to weed vineyards [6, 7], usually sheep, is an ancient practice used around the world. Animals grazing in vineyards feed from the unwanted weeds and fertilize the soil, in an inexpensive, ecological and sustainable way. However, this solution was progressively abandoned because it couldn't be used through all the year, since animals tend to feed from the vines and their fruits, causing troublesome production losses. To overcome that, sheep were traditionally used to weed vineyards only before the beginning of the growth cycle of grapevines, thus requiring the use of mechanical and/or chemical methods during the remaining part of the production cycle. Moreover, the lack of shepherds and the rise of their wages also contributed significantly to the reduction of the use of sheep to weed farmlands.

To overcome this scenario, the SheepIT project [8] came up, aiming at the development of an autonomous mechanism to control sheep's posture and location during vineyard grazing periods, allowing the use of this technique through all the year, without requiring systematic human supervision. The project includes an IoT-based solution to monitor and condition sheep's posture and location, being the gathered data related with the behaviour and physical condition of each one of the animals. The collected data is sent firstly to an aggregation gateway and then to a backend computational platform. This platform allows the human operator to oversee, in an easy and efficient way, the status of the entire flock, devices and network. It also permits the deployment of advanced algorithms to process data and detect abnormal situations, such as health conditions, lost animals or attacks from predators, generating automatically alarms when one of such events occurs.

The system architecture was designed in order to provide a flexible and adaptable solution, namely in what regards vineyard's size and shape. Moreover, the human intervention is maintained at a low level, being only required for installing the devices on the animals and place landmark poles to define the grazing areas. The system is composed of:

- a portable electronic collar, carried by the sheep, responsible for monitoring and controlling its behaviour;
- fixed devices, called beacons, installed in vineyards, responsible for interconnecting the network devices, defining the virtual fence placement and carrying out collar's relative localization;
- a gateway device, which aggregates, pre-analyses and uploads the data generated by collars to the computational platform; and
- a computational platform, responsible for gathering, processing, storing and make all the data available to the user.

The focus of this paper is on the description of the global system architecture of the SheepIT project, its functional blocks and interactions. Moreover, and due to its relevance, a special emphasis is given to the collars design and operation, particularly to the posture control mechanism. The reminder of this paper is organized as follows. Section 2 presents a review of the related work in the scope of animal monitoring and conditioning. Section 3 describes the SheepIT's overall system architecture while Sect. 4 addresses the posture control mechanism, particularly the posture detection, the conditioning mechanism and the hardware designed. Section 5 presents the implementation of the solution, including experimental results and finally, Sect. 6, concludes the paper and presents future work.

2 Requirements and Related Work

The requirements of the SheepIT project are detailed in [9] and summarized in Table 1. The main goal of the project is to provide an autonomous solution based on IoT technologies that should be capable of monitoring and conditioning sheep's posture and location while grazing in vineyards. To this end, the system shall include a virtual fence mechanism, to confine sheep within predefined areas, and a posture control mechanism, that senses sheep's head and neck position and triggers adequate actuators to revert undesired behaviours (*e.g.* feeding from vines and grapes).

Collars shall be carried by sheep and thus are subject to strict SWaP (Size, Weight and Power) requirements. Sheep are relatively small animals, thus any device carried by them must have small dimensions and be lightweight. Devices with dimensions and weight similar to the commercial solutions available for training dogs are recommended. Moreover, to minimize human intervention, collars should have a high autonomy (up to 4 months).

Farmers should be able to assess the system state. Moreover, if processed properly, sensor data generated by collars can be used to develop additional services that increase the system usefulness (*e.g.* predator attack detection, health issues). Thus, relevant data must be collected and transmitted, via a communication infrastructure, to a computational platform (*e.g.* in the cloud). This includes information regarding sensors, actuators, location of sheep and status of the devices. It should be remarked that, in virtue of the SWaP constraints above mentioned, the network should be highly energy-efficient.

Table 1. Comparison between the SheepIT requirements and the similar solutions available

Requirements/ Solution	SheepIT [8]	Brunberg et al. [21]	Thorstensen et al. [26]	Nadimi et al. [22]	Huircan et al. [24]	Jouven et al. [19]	Rutter et al. [18]
Small dimensions (<0,5 kg)	✓	✓	✓	✓	✓	✓	✗
Localization	✓	✓	✓	✓	✓	✗	✓
Data collection	✓	✓	✓	✓	✓	✗	✓
Communication infrastructure	✓	✓	✓	✓	✓	✗	✗
High autonomy (∼4 months)	✓	NA	✗	NA	✗	NA	✗
Virtual fence	✓	✓	✗	✗	✗	✓	✗
Posture control	✓	✗	✗	✗	✗	✗	✗
Pasture delimitation	✓	✓	✗	✗	✗	✗	✗
User interface	✓	✓	✗	✗	✗	✗	✗
Network scalability	✓	✓	NA	NA	NA	NA	NA

Finally, the system shall be scalable and flexible in order to be used in different scenarios, with a variable number of animals and different vineyard's size.

There are several research works and commercial products that are related with the scope of the SheepIT project. One topic with abundant research contributions concerns monitoring animal's location, behaviour and actions. The GPS (Global Positioning System) technology is the most common solution, often combined with additional sensors, as accelerometers. Experiments were made with cattle [10–14], white-tailed deer [15], griffon vultures [16], crocodiles [17] but also with sheep [18–21]. Most of these works are based on the off-line analysis of the data gathered by the sensors placed on animals, with further application of several Data Mining (DM) and Machine Learning techniques (ML).

Considering uniquely the use of GPS on cows, William et al. [14] tested several ML algorithms to distinguish three behavioural states: grazing, resting and walking. However, the results were discouraging, especially on distinguishing grazing and resting states. Thus, as expected due to its precision, GPS is not suitable to differentiate grazing behaviours.

A similar work for cows is presented in [13], although in this case the collars' sensors are a tri-axial accelerometer and a magnetometer. Several ML algorithms were tested to predict the activity of cows (grazing, walking, running, standing or lying), with accuracies around 90%.

In [20], authors applied supervised ML algorithms to differentiate active and inactive sheep. The former group includes behaviours as grazing, walking and running, while the latter one includes behaviours as standing and lying. The approach resorts on the use of GPS collars equipped with *pitch* and *roll* tilt sensors, albeit only tilt sensor data was used as attribute of the dataset. They achieved an accuracy of 92%, either using a decision tree or linear discriminant analysis. These works show the potential of using ML algorithms to predict animal's behaviours.

Regarding monitoring the absolute animal's location, most of the solutions described rely on GPS. However, even with the significant technological advances of such devices, specially concerning their autonomy and cost, they still incur in a high energy consumption, are expensive for these kind of solutions (due to the high number of devices needed to cover one flock) and take a significant amount of time to acquire satellites [22]. Hence, for application domains where the autonomy is expected to be large, the adoption of GPS still implies the use of high capacity batteries, rendering this approach unsuitable for small to medium size animals. Thus, alternative options were evaluated, namely the use of relative localization algorithms. Among them, the ones that rely on the Received Signal Strength Indicator (RSSI) must be highlighted, due to its simplicity. Moreover, since many low-cost wireless communication transceivers provide this parameter, a localization mechanism based on such method becomes very attractive, because it uses pre-existing hardware. There are abundant references on the literature regarding RSSI-based localization, particularly for indoor scenarios. Regarding outdoor RSSI-based localization, [22–24] assess its accuracy for animal's location monitoring. Although promising, the error associated is large and has a high variance, being significantly affected by obstacles and Radio Frequency (RF) noise. Thus, a less erratic solution based on this method must comprehend additional mechanisms as sensor fusion (for instance, using accelerometers or using advanced techniques as trilateration [25]).

Other approaches aim at the minimization of the GPS usage. E-shepherd [26] takes advantage of the gregarious behaviour of sheep to reduce the number of GPS devices, placing them only on the leaders of the herd. The remaining sheep were equipped with UHF radio tags and the location of these sheep evaluated relatively to the leaders. Notwithstanding, even if the cost of the solution could be highly reduced, the autonomy was still a problem.

Another relevant topic regards the concept of virtual fencing. It emerged as an alternative to classic physical fences (e.g. using wood and/or barbed wire), which are costly and inflexible. Virtual fences allow the definition of adjustable boundaries through electronic systems without requiring the installation of physical barriers. Independently of the electronic technology used, the basic concept is similar. Different cues/stimuli are used to condition animals when they approach the virtually defined fence boundary. These cues are usually composed by a pair of stimuli, namely a warning cue (e.g. sound, light, vibration) followed by an electrostatic discharge [27, 28]. The combination of these kinds of stimuli is known to be beneficial to animals since they have the ability to learn and associate the warning cue to the electrostatic cue, and consequently to a certain behaviour that shall be avoided [21, 29].

Using these kind of solutions raises ethical issues, essentially related to the animal well-being. In this context, some studies were carried out and it has been proved that the effects of these stimuli are similar to daily livestock activities as weighting or medical treatment processes [30]. Moreover, the *Electronic Collar Manufacturer's Association* (ECMA) defines the technical requirements that all training and conditioning electronic collars for domestic animal shall follow [31], characterizing the maximum stimuli admissible to maintain animal's well-being.

The approach most closely related with SheepIT is presented in [21], where a commercial collar (Nofence®), originally designed for goats, is used on sheep. This solution allows the definition of permitted grazing areas through a web application and conditions the animal's location through auditory and electrostatic cues generated by collars. The combination of both mechanisms allows the deployment of a virtual fence, where the animal's location is obtained by a GPS device incorporated on the collar, which is powered by a battery and a small solar panel.

Table 1 recaps the SheepIT requirements and cross-checks them with the features of the approaches found in the literature Albeit the solution presented in [21] fulfils most of the requirements, it does not incorporate any posture control mechanism, a critical feature of the SheepIT. Moreover, despite the high cost of each collar (189€ plus a fee of 0,51€ per day), there is no information about the autonomy of collar or efficiency of the integrated solar panel.

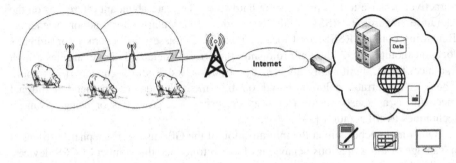

Fig. 1. Overall system architecture

3   System Architecture

SheepIT follows a typical IoT architecture [32], integrating a Wireless Sensor Network (WSN), a computational platform and an application layer (Fig. 1).

The WSN layer is responsible for implementing all local features, namely: (i) detection and conditioning of sheep's posture; (ii) implementation of the virtual fence and localization mechanisms, and; (iii) energy-wise efficient communication scheme between nodes.

Collars are the WSN mobile nodes, being carried by sheep. They contain the sensors and actuators necessary to implement the posture control mechanism (Sect. 4); a microprocessor, for carrying out local computations; a battery, to allow portability; and a radio transceiver, to allow communications between collars and the remaining network infrastructure.

Besides allowing the transport of sensor data to the computation platform, the radio link provides support to relative localization, through the measurement of the link's RSSI. Despite its relatively poor performance in terms of accuracy, this approach is very attractive because carrying out localization using the same radio infrastructure used for data collection contributes significantly to reduce the power consumption of collars, as well as its cost and size, which are critical requirements. Additionally, grazing areas are defined in a relatively gross way and collars contain additional sensors that can be combined, by means of suitable sensor fusion techniques, to improve the RSSI-based localization.

Grazing areas can be relatively large, exceeding the coverage of a single radio transceiver. Therefore, the communication infrastructure also contemplates beacon nodes, which receive data from collars and relay them, eventually through other beacons, to an aggregating gateway. This gateway can be seen as an extended version of a beacon, comprising additionally a Wide Area Network (WAN) interface (2G, 3G, 4G, etc.), used for sending the data to the computational platform.

Beacons define the grazing perimeter, as it is necessary to ensure connectivity to be able to collect sheep's data in real-time. As such, beacons also serve as landmarks for the RSSI-localization. When necessary, additional beacons can be disposed on the grazing area to create RF overlapping zones, with the objective of further increasing the accuracy and robustness of the RSSI-based localization mechanism. Thus, the placement of the beacons must involve a trade-off between the required effectiveness of the system, the dimensions of the area to be covered and the number of beacons to be installed.

Collars, beacons and the gateway share a communication infrastructure that allows the data exchanges between them. Different types of traffic coexist, with different purposes and characteristics, namely: periodic sensor data sent from collars to beacons; periodic synchronization and localization messages sent from beacons to collars; periodic relay traffic between beacons; and sporadic traffic related to system configuration and management, such as dynamic node registration. The network protocol plays a crucial role, as a significant part of the energy can be consumed by communication-related activities. Thus, a hybrid protocol was developed for SheepIT, based on a periodic superstructure that contains Time-Division Multiple Access (TDMA) phases, for carrying out periodic exchanges, combined with Carrier-Sense Multiple Access phases (CSMA) for the asynchronous communications. The rationale is using TDMA communications for normal communications, namely the ones related with collection of sensor data, because these communications are periodic, and so the TDMA scheme allows avoiding collisions and minimizes the time during which collars need to be active. The energy-wise less efficient CSMA phase is reserved for configuration and set-up events, which inherently occur at unpredictable time instants. As these latter activities shall occur sparsely, their impact on the collars' autonomy is marginal, despite the use of a less efficient MAC.

Finally, the computational platform processes and stores all the data, making it also available through web Application Programming Interfaces, so it can be conveniently presented to the user. SheepIT's communication infrastructure and computational platform are out of the scope of this paper, so the interested reader is referred to [9] and [33], respectively.

4 Posture Control

As discussed above, the objective of the SheepIT project is to let sheep autonomously weed vineyards without requiring continuous human supervision. To make it possible, it is mandatory to have a posture control mechanism, which shall continuously monitor sheep's posture and trigger warning cues or penalisations when undesired behaviours are detected.

4.1 Posture Detection

Identifying the sheep's posture, namely when it is armful for the vines, is not a trivial challenge. On the one hand, animals are individuals having distinct anatomical characteristics and behaviours. On the other hand, vineyards also present different features accordingly to their location, climate, slope or species cultivated. All these conditions introduce specific challenges that need to be handled by the posture control mechanism. Nevertheless, the detection of an offending posture is always dependent on the height of the vines and maximum height of sheep's head.

These two parameters define the maximum angle that the sheep neck may assume, and so the posture detection mechanism operation is based on these two entities, which are fused to reduce false offense detections caused by the different postures that sheep may adopt (*e.g.* the sheep may be laying on the ground and with the head lift up without endangering the vines).

Figure 2 illustrates the three most common behaviours taken by sheep. From those, the one represented on the rightmost picture is the only one that the system should differentiate, triggering a warning or penalization. It corresponds to an infraction situation, contrarily to the two other cases. While grazing, we can observe that the distance from the sheep's neck to the ground is slightly smaller than to the resting and infraction states distances. Also, the angle detected on the three states are different. Consequently, the problem of posture detection, particularly when in infraction, can be tackled thought the detection of suitable thresholds of both neck's distance to ground and tilt angles.

These thresholds may be obtained resorting on two different approaches. A theoretical one, through the definition of a mathematical model, or through experimental tests, measuring real values and analysing them through processing tools as DM and ML techniques. Considering the animals unpredictability, the latter method is potentially more attractive. In fact, as discussed in Sect. 2, classification-based ML algorithms revealed to be effective at differentiate animal's behaviour using several sensors. Thus, we adopt this approach, being particularly interesting the use of Decision Trees (DT) algorithms, since it allows an easier interpretation of the results, namely in the form of a tree of conditions that can be easily incorporated on the posture control mechanism.

Fig. 2. On the leftmost picture, the sheep is grazing from ground weed as intended, and thus presents the desired behaviour. On the centre, the sheep is on a resting position, that is considered correct but on the boundary of infraction. On the rightmost picture, the sheep is having food from a high place, hence in infraction.

4.2 Posture Conditioning

Upon detection of an undesired posture, the system should issue cues to induce the animal to revert its behaviour. Regarding animal conditioning, the literature shows that a sequence of cues, including warning signals before further penalization, are the most effective. Additionally, the literature also reveals that the conjugation of audio as a cue, eventually followed by a small electrostatic discharge, as penalization, is the most effective combination [34].

The effectiveness of using audio signals as warnings is closely dependent of a training process. During this process, sheep must learn to associate a forbidden behaviour to a specific penalization (electrostatic discharge), as well as this penalization to a previous warning signal (sound). When successful, this process allows sheep to revert the behaviour when facing a simple warning, minimizing the number of penalizations. It should be noted that sheep have a limited cognitive capacity, being crucial to the success of the learning process that cues and penalizations are always applied when appropriate (*i.e.*, with residual false positives and limited false-negatives) and with a small latency. This is essential to allow the animal to associate the behaviour with the corresponding warning and penalization signals.

Figure 3 presents a state machine that describes the high-level operation of the posture control mechanism. Periodically, sensors are read and their outputs analysed by the decision algorithm discussed in the previous section, to assess if the animal is incurring on an infraction situation ("INF" signal). While the animal is not in an infraction situation, the state machine remains on the "Idle" state. When the animal adopts an infraction posture, the state machine transits to the "Cue" state and starts applying the audio cue (sound sequence). If the animal reverts its behaviour, the state machine returns to the "Idle" and the audio cue is stopped. If the animal persists on the incorrect behaviour for a certain amount of time ("t_CUE") the state machine transits to the "Penal" state, and an electric discharge sequence starts to be applied. As previously, if the animal reverts is posture, the application of electric discharges is stopped, and the state chart returns to the "Idle" state. If the animal remains in the "Penal" state for a given duration ("t_PEN"), the system suspends all stimuli and remains blocked. This scenario corresponds to an abnormal situation, *e.g.* a system malfunction or improper

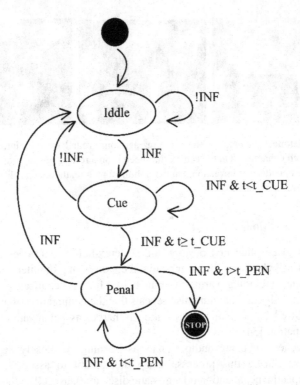

Fig. 3. Posture control mechanism state machine

training, being contemplated on the state machine to prevent the unnecessary application of penalizations that would otherwise overstress the animals.

4.3 Sensing and Actuation Hardware

Figure 4 illustrates the architecture of collars regarding the sensing and actuation blocks, required to implement the posture control mechanism. Collars contain an accelerometer, to measure the neck's tilt, and an ultrasound transceiver, to measure the distance between ground and sheep's neck.

The accelerometer allows measuring both static and dynamic accelerations. The static component is associated to the gravitational acceleration (also known as G-force), enabling the computation of tilt angles. Particularly, a tri-axial accelerometer permits obtaining the *pitch* and *roll*[1] angles through the three G components (G_x, G_y and G_z) as described in [35]. In turn, the ultrasound transceiver uses the propagation time of ultrasonic waves over the air (that is known) to estimate the distance between the emitting transceiver and the obstacle that reflects it.

---

[1] For the *pitch* and *roll* angles, we followed the definition given in [35].

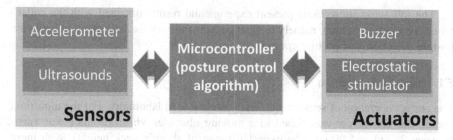

Fig. 4. Collar modules [36]

The conditioning mechanism is composed of an electromechanical audio transducer, to emit audio signals, and an electrostatic stimulation circuit, to apply electric discharges. Both actuators are controlled by software, which defines the duration and frequency of the cues.

Note that collars' hardware and firmware incorporate other functional blocks, *e.g.* related with communications, which are not represented here because they are not relevant to the posture control mechanism.

5 Implementation and Experimental Results

To validate the concepts developed on the scope of the SheepIT project, it was carried out a prototype implementation of the collars. It is based on the TI CC1110 SoC, which is a highly integrated, low-cost and low power device that contains all the peripherals necessary to interface with the sensors and actuators (e.g. digital I/O, timers, SPI, I2C), as well as an integrated radio module operating at the 433 MHz ISM band. This band was chosen because it is more suitable to the project constraints, namely presence of obstacles (*e.g.* trees, posts or metallic strings) and irregular slope.

It was also designed, on a 3D printer, the cover shown in Fig. 5, which accommodates the electronic components and places them on the desired position, at the sheep's neck. Despite being a prototype, the collar already contains all the necessary elements and its size and weight are suitable to be carried by sheep (Fig. 6).

Fig. 5. Prototype of the collar   **Fig. 6.** Sheep carrying a collar prototype

The following subsections present experimental results obtained with the collar's prototype implementation, namely in what concerns the sensor and actuation hardware, posture detection and posture control.

5.1 Sensors Evaluation

The correct operation of sensors was firstly evaluated in laboratory. For the ultrasound circuit, the transceiver was aimed to a moving obstacle, whose distance was varied between 25 cm and 90 cm (the expected range of sheep's neck height), with increments of 2.5 cm. The distance was measured with a measuring tape with 0.5 mm resolution and repeated 100 times for each distance. The whole testing procedure was repeated 10 times. A similar approach was followed for the accelerometer, in this case measuring the *pitch* and *roll* angles in the range [0, 90]° with intervals of 5°.

Table 2. Sensor testing results

Sensors/metric	Range	σ	Maximum Error
Ultrasounds circuit	[25;90] cm	1.5 mm	3.0 mm
Accelerometer	[0;90] °	0.75°	2°

Table 2 summarizes the experimental results in terms of range, standard deviation and maximum error. It is possible to observe that both sensors can measure within the required range with an acceptable error, therefore they are adequate for the project's objectives.

5.2 Posture Detection Decision Algorithm

For defining the appropriate thresholds to be integrated on the posture control mechanism, and in order to enable the application of DM and ML techniques, a testing scenario for gathering a large amount of sensing data in multiple environments (*i.e.* sheep grazing, resting, running, walking and being in infraction) with real sheep was devised. Collars were placed on sheep and their posture was monitored with a sampling frequency of 2 Hz for 3 h. The obtained dataset, after data clean-up, comprises 20555 entries and includes the raw sensor measurements and a corresponding times-tamp. Furthermore, to allow an ulterior classification of each entry, a timed video was also recorded.

Subsequently, the data was mined using the R language and RStudio[2]. Firstly, redundant or incoherent data was deleted through the analysis of the sequence number and timestamp (*e.g.* data with the same sequence number is considered duplicated information and thus not relevant). Then, each entry of the resulting dataset was manually classified with the supervision label *"Infraction"* or *"Not Infraction"*, considering the real posture observed through the recorded video. To evaluate the accuracy

---

[2] https://www.rstudio.com/.

of the supervised learning process, particularly the DT algorithm, the dataset was split in two, one for training (75%) and the other one for testing (25%). Several interactions were taken for tuning the algorithm using the *rpart* library.

It was possible to attain an accuracy of 96,56% using a tree depth of 5 and a *complexity parameter (cp)* of 0.0023163. While the *cp* parameter was chosen in order to minimize the cross-validation error value (*x-val relative error* in the *rpart* library) that can be obtained through the tool *printcp*, the depth of the tree was selected following a trial and error proceeding, seeking for the best accuracy value. Finally, to retrieve the intended thresholds, the generated tree was plotted using the *fancyRpartPlot*, on which each path from the root until a terminal leaf associated with an *Infraction* state represents a classification rule.

A detailed inspection of the records associated with classification errors, allowed to observe that most of them were related to transition states, probably due to misclassification during the supervision process.

5.3 Posture Control Mechanism Evaluation

To evaluate the overall performance of the posture control mechanism, it was realized a practical experiment using nine sheep with similar size and height, divided in three equal-sized groups. An area of 10 m² was enclosed by a fence and three volumes of fay (rich in nutrients) were suspended at a high of 50 cm from the ground, to simulate the vine's grapes (Fig. 7). To ensure the willingness of sheep in feeding themselves, they were kept in fast since the night before the test. Additionally, each group experiment lasted for 15 min.

During the learning phase, collars' were keep at high frequency operation mode (decisions with a frequency of 5 Hz), continuously measuring and immediately triggering the conditioning mechanism, when an infraction was detected.

Fig. 7. Scenario of tests on the field

The first group of sheep was used for control. They were not subject to the training process nor to posture control. As expected, this group of sheep feed from the fay.

The two remaining groups were used to evaluate the posture control mechanism. On both groups, it was verified the existence of a leader, *i.e.*, a sheep whose example was followed by the others. Leaders immediately tried to reach the fay, triggering the conditioning mechanism. Hence, they both received warning and penalization cues, immediately reverting their behaviour. For the first group the infraction situation happened four times, and then the leader sheep started to instantly revert the infracting behaviour after receiving the warning cue. The remaining sheep behaved similarly, but they did not attempt to feed from the fay as many times as the leader, probably because they were able to perceive the leader's behaviour. After reverting the behaviour, sheep started to look for food on the ground, behaving as it is intended to occur in a vineyard.

A similar behaviour was observed on the second group, except that the leader sheep took six conditioning cycles to start learning to associate the penalization to the warning cue. Remarkably, after this process, this sheep did not try to feed from the fay so regularly as the leader of the first group.

The practical results above presented clearly confirm that it is possible to condition the behaviour of sheep, namely preventing them from eating food placed at a minimum height from ground, and that the combination of sensors, actuators and decision algorithms chosen for SheepIT collars are suitable for the task. However, it was also noticed the presence of some issues. Particularly, it was observed that the defined thresholds were now suitable for all sheep, *i.e.*, the conditioning mechanism was not triggered at the exact moment for all sheep. After a rigorous analysis of the collected sensor data and footage, it was noticed that the pathological cases resulted from anatomical differences between the sheep used in this test and the ones used for the algorithm parametrization. As such, future work will address the development of an automatic calibration mechanism to adapt the algorithm thresholds to the anatomical characteristics of each sheep.

6 Conclusions

Wine production is a market with growing importance in Portugal, mainly due to its export capacity and high added value. Thereupon, wine sector companies are seeking for innovative techniques that could aid in the improvement of their production, either in terms of quantity or quality.

This paper presents the SheepIT project, which aims at developing a portable, adaptable, flexible and scalable solution for controlling the growth of infesting weeds in vineyards. In contrast to the solutions used nowadays, based in chemicals or plowing machinery, the solution developed in the scope of the ShepIT project relies on sheep, thus having several advantages, such as being environmentally friendly, contributing for the soil fertilization and being much less aggressive for the cultures.

Despite the inherent advantages of the solution proposed, many technical challenges arise. Controlling the animal's posture is essential for achieving the desired effects and hence, an IT solution based on sensors and actuators is presented. The hardware responsible for implementing the posture control mechanism is also described and evaluated to ensure its correct operation, considering the project requirements. For defining the suitable sensors' thresholds associated with infringing behaviours, ML techniques were used, namely the application of DT algorithms on a manually classified dataset. Finally, such conditions were implemented, and the mechanism was evaluated in practice.

Albeit confirmed that not all sheep react similarly, the mechanism revealed to be effective. However, since sheep have specific individual characteristics, and the terrains are not regular in terms of slope, the system needs, in the future, to automatically adapt to the anatomy of each individual sheep and terrain characteristics. Moreover, the tests were realized with the collars operating on a high frequency mode, resulting in a relatively high energy consumption. Thus, future work shall also include the evaluation of methods to minimize the periods in which collars operate in this mode, in order to attain the desired levels of autonomy.

Acknowledgments. This work is supported by the European Structural Investment Funds (ESIF), through the Operational Competitiveness and Internationalization Programme (COMPETE 2020) [Project Nr. 017640 (POCI-01-0145-FEDER-017640)].

References

1. Popović, T., Latinović, N., Pešić, A., Zečević, Ž., Krstajić, B., Djukanović, S.: Architecting an IoT-enabled platform for precision agriculture and ecological monitoring: a case study. Comput. Electron. Agric. **140**, 255–265 (2017)
2. Ojha, T., Misra, S., Raghuwanshi, N.S.: Wireless sensor networks for agriculture: the state-of-the-art in practice and future challenges. Comput. Electron. Agric. **118**, 66–84 (2015)
3. Monteiro, A., Moreira, I.: Reduced rates of residual and post-emergence herbicides for weed control in vineyards. Weed Res. **44**(2), 117–128 (2004)
4. Kennedy, M., Skinkis, P.: Are Your Weed-control Products Damaging Nearby Vineyards? Acts Congr. Oregon State Univ. (2016)
5. Carlos, C.: Spraying challenges in the Douro Wine Region of Portugal. DOURO Reg. WINE Clust. (2014)
6. Dastgheib, F., Frampton, C.: Weed management practices in apple orchards and vineyards in the South Island of New Zealand. New Zeal. J. Crop Hortic. Sci. **28**(1), 53–58 (2000)
7. Bekkers, T.: Weed control options for commercial organic vineyards. Wine Vitic. J. **4**, 62–64 (2011)
8. SheepIT Project (2017). http://www.av.it.pt/sheepit/
9. Nóbrega, L., Gonçalves, P., Pedreiras, P., Silva, S.: Energy efficient design of a pasture sensor network. In: The 5th International Conference on Future Internet of Things and Cloud- FiCloud 2017 (2017)
10. Turner, L.W., Udal, M.C., Larson, B.T., Shearer, S.A.: Monitoring cattle behavior and pasture use with GPS and GIS. Can. J. Anim. Sci. **80**(3), 405–413 (2000)
11. Kjellqvist, S.: Determining cattle pasture utilization using GPS-collars. slu (2008)
12. Augustine, D.J., Derner, J.D.: Assessing herbivore foraging behavior with GPS collars in a semiarid grassland. Sensors **13**(3), 3711–3723 (2013)
13. Dutta, R., et al.: Dynamic cattle behavioural classification using supervised ensemble classifiers. Comput. Electron. Agric. **111**, 18–28 (2014)

14. Williams, M.L., Mac Parthaláin, N., Brewer, P., James, W.P.J., Rose, M.T.: A novel behavioral model of the pasture-based dairy cow from GPS data using data mining and machine learning techniques. J. Dairy Sci. **99**(3), 2063–2075 (2016)

15. Bowman, J.L., Kochany, C.O., Demarais, S., Leopold, B.D.: Evaluation of a GPS collar for white-tailed deer. Wildl. Soc. Bull. **28**(1), 141–145 (2000)

16. Nathan, R., Spiegel, O., Fortmann-Roe, S., Harel, R., Wikelski, M., Getz, W.M.: Using tri-axial acceleration data to identify behavioral modes of free-ranging animals: general concepts and tools illustrated for griffon vultures. J. Exp. Biol. **215**(6), 986–996 (2012)

17. Hunter, J., et al.: OzTrack – E-infrastructure to support the management, analysis and sharing of animal tracking data. In: 2013 IEEE 9th International Conference on e-Science, pp. 140–147 (2013)

18. Rutter, S.M., Beresford, N.A., Roberts, G.: Use of GPS to identify the grazing areas of hill sheep. Comput. Electron. Agric. **17**(2), 177–188 (1997)

19. Jouven, M., Leroy, H., Ickowicz, A., Lapeyronie, P.: Can virtual fences be used to control grazing sheep? Rangel. J. **34**(1), 111–123 (2012)

20. Umstätter, C., Waterhouse, A., Holland, J.P.: An automated sensor-based method of simple behavioural classification of sheep in extensive systems. Comput. Electron. Agric. **64**(1), 19–26 (2008)

21. Brunberg, E.I., Bergslid, I.K., Bøe, K.E., Sørheim, K.M.: The ability of ewes with lambs to learn a virtual fencing system. Animal **11**(11), 2045–2050 (2017)

22. Nadimi, E.S., Søgaard, H.T., Bak, T., Oudshoorn, F.W.: ZigBee-based wireless sensor networks for monitoring animal presence and pasture time in a strip of new grass. Comput. Electron. Agric. **61**(2), 79–87 (2008)

23. Kwong, K.H., et al.: Practical considerations for wireless sensor networks in cattle monitoring applications. Comput. Electron. Agric. **81**, 33–44 (2012)

24. Huircán, J.I., et al.: ZigBee-based wireless sensor network localization for cattle monitoring in grazing fields. Comput. Electron. Agric. **74**(2), 258–264 (2010)

25. Oguejiofor, O.S., Okorogu, V.N., Adewale, A., Osuesu, B.O.: Outdoor localization system using RSSI measurement of wireless sensor network. Int. J. Innov. Technol. Explor. Eng. **2**(2), 1–6 (2013)

26. Thorstensen, B., Syversen, T., Bjornvold, T.-A., Walseth, T.: Electronic shepherd - a low-cost, low-bandwidth, wireless network system. In: MobiSys 2004: Proceedings of the 2nd International Conference on Mobile Systems, Applications, and Services, pp. 245–255 (2004)

27. Tiedemann, A., Quigley, T., White, L.: Electronic (fenceless) control of livestock. Res. Pap. PNWRP-510, Portland, OR. US For. Serv. Pacific Northwest Res. Station. Olympia, WA, USA., no. January 1999

28. Bishop-Hurley, G.J., Swain, D.L., Anderson, D.M., Sikka, P., Crossman, C., Corke, P.: Virtual fencing applications: implementing and testing an automated cattle control system. Comput. Electron. Agric. **56**(1), 14–22 (2007)

29. Fay, P.K., McElligott, V.T., Havstad, K.M.: Containment of free-ranging goats using pulsed-radio-wave-activated shock collars. Appl. Anim. Behav. Sci. **23**(1–2), 165–171 (1989)

30. Lee, C., Fisher, A.D., Reed, M.T., Henshall, J.M.: The effect of low energy electric shock on cortisol, [beta]-endorphin, heart rate and behaviour of cattle. Appl. Anim. Behav. Sci. **113**(1–3), 32–42 (2008)

31. ECMA: Technical Requirements for Electronic Pet Training and Containment Collars (2008)

32. Gubbi, J., Buyya, R., Marusic, S., Palaniswami, M.: Internet of Things (IoT): a vision, architectural elements, and future directions. Futur. Gener. Comput. Syst. **29**(7), 1645–1660 (2013)

33. Temprilho, A., Nóbrega, L., Gonçalves, P., Pedreiras, P., Silva, S.: M2M communication stack for intelligent farming. in Global Internet of Things Summit (GIoTS) (2018)
34. Umstatter, C., Brocklehurst, S., Ross, D.W., Haskell, M.J.: Can the location of cattle be managed using broadcast audio cues? Appl. Anim. Behav. Sci. **147**(1–2), 34–42 (2013)
35. Application note Using LSM303DLH for a tilt compensated electronic compass. - Pesquisa Google
36. Nóbrega, L., Pedreiras, P., Gonçalves, P., Temprilho, A., Morais, R.: SheepIT: automated vineyard weeding control system. In: INForum 2017 - Simpósio de Informática (2017)

Techniques for Plant Disease Diagnosis Evaluated on a Windows Phone Platform

Nikos Petrellis(✉) ⓘ

Computer Science and Engineering Department, TEI of Thessaly, Larissa, Greece
npetrellis@teilar.gr

Abstract. The recognition of plant diseases is a responsibility of professional agriculture engineers. Intelligent systems can assist plant disease diagnosis in the early stages with low cost. User descriptions and image comparison are exploited in some expert systems that are already available. More sophisticated techniques like the one presented in this paper are based on features extracted from the symptoms (e.g., lesions) of a plant disease that appear on the leaves, the fruits, etc. The color, the dimensions and the number of these lesion spots can be used in some cases to discriminate the disease that has mortified a plant. In this paper, we describe a smart phone application that measures the features of the plant lesions with higher than 90% precision. The accuracy in the recognition of grapevine or citrus diseases that have been used as case studies is higher than 70% in most of the cases using only 5 photographs for the definition of each disease. The most important advantage of the proposed method is that the set of the supported diseases can be easily extended by the end-user.

Keywords: Plant disease · Lesions · Image processing ·
Agricultural production

1 Introduction

The spread of a plant disease can dramatically increase the cost of agricultural production. The plants have to be continuously monitored for the detection of the first symptoms of a disease. Treating a disease at its early stages, before it is spread to the whole cultivation may reduce the cost of the medicine, minimize the environmental impact and prevent the destruction of the whole production. Small or isolated farms may not be able to support full monitoring by professional agriculturists. Monitoring the plants through expert systems that utilize machine vision and artificial intelligence techniques can offer an alternative lower cost option.

In the simplest case, the user can send photos to agriculturists and ask their opinion based on the visible symptoms. Additional molecular tests may be ordered if the visible symptoms indicate that a plant has been infected by a disease. The symptoms of a plant disease are described in [1] and can indicate underdevelopment, overdevelopment of tissues or organs and necrosis of

© Springer Nature Switzerland AG 2019
M. Salampasis and T. Bournaris (Eds.): HAICTA 2017, CCIS 953, pp. 148–163, 2019.
https://doi.org/10.1007/978-3-030-12998-9_11

plant parts. The progression of a disease drastically affects the appearance of the symptoms classifying them as primary and secondary. The symptoms are also different if more than one pathogen are active.

The symptoms of a disease in most of the cases appear as lesions on various plant parts: leaves, fruits, branches, root, etc. An image processing technique can be used to locate and qualify the lesions using the following features: number of spots, their area, color, etc. The texture of these lesions is also a very important feature revealing information in three dimensions, but it is more difficult to be characterized by a plain image.

Reviews of image processing techniques and molecular tests can be found in [2–4]. Image processing techniques can be applied in visual or infrared light. Spectroscopic techniques can also be employed for plant disease diagnosis based on its symptoms. For example, spectroscopic techniques can identify water stress levels and nutrient deficiency. They can also be used to measure the fruit quality during or after the harvest. Infrared spectroscopy is described in [5]. Multispectral image and thermal view using drones was applied to detect if a plant with opium poppy is affected by Downy Mildew in [6]. In [4] an image segmentation takes place in the CIE L*a*b color spaces where each pixel is described by three components: its brightness (L), its position between red and green (*a) and its position between yellow and blue (*b) in the color palette wheel. A neural network classifies the image in one of the potential diseases. Other color spaces like Citrus Color Index have also been used in similar applications like citrus harvest [7]. Additional features that have been used in the plant disease classification include the shape of a plant part, its texture, fractal dimensions, lacunarity, dispersion, grey levels, grey histogram discrimination and the Fourier descriptors.

An expert system based either on graphical representation or a step-by-step descriptive method is discussed in [8]. In the graphical representation, photographs are interactively compared to find the matching disease while in the descriptive mode the user answers a list of questions set by the system. In [9], a low cost advanced machine vision method is described to detect Citrus Huanglongbing (HLB) disease. The Gaussian mixture density is used to extract the leaf object from the citrus image, followed by the feature extraction and recognition of the existence of HLB in the leaf based on scalable vocabulary tree. Corn diseases are diagnosed using the system presented in [10]. A quantification technique for fruit traits is presented in [11]. Pine-apples and bitter melons were used in [12] to evaluate a texture analysis technique for detecting green fruits on plants. The extracted features are classified using support vector machines. Most of the image processing and spectroscopic techniques presented in the literature require high cost equipment or computational intensive operations.

The image processing analysis may indicate that additional molecular tests have to be performed to confirm the detected disease. A popular molecular test is called ELISA. It is based on the use of a microbial protein associated with the plant disease. The antibodies are produced by an animal after this protein is injected to it. Another popular technique based on DNA analysis is Polymerase

Chain Reaction (PCR) that is employed in [13]. A portable DNA analysis tool has also been presented recently by the author in [14].

A plant disease diagnosis method appropriate for implementation on mobile platforms is presented in this paper. It employs a low complexity image processing technique that distinguishes regions of special interest on a plant part: it isolates the normal leaf area from the sick lesions and the potential halo that surrounds them. The developed system can operate in standalone mode as an autonomous smart phone application or in cooperation with remote clouds or databases. Such an extended configuration can support additional plant diseases or can be offered as an advanced more accurate option to the users with higher cost. Portable molecular analysis equipment like the one described in [14] can also provide additional features to the plant disease method presented here for higher precision diagnosis.

The developed application extracts a number of features from the image including the number of spots in the displayed plant part, their area and their grey level. The grey level of the normal leaf and the halo around the spots is also estimated. Moreover, the positions of the lobes in the color histograms of each one of the distinguished plant part are used as additional features. In real time operation, the user can analyse photographs of mortified plant parts (leaves, fruits, etc.) in situ. The application may also ask additional information useful for a reliable diagnosis. However, in the present version the plant disease diagnosis is based merely on the image processing analysis. In its current form the application has been tested for the precision in the measurement of the spot features that appear in pear, citrus or grapevine leaves. The application has also been evaluated in the diagnosis of citrus and grapevine diseases. The measurement of the number of spots and their area in any plant part photo can be achieved with a precision higher than 90% while most of the supported diseases were recognized with an accuracy higher than 70% using only 5 photographs for the definition of the disease diagnosis rules. The most important advantage of the proposed method is that the end user can easily extend the supported set of diseases by analysing a few photographs.

The proposed plant disease classification method is described in Sect. 2. The implementation of this method as a Windows Phone application is presented in Sect. 3 and experimental results are discussed in Sect. 4.

2   Extraction of Features Useful in Plant Disease Diagnosis

The proposed plant disease recognition method is based on the extraction of a number of features from a photograph of a plant part. It can be implemented as an autonomous smart phone application due to its low complexity. The mobile phone where the application is installed needs to be connected to the internet only if plant disease recognition rules stored in remote databases or clouds have to be accessed. Such a connection would also be useful if the photographs taken by the smart phone camera have to be inspected by agriculturists or if they have to be stored in agricultural databases with information about the diseases that occurred in specific regions. In the autonomous operating mode the application can support a restricted number of plant diseases only if this is dictated by the financial policy of the provider. The resources required to support a specific disease recognition are negligible and they do not pose a significant restriction concerning the number of supported diseases.

During real time operation the user, can take photographs of plant parts with lesions like leaves and fruits which are analysed by the plant disease recognition application. The application may also ask the user additional questions like: what is the type of the plant, which plant part is displayed, how far was the plant when it was photographed, an estimation of how many leaves have been affected in a single plant or how many plants have been mortified, information about the speed of the disease progression, etc. Very important features needed for plant disease recognition can also concern environmental conditions like temperature, moisture, etc. This kind of information can be downloaded from websites that provide such historical weather data for specific geographical coordinates that can be estimated by the GPS sensor of the smart phone. The experimental results presented in this paper have been based only on features extracted by the proposed image processing procedure as well as weather data. For this reason, it is obvious that higher accuracy is expected in the diagnosis if the additional information given by the user is also taken into account in the future versions of our application. The proposed image processing technique extracts a number of features including the number of lesion spots, their grey level and area using an algorithm that has already been described in [15]. This set of features is extended here with color features of the normal leaf parts as well as the leaf spots. A third region of interest is also de-fined: halo around the spots. A fuzzy-like classification method is used to rank all the supported diseases, weighting appropriately the feature values. The main advantage of the proposed method is its extendibility since new disease recognition rules can be added by

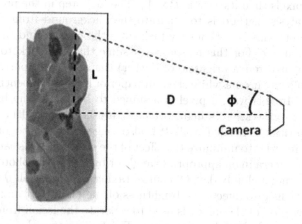

Fig. 1. Measurement of the leaf or lesion size [15].

the end-user. The end-user can be an agriculturist not necessarily qualified in computer science. Neural networks that accept as input the features described in this paper can also be tested in future versions of the application achieving even better accuracy but they will probably lack the advantage of the extendibility. In a more advanced setup, the mobile phone can communicate (e.g., through USB, bluetooth, WiFi, etc.) with a portable device that can perform molecular analysis like the biosensor readout circuit described in [14] that has been developed for the Corallia/LabOnChip project. These biosensor values can also be treated as additional features taken into consideration by the proposed disease recognition method. The absolute size of a lesion can be estimated if the distance D of the camera from the plant is known (Fig. 1). Some tricks can be used to take photographs from known distance like for example to fit a leaf or a fruit exactly within the borders of a photograph or take photographs with a distance of one palm or one finger. The angle ϕ of Fig. 1 is camera-specific and the user may find its value in the smart phone specifications. The leaf length L is estimated by:

$$L = 2 \times D \times tan(\phi) \tag{1}$$

If P is the number of pixels corresponding to a known distance L, then a scaling can be performed by the ratio $S = L/P$ to estimate another distance L' from a different number of pixels P':

$$L' = P'\frac{L}{P} \tag{2}$$

The area A_p occupied by a single pixel can be estimated if P_x and P_y pixels correspond to the length L_x, L_y of the sides of a rectangle:

$$A_p = \frac{1}{S^2}\frac{L_x L_y}{P_x P_y} \tag{3}$$

It can generally be stated that if a lesion with either regular or irregular shape consists of P pixels then its area is $P \times A_p$. The first step in the proposed image processing analysis method is to separate the background from the displayed part of the plant. This is not an easy task since the background can be the rest of the plant, soil, etc. For this reason, we assume that the background is white or at least that it is much brighter (or darker) than the plant part. This can be reassured by placing it on a white sheet of paper or on a white bench or a marble in the garden. In this way, a pixel is assumed to belong to the background if its brightness in grey scale is higher than a threshold B_g and no complicated separation algorithm is needed at all. It is also suggested to photograph the plant appropriately in order to minimize the effect of the shadows. This can be achieved by placing the camera in an appropriate angle or by taking the photograph under a canopy or during a cloudy day. Of course, taking a photograph under different lighting conditions also affects the brightness of the plant part and the lesion.

The grey version of the image is used to separate the lesion from the normal plant part which may be a leaf or a fruit. The lesion can either be brighter or darker than the normal plant part. The grey level of all the pixels that belong to the plant part are averaged (A_g). It is assumed that the grey level of a pixel i that belongs to the lesion has an absolute difference from the A_g higher than a threshold T_h:

$$|G_i - A_g| > T_h \tag{4}$$

A matrix $M1$ that has the same size with the original image is constructed. Each cell in $M1$ is initially marked with 'B' or 'N' according to whether the pixel that corresponds to this specific cell belongs to the background or the plant part (Fig. 2a). The grey level of the pixels in the original image that have been marked as 'N' in $M1$ is averaged to estimate A_g. Then, $M1$ is scanned from top to the bottom and from left to right in order to find the pixels marked as 'N' that fulfil the condition of Eq. (4) and thus belong to a lesion spot. These cells are replaced in $M1$ with an identity I that is initially set to 1. The identity I of the neighbouring spot pixels that have already been visited (top left, top, top right, left) is also assigned to the current pixel. If no neighbouring pixels belong to a lesion spot, then the current pixel is assigned with the maximum I value increased by 1 ($I + 1$). The resulting matrix after these modifications is $M2$ (Fig. 2b). Some spot pixels although they are adjacent may be initially assigned with a different I value as shown in the cell (6,8) of $M2$ in Fig. 2b. This cell can be assigned either with the identity 1 or 3. This pixel is both adjacent to pixels marked with $I = 1$ and $I = 3$, meaning that it links two spots that must be handled as a single one. For this reason, $M2$ must be repeatedly scanned merging any adjacent spots and shifting appropriately the spot identities to fill the resulting gaps. Moreover, the pixels surrounding the spots in a zone of pixel width H_p that do not belong to the back-ground are marked as Halo ('H'). The resulting matrix after these modifications on $M2$ is the $M3$ shown in Fig. 2c where the halo zone has a width of one pixel ($H_p = 1$). Of course, the halo could have been separated by the other regions through its color features.

The matrix $M3$ serves as a map of the three regions of interest distinguished in the photograph of a plant part (Normal, Lesion, Halo). Some useful features can be easily extracted using $M3$. The highest I value corresponds to the number of spots (F_{ns}). The ratio of the number of the pixels found in the Normal, Lesion and Halo region (N_N, N_L, N_H, respectively) to the total number of pixels ($N_N + N_L + N_H$) in the displayed plant part is the relative area of each region (F_{NA}, F_{LA}, F_{HA}, respectively):

$$F_{NA} = \frac{N_N}{N_N + N_L + N_H} \tag{5}$$

$$F_{LA} = \frac{N_L}{N_N + N_L + N_H} \tag{6}$$

$$F_{HA} = \frac{N_H}{N_N + N_L + N_H} \tag{7}$$

The average grey level of the Normal, the Lesion and the Halo region (F_{NG}, F_{LG}, F_{HG}, respectively) can be estimated by the grey level G_i of the pixels i

B	B	B	B	B	N	N	B	B	B	B
B	N	N	N	N	N	N	N	N	N	B
B	N	N	N	N	N	N	N	N	N	N
B	N	N	N	N	N	N	N	N	N	N
B	B	B	N	N	N	N	N	N	N	N
B	B	B	B	N	N	N	N	N	B	B
B	B	B	B	N	B	B	B	B	B	B

(a)

B	B	B	B	B	N	N	B	B	B	B
B	N	N	N	N	N	N	N	N	N	B
B	N	N	N	N	1	1	N	N	2	2
B	N	N	N	N	1	1	N	N	N	N
B	B	B	N	N	1	N	N	3	N	N
B	B	B	B	N	1	1	1 or 3	N	B	B
B	B	B	B	N	B	B	B	B	B	B

(b)

B	B	B	B	B	N	N	B	B	B	B
B	N	N	N	N	H	H	H	H	H	B
B	N	N	N	H	1	1	H	H	2	2
B	N	N	N	H	1	1	H	H	H	H
B	B	B	N	H	1	H	H	1	H	N
B	B	B	B	H	1	1	1	H	B	B
B	B	B	B	H	B	B	B	B	B	B

(c)

Fig. 2. In $M1$ matrix the background is separated by the normal plant (a), in $M2$ the lesion spots are separated by the normal plant part and are numbered (b) while in $M3$ neighboring spots are merged and a Halo zone of 1 pixel width is defined around each spot (c).

marked in $M3$ as 'N', I, and 'H', respectively:

$$F_{NG} = (\sum_i G_i)/N_N, M3[i] = 'N' \tag{8}$$

$$F_{LG} = (\sum_i G_i)/N_L, 0 < M3[i] \leq I \tag{9}$$

$$F_{HG} = (\sum_i G_i)/N_H, M3[i] = 'H' \tag{10}$$

Additional important features can be extracted using the histograms of each region and each basic color in Red-Green-Blue (RGB) color space. The horizontal axis in each histogram has 256-positions corresponding to the level of each color. Each value $H(L)$ of the Red, the Green or the Blue histogram in the position L corresponds to the number of pixels in the specific region that have this exact color level L. For example, if $H_{RL}(100) = 150$ in the Red histogram of the Lesion region then, there are 150 lesion pixels that have Red color level equal to 100. In Fig. 3a, a grapevine leaf infected by Downy Mildew is displayed. The corresponding $M3$ matrix is displayed in Fig. 3b with four levels of grey. The Background is displayed in white, the Lesion spots in black and the normal leaf in grey. Brighter grey is used to display a Halo zone of 3 pixels wide around the lesion spots. The three color histograms derived from the pixels of the Lesion spots are displayed overlapped in Fig. 3c. As can be seen from this figure, all of the histograms consist of a single lobe. This is also true for the three histograms of the Normal region. The Halo histograms can consist of two lobes if there is actually no distinct halo region with different color. Nevertheless, if the user defines a Halo zone that consists of pixels from both the Normal and the Lesion region then, its histogram may have one lobe derived from the lesion and one from the normal region since the pixels within these regions have similar color. The starting (b), the ending (e) and the peak position (p) of each histogram lobe are used as features (F_{RCb}, F_{RCe}, F_{RCp}, respectively) that can be checked against strict and loose limits during the disease diagnosis. The strict and loose limits of these features can be denoted as (S_{RCh_n}, S_{RCh_x}) and (L_{RCh_n}, L_{RCh_x}) respectively, where the index R is the region (Normal-N Lesion-L, Halo-H), C is the color (Red-R, Green-G, Blue-B) and h is the histogram lobe positions (Begin-b, End-e, Peak-p). The strict and loose limits of all the supported features form a Disease Identity (DI). The employed fuzzy-like classification method ranks each potential disease according to whether an estimated feature falls within (a) the strict, (b) the loose or (c) none of the limits that have been defined for this feature in the specific DI. A different grade is taken into account in each one of these three cases and the overall disease rank G_d for a disease d, is estimated by the weighted sum of the individual feature grades:

$$G_d = \sum_{\substack{R = N, L, H \\ C = R, G, B \\ h = b, e, p}} (W_{S\_RCh} G_{S\_RCh} x_{S\_RCh} + W_{L\_RCh} G_{L\_RCh} x_{L\_RCh}) \qquad (11)$$

The grades G_{S_RCh} and G_{L_RCh} are added after they have been multiplied by the corresponding weights W_{S_RCh} and W_{L_RCh} if the feature F_{RCh} is found within the strict ($x_{S\_RCh} = 1$) and loose ($x_{L\_RCh} = 1$) limits respectively:

$$x_{S\_RCh} = \begin{cases} 1, S_{RCh\_n} \leq F_{RCh} \leq S_{RCh\_x} \\ 0, otherwise \end{cases} \qquad (12)$$

$$x_{L\_RCh} = \begin{cases} 1, L_{RCh\_n} \leq F_{RCh} \leq L_{RCh\_x} \\ 0, otherwise \end{cases} \qquad (13)$$

The Eqs. (11)–(13) that were defined for the histogram features are extended to also encounter the features: F_{ns}, F_{NA}, F_{LA}, F_{HA}, F_{NG}, F_{LG}, F_{HG}. The rest of the features used in the proposed plant disease diagnosis method are

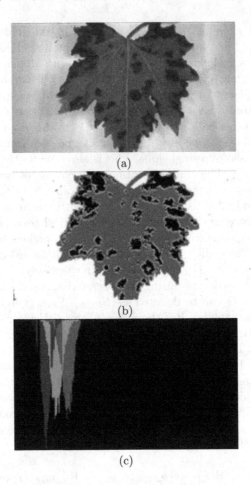

Fig. 3. The photograph of a grapevine leaf infected by Downy Mildew (a), the representation of its $M3$ matrix in four grey levels (b) and the three color histograms corresponding to the lesion spots (c). (Color figure online)

weather data that have been retrieved by web sites that provide such information for given geographical coordinates ([16,17], etc.). The most important weather information required for plant disease diagnosis concerns the moisture and the temperatures in specific time intervals in the past e.g., in the spring months. In our approach, we employed the average moisture F_M, as well as the average minimum and maximum daily temperatures (F_{TN}, F_{TX} respectively). These three weather features are estimated by averaging the corresponding daily parameters from past time intervals (or individual dates) defined by the user. Features with Boolean or discrete values have also been employed like the plant part selection (F_{PT}) i.e., whether the photograph displays leaf, fruit, etc. These features can also be compared with strict and loose limits in the broader sense.

A slightly different plant disease classification method could use multiple strict and loose limits to compare each feature. In a pure fuzzy-logic classification each features would be assigned with a grade proportional to the distance of the estimated feature from a reference value defined in the DI. Alternative classification methods like these will be examined in our future application versions. The DI of a specific disease d in the proposed method includes the following values concerning each feature f:

$$DI_{d,f} = \{G_{S\_f}, G_{L\_f}, W_{S\_f}, W_{L\_f}, S_{f\_n}, S_{f\_x}, L_{f\_n}, L_{f\_x}\} \tag{14}$$

where $[S_{f\_n}, S_{f\_x}]$ are the strict and $[L_{f\_n}, L_{f\_x}]$ are the loose limits of the feature f, G_{S_f}, G_{L_f} are the grades and W_{S_f}, W_{L_f}, are the weights corresponding to these strict and loose limits. If a new disease has to be supported, the user can analyse a few photographs (5–10) of the same disease using the developed application. The values of all the aforementioned features are listed to the user who can determine the draft range of each feature. Based on these ranges he can heuristically define strict and loose limits for each feature as well as the grades and potentially different weights in a new DI. This DI may be stored in a special format (e.g., JavaScript Object Notation-JSON) and loaded dynamically by the application. In such a dynamic configuration, the software of the plant disease diagnosis application does not have to be altered.

3   Implementation as a Smart Phone Application

The proposed plant disease diagnosis method has been implemented in Microsoft® Visual Studio as a Windows Phone application (Plant Disease) and tested on a Lumia 535 smart phone. The main page of the Plant Disease application is shown in Fig. 4a. The user can select a stored photograph from this page and analyse it. He can potentially modify three thresholds: (a) B_g in the field "Background" separates the Background from the plant part, (b) T_h in the field "Threshold" separates the Lesion from the Normal plant part and (c) the field "Min Spot Area" determines the minimum number of pixels that a lesion spot should consist of. If a spot consists of fewer pixels than the number defined in the "Min Spot Area" field, it is considered as noise and it is ignored. The user has the option to let the system select automatically the thresholds T_h and B_g based on the grey histogram of the all the photograph pixels which is expected to have a shape like the one shown in Fig. 5a. The lobe at higher grey levels is derived by Background pixels that are white or generally much brighter than the plant part. The other two lobes correspond to the Normal plant part and the Lesion. If the Lesion is darker than the Normal plant part then, the Lesion lobe is at the lower grey levels. Although this method may work well in many cases, it may not select appropriate thresholds T_h and B_g if the grey histogram of the photograph is like the one shown in Fig. 5b. However, the user may try an automatic threshold selection and interactively evaluate if the Lesion and the Background are correctly separated otherwise he may experiment himself with these thresholds to find their optimal value.

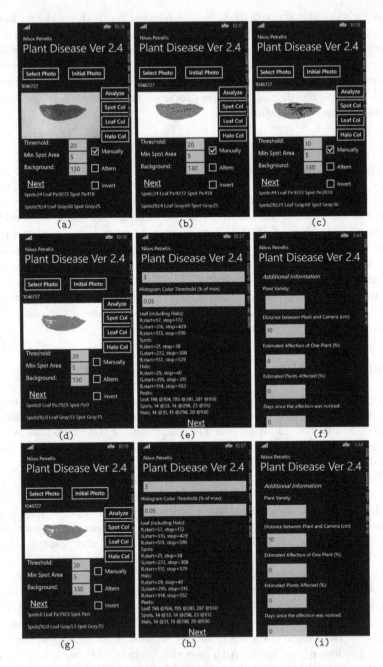

Fig. 4. The main application page displaying a citrus leaf (a), image analysis with $T_h = 20$ (b) $T_h = 10$ (c), $T_h = 30$ (d), detailed histogram features (e), insertion of additional information (f), plant part selection (g), geographical location (h) and weather data retrieval (i).

The draft color histograms of all the regions of interest (Normal, Lesion spots, Halo) like the one already shown in Fig. 3c can be displayed in the main page of the application (Fig. 4a). In the photograph of Fig. 4a, a lemon leaf infected by Melanose is displayed and Fig. 4b, c, and d show the results of the analysis if T_h has the values: 20, 10 and 30 respectively. Setting $T_h = 20$ seems to be a good option since the spots appear to be recognized accurately. Using a lower threshold as in Fig. 4c, Normal area is falsely recognized as Lesion. On the contrary, a higher threshold fails to recognize any Lesion spots as shown in Fig. 4d.

The features: F_{ns}, F_{LA}, F_{NG}, F_{LG}, are displayed at the bottom of the main application page as shown in Fig. 4a–d. The features extracted from the color histograms are listed to the user in the following application page as shown in Fig. 4e. In this page the user can also determine the Halo zone width (H_p) and where the histogram lobes are assumed to start and end (e.g., at the 5% of the lobe peak). The user can also provide additional information (Fig. 4f) about the status of the plant or the cultivation but this type of information is

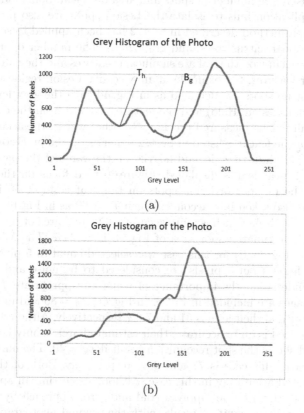

(a)

(b)

Fig. 5. The grey histogram of a plant part photo with distinct T_h and B_g thresholds (a) and a grey histogram where the T_h and B_g thresholds cannot be easily discriminated (b).

not taken into consideration in the present version of the application. It is also necessary to determine the type of the plant and the plant part (feature FPT) that is displayed in the selected photograph (Fig. 4g). Weather historical data are necessary to determine the features F_M, F_{TN} and F_{TX}. In Fig. 4h, the user selects interactively the geographical region where the plant exists or he may insert the precise coordinates (longitude, latitude). Then, in the page of Fig. 4i, the user can select individual dates that are going to be used for averaging the daily moisture and minimum/maximum temperatures during the estimation of the features F_M, F_{TN} and F_{TX} respectively. The application then, lists the three diseases with the highest rank. Instructions may also be given on how to treat each disease.

4   Experimental Results - Discussion

In this section, we initially test if the developed Plant Disease application can estimate precisely the number of spots and area on a leaf. Some indicative cases where the application fails to isolate the Lesion spots are also presented. The spot recognition method described in Sect. 2 has been applied to several photos of leaves from pear, citrus trees, and grapevines. The number of spots and the area that they occupy on the leaf are significant features and they affect the value of many other features. For example, if an excessive Lesion region is recognized as in Fig. 4c or no spots are detected as in Fig. 4d then the grey level of all the regions (Normal, Lesion, Halo) and the features derived from the corresponding histograms will not be measured precisely. In other words, the accurate estimation of most of the features listed in Sect. 2 depends on the precision of the F_{ns}, F_{LA} features, which in turn depend heavily on the value of the parameter T_h.

In Fig. 6a a pear leaf is displayed. Figure 6b to d focus on the lesion spot recognition. The number of lesion spots on this leaf is 45 or 50 if some very small ones are also taken into account. When $T_h = 60$ as in Fig. 6b, the number of estimated spots is 49 which is quite accurate. The real area of the spots is 14% of the leaf. The estimated spot area of Fig. 6b is 12.34%. The Min Spot Area parameter (see Fig. 4a–d) for this case was selected equal to 5 pixels i.e., spots consisting of fewer than 5 pixels are considered to be noise and are ignored. In order to understand the importance of using an appropriate T_h value, two additional images are included in Fig. 6. In Fig. 6c, $T_h = 80$ and in this case the number of spots and their area is 51 and 7.6% respectively. Although the number of spots recognized is quite accurate, their estimated area is only half of the real one. Figure 6d shows the spot recognition result if $T_h = 40$. The number of spots and their area in this case is 77 and 20% respectively. Both of these features are not estimated accurately in this case. Although selecting an appropriate T_h value is critical, the user can apply a trial and error approach by interactively comparing the spot recognition results with the original photograph.

In the experiments conducted in the framework of this paper, the average error measured in the number of spots and the spot area is 7% and 11% respectively. This error was measured by interactively finding a T_h value multiple of

10 that produced the best spot recognition in each photograph. About 100 photographs were used, with pear, grapevine and citrus leaves that had distinct spots with clearly measurable area.

The proposed spot recognition method is not always successful whatever value is selected for the T_h threshold as shown in Fig. 7 where a grapevine leaf is displayed. One reason for this unsuccessful spot recognition attempt is the fact that the background is not bright enough and has some dark lines that are confused with the leaf color thus, it is difficult to select an appropriate B_g threshold. Moreover, the color of the spots is the same as the one of the leaf veins.

Despite these problems, the proposed method can achieve a good accuracy as shown in Table 1 where the developed Plant Disease application is tested on grape-vine diseases and Table 2 where citrus diseases are used. Five only photographs of each disease were used during the definition of the corresponding DIs. The number of test photographs used per disease, ranges between 14 and 40 (please see the third column of Tables 1 and 2). The photographs used during the experimentation were taken in the field, half of them under direct sunlight and the rest of them in a canopy to minimize the effect of the shades. Although there are a few particular diseases that cannot achieve an acceptable accuracy (like Powdery Mildew), most of the diseases are recognized with an accuracy higher than 70% which is a quite good taking into consideration the small number of photographs used for the definition of the DIs. The accuracy measured in some of

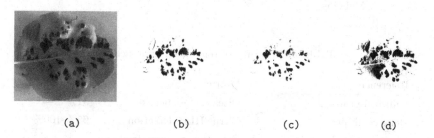

(a)   (b)   (c)   (d)

Fig. 6. Original image of a pear tree leaf (a), and the isolation of the spots with $T_h = 60$ (b), $T_h = 80$ (c) and $T_h = 40$ (d).

(a)   (b)   (c)

Fig. 7. A grapevine leaf with Powdery Mildew (a), spot isolation with $T_h = 80$ (b) and $T_h = 70$ (c).

the referenced approaches is listed in Table 3. Although these approaches achieve an accuracy higher than 85%, they are exploiting classification methods like neural networks that require a large number of training photographs. Moreover, the set of the supported diseases cannot be extended by the end user.

Table 1. Accuracy in the recognition of grapevine diseases.

Grapevine disease	Recognition accuracy	Tested photos
Downy Mildew	73%	40
Powdery Mildew	35%	14
Phomopsis	89%	35
Esca	50%	16

Table 2. Accuracy in the recognition of citrus diseases.

Grapevine disease	Recognition accuracy	Tested photos
Alternaria	78%	30
Anthracnose	81%	32
CCDV	75%	22
Deficiency	55%	38
Melanose	95%	23

Table 3. Accuracy of referenced approaches.

Reference	Metric	Accuracy
Kulkarni et al. [4]	Disease classification	91%
Deng et al. [9]	Citrus HLB detection	95%–100%
Chaivivatrakul and Dailey [12]	Detection of green fruits on - pineapples - bitter melons	85% 100%
This approach	Disease classification	35%–95%

5   Conclusion

A low complexity image processing technique that can be used for the estimation of features useful in plant disease diagnosis was presented in this paper. The number of spots and their area on plant leaves is measured with an accuracy higher than 90%. The disease diagnosis was tested with grape and citrus leaves with an accuracy in the classification higher than 70%, in most of the cases using only 5 photographs as a training set. The most important advantage of the proposed method is that it can be easily extended by the end-user to support new diseases.

Future work will focus on testing different classification methods without sacrificing extendibility. The developed applications will also be ported on different platforms. Finally, the proposed diagnosis method will also be tested on different applications like human and animal skin diseases.

Acknowledgement. This work is protected by the provisional patents 1009346/13-8-2018 and 1008484/12-5-2015 (Greek Patent Office).

References

1. Riley, M.B., Williamson, M.R., Maloy, O.: Plant disease diagnosis. Plant Health Instructor (2002). https://doi.org/10.1094/PHI-I-2002-1021-01
2. Sankaran, S., Mishra, A., Eshani, R., Davis, C.: A review of advanced techniques for detecting plant diseases. Comput. Electron. Agric. **72**(1), 1–3 (2010)
3. Patil, J., Kumar, R.: Advances in image processing for detection of plant diseases. J. Adv. Bioinform. Appl. Res. **2**(2), 135–141 (2011)
4. Kulkarni, A., Patil, A.: Applying image processing technique to detect plant diseases. Int. J. Mod. Eng. Res. **2**(5), 3361–3364 (2012)
5. Purcell, D.E., O'Shea, M.G., Johnson, R.A., Kokot, S.: Near infrared spectroscopy for the prediction of disease rating for Fiji leaf gall in sugarcane clones. Appl. Spectrosc. **63**(4), 450–457 (2009)
6. Calderon, R., Montes-Borrego, M., Landa, B.B., Navas-Cortes, J., Zarco-Tejada, P.J.: Detection of Downy Mildew of opium poppy using high-resolution multispectral and thermal imagery acquired with an unmanned aerial vehicle. Precision Agric. **15**(6), 639–661 (2014)
7. Cubero, S., et al.: Optimised computer vision system for automatic pre-grading of citrus fruit in the field using a mobile platform. Precision Agric. **15**, 80–94 (2014)
8. Abu-Naser, S.S., Kashkash, K.A., Fayad, M.: Developing an expert system for plant disease diagnosis. J. Artif. Intell. **1**(2), 78–85 (2008)
9. Deng, X.-L., Li, Z., Hong, T.S.: Citrus disease recognition based on weighted scalable vocabulary tree. Precision Agric. **15**, 321–330 (2014)
10. Lai, J.C., Ming, B., Li, S.K., Wang, K.R., Xie, R.Z., Gao, S.J.: An image-based diagnostic expert system for corn diseases. Agric. Sci. China **9**(8), 1221–1229 (2010)
11. Mix, C., Picó, F.X., Ouborg, N.J.: A comparison of stereomicroscope and image analysis for quantifying fruit traits. SEED Technol. **25**(1), 12–19 (2003)
12. Chaivivatrakul, S., Dailey, M.: Texture-based fruit detection. Precision Agric. **15**(6), 662–683 (2014)
13. Schaad, N.W., Frederick, R.D.: Real time PCR and its application for rapid plant disease diagnostics. Can. J. Plant Pathol. **24**(3), 250–258 (2002)
14. Georgakopoulou, K., Spathis, C., Petrellis, N., Birbas, A.: A capacitive to digital converter with automatic range adaptation. IEEE Trans. Instrum. Meas. **65**(2), 336–345 (2016)
15. Petrellis, N.: Plant disease diagnosis based on image processing, appropriate for mobile phone implementation. In: 7th HAICTA 2015 Conference Proceedings, Kavala, Greece, pp. 238–246, 17–20 September 2015
16. Dark Sky weather information. https://darksky.net/forecast/40.7127,-74.0059/us12/en. Accessed 15 Mar 2018
17. Open Weather Map weather information. https://openweathermap.org/api. Accessed 15 Mar 2018

Different Remote Sensing Data in Relative Biomass Determination and in Precision Fertilization Task Generation for Cereal Crops

Jere Kaivosoja[1]([⊠]) [iD], Roope Näsi[2] [iD], Teemu Hakala[2] [iD],
Niko Viljanen[2] [iD], and Eija Honkavaara[2] [iD]

[1] Natural Resources Institute Finland (LUKE), Korkeakoulunkatu 7,
33720 Tampere, Finland
jere.kaivosoja@luke.fi
[2] Finnish Geospatial Research Institute, Geodeetinrinne 2,
02430 Masala, Finland

Abstract. Recently, the area of passive remote sensing in agricultural fields has been developing fast. The prices of RPAS (remotely piloted aircraft system) equipment has gone down, new suitable sensors are coming into markets while simultaneously new and free relevant satellite data has become available. One of the most used applications for these methodologies is to calculate the relative biomass as a basis for additional nitrogen fertilization. In this work, we study the difference of biomass estimations based on Sentinel-2 imagery, tractor implemented commercial measurement system, a low-cost RPAS equipment with commercial software and a hyperspectral imaging system implemented in a professional RPAS system in the fertilization planning. There was a 23% spatial variation in our malt barley yield. Different relative biomass estimations produced similar and sufficient results and the observation time or the used methodology was not very critical. Also none of the methodologies were remarkably better. When we generated the nitrogen fertilization application tasks, different reasonable parameters conducted very different application tasks. This means that in our case, the relative biomass does not provide sufficient information for nitrogen shortage variation. Knowledge of the local conditions is essential.

Keywords: Sentinel-2 · RPAS · UAV · Variable Rate Application (VRA)

1 Introduction

The basic idea of precision farming is to spatially and timely optimize the farming inputs to maximize the farming outcomes while reducing the environmental stress. Nitrogen fertilizers are one of the core inputs in plant production. An insufficient dosage of the nitrogen fertilizer for cereal crops can decrease the amount and quality of the yield. Too much nitrogen fertilization degreases the quality and causes risk of flattening of the growth causing yield losses. Also unused nitrogen in the soil leaches to the environment throughout the growing period and after. The growing conditions within a field vary quite a lot and a smart spatial variation in the fertilization amount

© Springer Nature Switzerland AG 2019
M. Salampasis and T. Bournaris (Eds.): HAICTA 2017, CCIS 953, pp. 164–176, 2019.
https://doi.org/10.1007/978-3-030-12998-9_12

could have a great impact for economics and the environment. For this, it is necessary to detect the different nitrogen needs around the field.

There are several methodologies developed for precision nitrogen management. Already developed applications for cereal crops utilize an optical sensing of the growth status during the growing season to determine how much additional nitrogen is needed. Sensing may take place from satellites, aircrafts, RPAS's (remotely piloted aircraft system) also called UAV (Unmanned Aerial Vehicle), working machinery such as Yara-N-sensor and Trimble GreenSeeker or handheld devices. Recently there has been a fast development in this area of passive and active remote sensing and the productization is in progress. The prices of RPAS equipment have gone down and new sensor technologies are coming into markets. Also new, free and relevant satellite technology has become available for the environmental mapping. The Sentinel-2 satellites are providing useful data several times per week with up to 10×10 m accuracy if the weather is cloud free.

One of the most common applications for those methodologies is to calculate relative biomass as a basis for additional nitrogen fertilization. Typically different remote sensing data are used by comparing a red and near infrared wavelengths by measuring a normalized difference vegetation index (NDVI) or its variants. Then an implemented decision support system (DSS) produces an estimate for the required nitrogen fertilization need. This DSS system requires calibration information about crop's remaining nitrogen needs and responsiveness according to the predicted yield potential [1, 2] being an important factor for the nitrogen fertilization. There are mobile applications and web services which can calculate a suggested fertilization rate for the specific crops based on NDVI-measurements from single spots, or the application shows a NDVI map based on the latest satellite images and the farmer decides the exact application rates [3].

In practice, the basic NDVI maps indicate the amount of green mass in the field. However, the method is not able to differentiate situations of a low growth density with high nitrogen content from those of high growth density and low nitrogen content. Thus, generating nitrogen fertilization plans based only on NDVI map might not be the best solution in all of the cases so many supporting optical methodologies has been developed. Pena-Yewtukhiw et al. [4] found out that even the sensor output difference of 0.05 NDVI units could strongly affect the resulting nitrogen rate prescription, depending on the selected algorithms. Křížová [5] got conflicting results between different remote sensing data and yields. Also image mosaics that are mandatory with passive RPAS sensing may create large radiometric errors that effect on spectral vegetation indices [6].

There are also other potential vegetation indices. Dong et al. [7] presented 28 chlorophyll-related vegetation indices suitable to be applied with Sentinel-2 data and by simulation studies; they found out that incorporating red-edge reflectance (around 700 nm) improved the estimates for assessing vegetation growth rate and predicting crop productivity. Also, Hunt et al. [8] noted that assessing red-edge detection could make a difference in determining nitrogen applications to potato. In their study, they did not found RPAS beneficial to the WorldView-2 satellite data.

Multispectral and hyperspectral imaging was found to be a promising method for agricultural purposes [9] and obtaining separate biomass and nitrogen content [10–13] for additional fertilization need determination. This is also what current commercial solutions support. The tractor implemented YARA N-Sensor five spectrometer detects the wavelengths of 550 nm, 650 nm, 700 nm, 710 nm and 840 nm [14]. The gained economic benefits of this tractor implemented solution have been around 5% [15]. Typically RPAS installed Parrot Sequoia multispectral camera measures the wavelengths of RGB, 550 nm, 660 nm, 735 nm and 790 nm. The most accurate wavelengths of Sentinel-2 satellite are 490 nm, 560 nm, 665 nm, 842 nm with 10 m spatial resolution and 705 nm, 740 nm, 783 nm, 865, 1610 nm, 2190 nm with 20 m spatial resolution. In Finland, the average field size is less than 4 hectares which may make it challenging to exploit coarser data efficiently.

There is also other ways how to apply image data. The RPAS based photogrammetric point clouds have also shown potential in agricultural crop biomass estimations [16–18]. These methodologies could even provide absolute values [18] but they require high overlapping between images and information about the bare soil level.

Data from other sources can be combined with remote sensing as inputs to decision support systems for determining nitrogen application rates [13, 19, 20]. Such data can be for example as previous yield maps, earlier fertilization amounts, soil nutrition samples, elevation models and slope models. Many new technologies are coming available, but since the commercialization for agricultural purposes is continuously developed, the farmers are somewhat left alone on how to really apply them and how to get the benefits out of them and which methods would be the most suitable for their purpose.

So, there are many ways how to map the field and how to develop the fertilization plan. Although there have been studies on comparing different methodologies [5, 7], the actual real world case or variation between different methodologies has not been studied, also conducting the final fertilization task has not been studied and there has not been a ground zero for what those differences mean. The aim of this paper is to present these variations by using case studies. This paper has three research questions: (1) how much there is variation in our field yields, meaning that how much there is potential on adjusting the amount of fertilizers? (2) How much there is variation of relative biomass estimations based on different remote sensing data obtained for the same purpose in our 20 ha test field 2016? (3) Based on different source data, how different are the application tasks made for the same purpose?

2   Materials and Methods

We developed a case study where we studied a regular barley field and its additional fertilization planning during a single growing season. We used relevant and real remote sensing data from the barley field. The test area was about 20 ha malt barley Trekker field in southern Finland in Vihti, sowed at 2016/5/29. The overview picture of the field during the 2016 growing season is presented in a Fig. 1. The field was evenly treated although a 12 m wide not treated stripe was left in the middle of the field to have a bare soil reference.

Fig. 1. A slant view of the test field showing the high biomass area in the left size and the not seeded stripe in the middle (2016/7/5).

The agricultural sample reference measurements of a single barley field were carried out in 2016/7/8 by taking 25 sample areas of size of 50 cm × 50 cm. The measurements included the average plant height (cm), dry biomass and amount of nitrogen. The coordinates of the sample areas were measured using differentially corrected Trimble GeoXH GPS with post-processed accuracy of about 10 cm. Three of the samples were in the bare soil reference area. The other sample plots were selected so that the vegetation was as homogeneous as possible inside and around the sample areas.

2.1 Yield Variation

First, to measure the variations in our field, we analyzed our combine harvester data to measure the yield variation in the selected test field and in the fields nearby. We analyzed the yield data of barley and wheat from the years 2015–2013. In total, 20 harvestings with an average field plot size of 6.4 ha was evaluated. Those fields were evenly threated. The harvesting was done with Sampo Comia C4 combine harvester with Ceres 8000 yield monitor, which logged position and filtered yield data with 5 Hz interval. We also filtered out less than 900 kg/ha measurements and exceptionally high yield values (peak data) from the yield data. Next, we calculated the variance for each harvesting operation.

For the study field harvesting data, we also added a moving average of five. Also the minimum value was excluded for each moving average calculation; this gave slightly better correlation with all of the remote sensing datasets. This addition was based on the assumption that there might be moments when the cutting width is not the whole table because of the driving accuracy and there was no automatic cutting width measurement in the combine harvester.

2.2 Remote Sensing Data Variations

Next we studied different remote sensing data. Figure 2 presents relative biomass maps based on different remote sensing technologies: Sentinel-2 satellite images, Yara-N-sensor measurements, a consumer level Phantom 4 UAV with RGB (red, green, blue)-camera a professional UAV with FPI (Fabry Perot Interferometer)-hyperspectral camera (FPI2012b sensor with 36 spectral bands in 500 nm to 900 nm spectral range) and RGB camera system, more detailed descriptions of data processing of the professional UAV data are presented by Näsi et al. [18]. These maps represented the starting point of this work. To calculate the relative biomass from the remote sensing data, these methodologies were used:

NDVI, Normalized Difference Vegetation Index [21], most commonly used vegetation index (NIR − R)/(NIR + R).

NDII, Normalized Difference Infrared Index [22], sensitive to changes in water content of plant canopies. Sentinel-2: (842 nm − 1610 nm)/(842 nm + 1610 nm). The 1610 nm data resolution is 20 × 20 m.

SAVI, Soil Adjusted Vegetation Index [23], (1 + L) * (800 nm − 670 nm)/ (800 nm + 670 nm + L), L = 0.5. This index tries to minimize soil brightness influences from spectral vegetation indices.

VARI, Visible Atmospherically Resistant Index (G − R)/(G + R − B), practical index when only RGB data is available [24].

CHM Canopy height model was extracted from photogrammetric point clouds [18] based on RGB data.

FPI Fabry Perrot Interferometer hyperspectral imaging based biomass estimation using linear regression models [18].

The specific datasets (Fig. 2) are presented below including the name of data, used calculation methods and remote sensing platform, the date of the remote sensing and a short argument why the dataset was studied:

1. Satellite1: NDII, Sentinel-2, 2016/5/23. Entirely bare soil
2. Satellite2: NDII, Sentinel-2, 2016/7/2. For comparison to first dataset
3. Satellite3: NDVI, Sentinel-2, 2016/7/2. Typical dataset
4. Satellite4: SAVI, Sentinel-2, 2016/7/2. Reduced soil reflectance
5. Satellite5: VARI, Sentinel-2, 2016/7/2. Comparison to UAV data
6. Satellite6: NDVI, Sentinel-2, 2016/7/29. Temporal aspect
7. ProUAV1: NDVI, FPI-UAV, 2016/7/4. Index based on FPI sensor
8. ProUAV2: FPI, FPI-UAV, 2016/7/4. Biomass estimation based on FPI
9. ProUAV3: CHM, FPI-UAV, 2016/7/4. Crop height
10. Tractor: Yara-N-Sensor, 2016/7/16. Biomass estimation
11. UAV1: VARI, Phantom 4, 2016/7/4. Common UAV data
12. UAV2: VARI, Phantom 4, 2016/7/16. Temporal aspect
13. UAV3: VARI, Phantom 4, 2016/7/16. Constantly changing cloud cover
14. Yield map 2015: Combine harvester. Seasonal variation
15. Yield points 2016: Combine harvester. Field performance.

The yield map 2015 was based on combine harvester point data and a surface fitting by using inverse distance weighting (5 m circle search distance and weighting power of 1). The yield points 2016 processed data from the combine harvester.

The 2016 yield points were used as a basis for the correlation analyses. There were about 14 000 accepted yield points. The corresponding values of each dataset (1–14) were connected to the yield points. This 15 × 14000 table was used for the correlation analysis between different datasets.

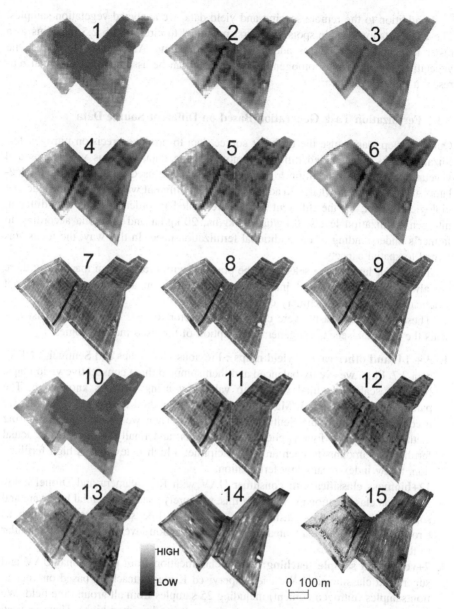

Fig. 2. Relative biomass estimations based on Sentinel-2 satellite images (1–6), consumer level Phantom 4 drone with RGB-camera (7–9), tractor implemented Yara N-sensor (10), professional UAV with FPI-camera (11–13) and measured yield maps (14–15).

As the correlation analysis, we used the most common Pearson product-moment correlation coefficient, also known as R. It is a measure of the strength and direction of the linear relationship between two variables that is defined as the covariance of the variables divided by the product of their standard deviations.

In addition to the remote sensing and yield data, we analyzed vegetation samples. The 25 vegetation sample spots were first modelled to circles with 2.5 m radius as a raster map and this data was added to the yield points. As we tried to collect the vegetation samples from homogenous locations it can be assumed that they can represent a larger local area.

2.3   Fertilization Task Generation Based on Different Source Data

Our next step was to use the different source data to produce precision nitrogen fertilization tasks. We applied different remote sensing data, previous yield maps and vegetation samples. In addition to different datasets, we used nitrogen amount calculators and farmer's knowledge to adjust the tasks in different ways. To exclude a deeper biological aspect, all the different tasks were scaled in order to have four different nitrogen fertilization levels: 0 kg/ha, 10 kg/ha, 20 kg/ha and 30 kg/ha according to farmer's understanding of the additional fertilization need. In this way, the focus was turned to spatial aspects.

Those four levels were selected to be practical with present farm machinery: there are always some delays and inaccuracies with precision adjustments, so it is not practical to adjust the machinery continuously.

These fertilization tasks were calculated in vector format. The following list presents the used datasets and a general description of the used methodologies:

1. **3 + 14 (and other earlier yield maps):** Previous yield maps and Sentinel-2 NDVI data 2.7. First, we evenly balanced and then summed three consecutive yield maps. Next we scaled the final yield map values by using farmer's knowledge. The parameters were: min 0.4, Max 1.6, Mean 1.07, standard deviation 0.19. Then we used this to multiply the Sentinel-2 NDVI-map. Then we applied the contouring method to generate four application rate levels, and finally we added the actual fertilization amounts to each area in discipline: a high index means high fertilization, a low index means low fertilization.
2. **12+biomass classification:** consumer UAV with RGB-camera and DroneDeploy vegetation classification (VARI). For this, we purely used commercial hardware and software to produce the task sketch. Similar to free satellite services such as CropSAT, the farmer estimated the actual fertilization levels for each class similar to the first case.
3. **7+vegetation sample teaching:** NDVI classification from professional UAV and supervised classification. We used supervised K-means teaching based on vegetation samples (nitrogen content) including 25 samples from all around the field. We categorized nitrogen samples into four classes (none-low-med-high). Then we used that data to supervise NDVI data to four classes. Then actual fertilization amounts were decided according to farmer's knowledge as previously.
4. **12+biomass classification+farmer teaching:** consumer UAV with RGB-camera, VARI calculated with DroneDeploy software, added with farmer teaching (polygons drawn by the farmer including wanted nitrogen input) by using K-means

methodology. In this study, the farmer drew circles representing the wanted fertilization amounts to top of the RGB-map. Then these areas were used to teach the VARI raster map. Finally, the contouring method was applied as in previous cases.

5. **5+calculator:** Sentinel-2 data (VARI, 2.7) and applied nitrogen rate calculator results. In this case, we linearly adapted the nitrogen calculator recommendations: the high index means that there are already enough nitrogen resources, the low means that there is lack of nitrogen.

6. **Vegetation samples:** no remote sensing data was used in this analysis. We adapted vegetation sample interpolation: high biomass and low nitrogen equals high nitrogen need, high nitrogen content or low biomass equals low nitrogen need, low nitrogen level means a medium nitrogen need [13]. Surface modelling for the vegetation sample data was made with minimum curvature methodology [25].

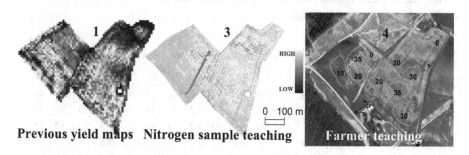

Previous yield maps   Nitrogen sample teaching   Farmer teaching

Fig. 3. Different interphases in task generation processes for tasks 1, 3 and 4.

Figure 3 shows the weighted sum of previous yield maps used in task generation 1, nitrogen sample point teaching of NDVI data in task generation 3 and farmer teaching areas in the task generation 4. After the task generations, we visually studied the different tasks aimed for same additional nitrogen fertilization.

3   Results

The average of the yield amount variance in our fields was 32.7%. Our test field yield had a variance of 23.3%, the histogram is presented in Fig. 4. By applying the moving average of five, the variance was lowered by 0.5 percentage points. These are indicating at least a 30% variance in the yields on average in our test fields in Finland. The total yields of our fields were 4.6 t/ha on average and the average variance was 1.8 t/ha. During the summer 2016, our test field had an exceptionally low yield on average.

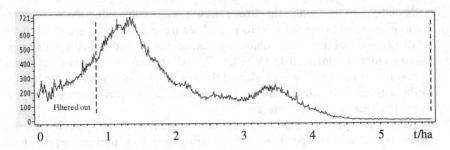

Fig. 4. Test fields yield histogram (yield amount and number of measurement points)

Next we present Table 1 illustrating the correlations between different remote sensing data, yield measurements and vegetation samples. The highest correlation witch each dataset were highlighted.

Table 1. Correlation between different remote sensing datasets

	1	2	3	4	5	6	7	8	9	10	11	12	13	14	15
1. Sat1NDII	1	**.61**	.60	.58	.56	.62	.44	.39	.48	.58	.44	.56	.52	.36	.46
2. Sat2NDII	.61	1	.97	**.97**	.94	.85	.69	.62	.72	.79	.74	.83	.75	.29	.72
3. Sat3NDVI	.60	.97	1	**.99**	.96	.88	.70	.62	.73	.80	.76	.85	.78	.30	.75
4. Sat4SAVI	.58	.97	**.99**	1	.95	.89	.70	.62	.73	.81	.76	.86	.78	.30	.75
5. Sat5VARI	.56	.94	**.96**	.95	1	.81	.67	.60	.70	.75	.76	.80	.72	.29	.69
6. Sat6VARI	.62	.85	.88	**.89**	.81	1	.66	.55	.66	.85	.69	.87	.83	.30	.81
7. Pro1NDVI	.44	.69	.70	.70	.67	.66	1	.89	**.92**	.62	.79	.72	.68	.20	.61
8. Pro2FPI	.39	.62	.62	.62	.60	.55	**.89**	1	.88	.54	.71	.62	.58	.17	.51
9. Pro3CHM	.48	.72	.73	.73	.70	.66	**.92**	.88	1	.62	.79	.73	.67	.21	.58
10. Tractor	.58	.79	.80	.81	.75	.85	.62	.54	.62	1	.67	**.87**	.85	.28	.82
11. UAV1VARI	.44	.74	.76	.76	.76	.69	**.79**	.71	.79	.67	1	.78	.75	.19	.64
12. UAV2VARI	.56	.83	.85	.86	.80	.87	.72	.62	.73	.87	.78	1	**.90**	.26	.81
13. UAV3VARI	.52	.75	.78	.78	.72	.83	.68	.58	.67	.85	.75	**.90**	1	.25	.82
14. Yield2015	**.36**	.29	.30	.30	.29	.30	.20	.17	.21	.28	.19	.26	.25	1	.29
15. Yield2016	.47	.72	.75	.75	.69	.81	.61	.51	.58	.82	.64	.81	**.82**	.29	1
Average	.52	.75	.76	**.76**	.73	.73	.66	.59	.67	.70	.68	.75	.71	.26	.66
Nitrogen	.24	.40	.45	.44	.41	.50	.70	.56	.56	.38	**.74**	.53	.49	.34	.49
Biomass	.34	.66	.67	.66	.65	.48	.79	.73	**.81**	.47	.81	.69	.69	.54	.61

The average correlation of all data was 0.66, the average correlation of the most common remote sensing data for biomass mapping (3, 7, 10 and 11) was 0.72, the same day consumer UAV correlation (12 and 13) was 0.90. The correlation with Sentinel-2 based NDVI maps with 27 day difference (3 and 6) was 0.88. The commercial UAV (13) had the highest correlation with the yield. The canopy height model (9) had the highest correlation with the biomass sample. The correlation between biomass and nitrogen samples (Fig. 5) was 0.51. Three examples of the correlation are illustrated in the following Fig. 4: biomass and nitrogen samples, Sentinel-2 VARI index to yield map 2016, and the Sentinel-2 SAVI map to consumer UAV VARI.

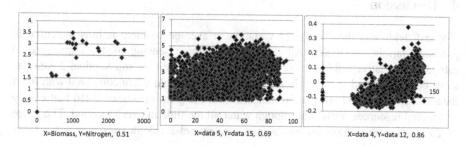

X=Biomass, Y=Nitrogen, 0.51   X=data 5, Y=data 15, 0.69   X=data 4, Y=data 12, 0.86

Fig. 5. Correlation between different datasets.

Next we present the demonstrative task maps which combined other data to remote sensing with the following early presented methodologies:

1. Previous yield maps and Sentinel-2 NDVI data 2.7
2. Consumer UAV with RGB-camera and DroneDeploy
3. NDVI classification from professional UAV and supervised classification
4. Consumer UAV with RGB-camera with farmer teaching
5. Sentinel-2 VARI, 2.7 and applied nitrogen rate calculator results
6. Vegetation sample interpolation

The following Fig. 6 illustrates the different generated tasks.

Additional nitrogen fertilization input

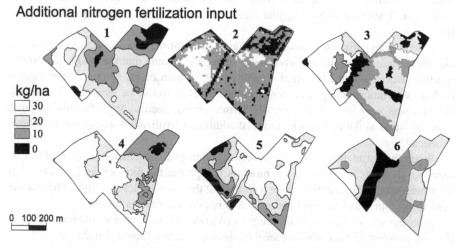

kg/ha
☐ 30
☐ 20
☐ 10
■ 0

0 100 200 m

Fig. 6. Different fertilization tasks based on remote sensing and external data.

The nitrogen fertilization tasks were clearly deviating even when the application rates were equalized.

4 Discussion

Our test fields had the 30% yield variation in average so there is huge potential in precision farming activities. All the relevant remote sensing methods managed to estimate the relative differences of the biomass. Even the bare soil Sentinel-2 data had some correlation and visually similar variations in the field when compared with other datasets. The bare soil correlation indicates that the growing season 2016 had evenly distributed resources: there was enough water all the time in every location. The usage of 20×20 m resolution images as part of Sentinel-2 calculations was not notably weakening the results.

The optimal timing for the additional fertilization would have been in the early July, all the evaluations estimated visually correctly the relative biomass. However, when developed into precision fertilization tasks, the differences between different tasks were phenomenal, even opposite between each other. This comes back to trivially sound questions in fertilization planning: should the farmer put more fertilizers to the weak or high biomass areas? Which parts of the growth are limited by the lack of nitrogen and which parts are limited by other resources? The relative biomass estimations in our malt barley case, no matter which methods were used, were not providing sufficient information for the determination of nitrogen fertilization variations. In addition, local and crop specific calibrations are needed together with spatial information about nitrogen variations.

The coefficient of determination R^2 of two one after the other measured commercial UAV VARI maps (datasets 12 and 13 in Fig. 2) was 0.81 and that was one of the highest coefficients in our datasets. Measurements taken by different time had a smaller coefficient. These are indicating that there is always certain noise in passive remote sensing methods.

When the hyperspectral imagery was used only for the biomass estimations as we did, there were no significant advantages seen. We assume that the usage of a multispectral camera would have similar results here. In both cases, additional estimations such as vegetation nitrogen content estimations [13] would be essential. The actual biomass was very low for the Yara-N-Sensor measurements. Actually, this was true since the yield in the end was so low that additional fertilization would not have been beneficial.

When the correlation between biomass and nitrogen is evaluated (Fig. 5), it can be seen that there are areas where the biomass is high but the nitrogen level is low, also there are spots where the biomass is average but the nitrogen level is high. These areas need to be found and the application task 6 is purely based on those.

After the visual evaluation of different tasks (Fig. 6) the farmer would have selected the task number 4. That was foreseeable since the farmer taught that dataset.

5 Conclusions

As the main conclusions of this work, there is a large variation within cereal fields in Finland, the relative difference was easy to determine with different remote sensing methods during the growing season, but there is huge step needed to use these biomass variations in a consistent way. Sentinel-2 and cheap drones are temptating to be used straight forward in fertilization execution planning but the typical biomass estimation might be unusable without external data or local knowledge. Neither helps the more expensive hyperspectral technologies if case specific parameters and calibrations are not available.

We should also note that the yield of our test field was low and the areal differences between crops were very similar during the entire growing season. These factors can be very different in different years when there is for example lack of water, so the very generalizing conclusions of the goodness of the relative biomass estimations cannot be drawn.

As long as the studied vegetation is such that its greenness and high NIR indicates high biomass we consider that our results are rather general in terms of passive remote sensing, relative biomass estimations and difficulties of transferring observations into the absolute values and decisions.

In the end, the lack of sensors might not be the limiting element in precision agriculture but the usage of the sensor data is still in its very early stages.

Acknowledgments. We acknowledge ESA (ESRIN/Contract No. 4000117401/16/I-NB) and Business Finland (1617/31/2016) for funding the project.

References

1. Raun, W., et al.: Optical sensor based algorithm for crop nitrogen fertilization. Commun. Soil Sci. Plant Anal. **36**, 2759–2781 (2005). https://doi.org/10.1080/00103620500303988
2. Lukina, E., et al.: Nitrogen fertilization optimization algorithm based on in-season estimates of yield and plant nitrogen uptake. J. Plant Nutr. **24**, 885–898 (2001). https://doi.org/10.1081/PLN-100103780
3. Söderström, M., Stadig, H., Martinsson, J., Piikki, K., Stenberg, M.: CropSAT – a public satellite-based decision support system for variable-rate nitrogen fertilization in Scandinavia. In: 13th International Conference on Precision Agriculture (ICPA)At, St Louis, MI, USA (2016). https://doi.org/10.13140/RG.2.2.13250.99520
4. Pena-Yewtukhiw, E., Grove, J., Schwab, G.: Fertilizer nitrogen rate prescription, interpretational algorithms, and individual sensor performance in an array. Agron. J. **107**, 1691–1700 (2015). https://doi.org/10.2134/agronj14.0573
5. Křížová, K., Kumhálová, J.: Comparison of selected remote sensing sensors for crop yield variability estimation. Agron. Res. **15**(4) (2017). http://dx.doi.org/10.15159/ar.17.016
6. Rasmussen, J., Ntakos, G., Nielson, J., Svensgaard, J., Poulsen, R.N., Christensen, S.: Are vegetation indices derived from consumer-grade cameras mounted on UAVs sufficiently reliable for assessing experimental plots? Eur. J. Agron. **74**, 75–92 (2016)
7. Dong, T., Meng, J., Shang, J., Liu, J., Wu, B.: Evaluation of chlorophyll-related vegetation indices using simulated Sentinel-2 data for estimation of crop fraction of absorbed photosynthetically active radiation. IEEE J. Sel. Top. Appl. Earth Obs. Remote. Sens. **8**(8), 4049–4059 (2015)

8. Hunt, E., et al.: Monitoring nitrogen status of potatoes using small unmanned aerial vehicles. Precis. Agric., 1–20 (2017). https://doi.org/10.1007/s11119-017-9518-5
9. Bareth, G., et al.: Low-weight and UAV-based hyperspectral full-frame cameras for monitoring crops: spectral comparison with portable spectroradiometer measurements. Photogramm. - Fernerkund. - Geoinformation PFG **2015**(1), 69–79 (2015). https://doi.org/10.1127/pfg/2015/0256
10. Raun, W., Solie, J., Stone, M.: Independence of yield potential and crop nitrogen response. Precis. Agric. **12**(4), 508–518 (2011). https://doi.org/10.1007/s11119-010-9196-z
11. Honkavaara, E., et al.: Processing and assessment of spectrometric, stereoscopic imagery collected using a lightweight UAV spectral camera for precision agriculture. Remote. Sens. **5** (10), 5006–5039 (2013)
12. Pölönen, I., Saari, H., Kaivosoja, J., Honkavaara, E., Pesonen, L.: Hyperspectral imaging based biomass and nitrogen content estimations from light-weight UAV. In: Proceedings of SPIE 2013, vol. 8887, p. 88870J (2013)
13. Kaivosoja, J., et al.: A case study of a precision fertilizer application task generation for wheat based on classified hyperspectral data from UAV combined with farm history data. In: Proceedings of SPIE 2013, vol. 8887, p. 88870H (2013)
14. Varco, J.: Sensor Based Fertilizer Nitrogen Management. Crop Management Seminar, Memphis, TN, USA, 9–11 November 2010
15. Nissen, K.: Yara N-Sensor – sensible sensing, testing and certification of agricultural machinery, Riga, Latvia, 16–18 October 2012. Bjugstad, N., Nilsson, E., Birzietis, G. (eds.) NJF Report 8 6: 69-70 (2012)
16. Bendig, J., Bolten, A., Bareth, G.: UAV-based imaging for multi-temporal, very high resolution crop surface models to monitor crop growth variability. Photogramm. - Fernerkund. - Geoinformation **2013**(6), 551–562 (2013)
17. Li, W., Niu, Z., Chen, H., Li, D., Wu, M., Zhao, W.: Remote estimation of canopy height and aboveground biomass of maize using high-resolution stereo images from a low-cost unmanned aerial vehicle system. Ecol. Indic. **67**, 637–648 (2016). https://doi.org/10.1016/j.ecolind.2016.03.036
18. Näsi, R., Viljanen, N., Kaivosoja, J., Alhonoja, K., Markelin, L., Honkavaara, E.: Estimating biomass and nitrogen amount of barley and grass using UAV and aircraft based spectral and photogrammetric 3D features. Remote. Sens. **10**(7), 1082 (2018). https://doi.org/10.3390/rs10071082
19. Shanahan, J., Kitchen, N., Raun, W., Schepers, J.: Responsive in-season nitrogen management for cereals. Comput. Electron. Agric. **61**, 51–62 (2008)
20. Van Evert, F., et al.: Using crop reflectance to determine side dress N rate in potato saves N and maintains yield. Eur. J. Agron. **43**, 58–67 (2012)
21. Rouse, J., Hass, R., Deering, D., Sehell, J.: Monitoring the vernal advancement and retrogradation (Green wave effect) of natural vegetation. Texas A&M university. Type I progress report-number 7 (1974)
22. Hardisky, M., Klemas, V., Smart, R.: The influence of soil salinity, growth form, and leaf moisture on-the spectral radiance of partina alterniflora canopies. Photogramm. Eng. Remote Sens. **49**, 77–83 (1983)
23. Huete, A.: A soil-adjusted vegetation index (SAVI). Remote Sens. Environ. **25**(3), 259–309 (1988). https://doi.org/10.1016/0034-4257(88)90106-x
24. Gitelson, A., Kaufman, Y., Stark, R., Rundquist, D.: Novel algorithms for remote estimation of vegetation fraction. Remote Sens. Environ. **80**, 76–87 (2002)
25. Microimages TNTGIS, Surface modeling tutorial. http://www.microimages.com/documentation/Tutorials/surfmodl.pdf. Accessed 21 Nov 2016 (2013)

Unmanned Ground Vehicles in Precision Farming Services: An Integrated Emulation Modelling Approach

Dimitrios Bechtsis[1](✉) [iD], Vasileios Moisiadis[2] [iD],
Naoum Tsolakis[3] [iD], Dimitrios Vlachos[4] [iD], and Dionysis Bochtis[2] [iD]

[1] Department of Automation Engineering, Alexander Technological Educational
Institute of Thessaloniki, Thessaloniki, Greece
dimbec@autom.teithe.gr
[2] Institute for Bio-Economy and Agri-Technology (IBO), Centre for Research
and Technology Hellas (CERTH), 10th Km Thessalonikis-Thermis Rd,
BALKAN Center, BLDG D, 57001 Thessaloniki, Greece
[3] Centre for International Manufacturing, Institute for Manufacturing,
Department of Engineering, School of Technology, University of Cambridge,
Cambridge, UK
[4] Department of Mechanical Engineering, Aristotle University of Thessaloniki,
Thessaloniki, Greece

Abstract. Autonomous systems are a promising alternative for safely executing precision farming activities in a 24/7 perspective. In this context Unmanned Ground Vehicles (UGVs) are used in custom agricultural fields, with sophisticated sensors and data fusion techniques for real-time mapping and navigation. The aim of this study is to present a simulation software tool for providing effective and efficient farming activities in orchard fields and demonstrating the applicability of simulation in routing algorithms, hence increasing productivity, while dynamically addressing operational and tactical level uncertainties. The three dimensional virtual world includes the field layout and the static objects (orchard trees, obstacles, physical boundaries) and is constructed in the open source Gazebo simulation software while the Robot Operating System (ROS) and the implemented algorithms are tested using a custom vehicle. As a result a routing algorithm is executed and enables the UGV to pass through all the orchard trees while dynamically avoiding static and dynamic obstacles. Unlike existing sophisticated tools, the developed mechanism could accommodate an extensive variety of agricultural activities and could be transparently transferred from the simulation environment to real world ROS compatible UGVs providing user-friendly and highly customizable navigation.

Keywords: Precision farming · Robot Operating System · UGV simulation · Real-time navigation · Orchard field

© Springer Nature Switzerland AG 2019
M. Salampasis and T. Bournaris (Eds.): HAICTA 2017, CCIS 953, pp. 177–190, 2019.
https://doi.org/10.1007/978-3-030-12998-9_13

1 Introduction

Intelligent automation tools are systematically reported to promote operations excellence and foster structural configurations in industrial supply networks [1, 2]. To this end, mechanization and automation in agriculture have resulted in increased productivity both in terms of quality and quantity [3]. However, the proactive analysis and assessment of Unmanned Ground Vehicles (UGVs) is still being neglected [4], while for the particular agricultural sector the majority of related research efforts focuses on the direct implementation and testing of real-word physical systems in agrifield operations. In this context, the objective of the present study is to provide a simulation tool for the dynamic navigation of UGVs in custom agricultural fields for accurately performing optimal precision farming activities, hence leading to improved farming output and efficient agrifood supply chains (SCs). In particular, we provide an emulation validation and verification tool for capturing and assessing a UGV's capabilities on performing precision farming activities at custom agricultural fields, under the occurrence of any geomorphological and environmental conditions and under dynamically evolving uncertainties at operational and tactical levels.

In traditional agriculture activities, limited accuracy on farming operations in tandem with the lack of real-time information feedback leads to: (i) loss of situation awareness [5], (ii) vigilance decrement [6], (iii) complacency [7], and (iv) skill degradation and human errors [8]. In this regard, semi- or fully-autonomous vehicles that are controlled by computers [9] are being used to address such challenges and increase efficiency in agricultural operations [10]. More specifically, autonomous systems are a promising alternative for translating agrifield management strategies into effective agricultural operations considering that UGVs: (i) provide business intelligence with real-time feedback on field's parameters, (ii) can efficiently handle throughput volatility, (iii) can optimally operate autonomously on a 24/7 shift with reliable performance, (iv) save energy compared to conventional man-driven farming vehicles, (v) promote the smart agriculture vision, and (vi) increase safety at the field level.

Despite the evident benefits of UGVs in agriculture, the application of autonomous mechanization in the sector is primarily challenged by inherent factors including crop characteristics [11] and field geographical/geometric/geological particularities [12]. Environmental uncertainties like volatile climatic and meteorological conditions along with encounters with random objects and obstacles [13] comprise an additional level of challenges. This calls for automated systems with dynamic scheduling and control intelligence capabilities able to evaluate alternative navigation decisions based on real-time sensory-driven information about fields' and crops' states [14]. However, the limited standardization of UGV systems along with the high cost and the range of possible technical issues such as low resolution maps, low positioning accuracy, low grade process automation and incorrect or incomplete measurements, dictate the need for the proactive assessment of these systems prior to any substantial investment. Emulation comprises a set of software and sometimes hardware layers that enable practitioners to simulate, mimic and proactively assess the behavior of real-life intelligent systems [15].

The present research principle relies on the basic hypothesis that an agricultural field presents obstacles (both random and static) that an UGV should detect and re-evaluate an alternative routing pathway to perform the required precision farming activities. A key theoretical contribution in the existing body of literature is the proposition of an agricultural UGV-centric framework and software tool for emulating the autonomous navigation of a vehicle enabled by real-time agrifield recognition, whilst allowing for the optimal usage of resources and potentially a better harvest.

The aim of this paper is to present an engineering-driven approach for the early scheduling and control of agricultural UGVs with the objective of executing precision farming activities in an optimal manner, via attempting to tackle the following research questions (RQs):

- RQ#1 – Which are the main components of an emulation-based agricultural UGV's system that can ensure the proactive assessment of the respective operations?
- RQ#2 – How is the emulation framework and its components integrated in a functional emulation tool?

2 Intelligent Vehicles in Agriculture: Background

In this section, we briefly review the extant literature concerning the use of autonomous vehicles in precision agriculture to identify the level of analysis. The provided taxonomy is based on the methodological approach developed by Tsolakis et al. [4] who propose a theoretical and empirical evidence-based methodological framework for the integrated application of conceptualization, simulation, emulation and physical application of intelligent autonomous vehicles for the effective design of digital supply networks.

Auat Cheein and Carelli [16] provide a detailed discussion about the four core abilities of unmanned service units in agricultural operations, namely: (i) guidance, (ii) detection, (iii) action, and (iv) mapping. The authors demonstrate the interdependency of these capabilities through the case study of an unmanned service unit used for supervising an olive grove in San Juan, Argentina. In terms of guidance, Cariou et al. [17] experimentally demonstrate a high-precision path tracking system for a generic four-wheel-steering mobile robot navigating on slippery ground to perform agricultural operations. In particular, the authors' guidance algorithmic approach enables the robotic system to automatically and accurately achieve a desired path, despite an agrifield's morphology, terrain conditions and any sliding phenomena.

Following that, Christiansen et al. [18] introduce the "DeepAnomaly" algorithm for the fast detection of distant and heavily occluded obstacles in agricultural fields. Eaton et al. [19] describe a system-of-systems architecture that could facilitate the implementation of autonomous precision farming operations. More specifically, the authors propose and test through simulation analysis a kinematic model for the guidance of a tractor, under sliding phenomena and terrain disturbances.

In terms of action, Garcia-Perez et al. [20] present AGROAMARA, an agent with behavior based architecture, for navigating an autonomous vehicle in an olive tree area at the Industrial Automation Institute campus in Madrid, Spain; a sensor-fusion algorithm is also developed for enabling real-time data gathering and sharing to navigate the vehicle under dynamic conditions.

Moreover, Bengochea-Guevara et al. [21] test and apply an integrated approach combining camera-acquired images and a GPS receiver to effectively navigate an autonomous vehicle for the inspection of a maize field in Madrid, Spain. The aim is to achieve complete coverage in field inspection and minimized impact of the scouting on the crop and soil compaction through: (i) tracking of crop rows, (ii) detection of the end of crop rows, and (iii) transition between crop rows. Finally, Duggal et al. [22] propose an approach for pomegranate plantation monitoring and yield estimation by applying supervised learning analysis over data collected by a quadcopter. The autonomous aerial vehicle is navigated through the plantation's inter-row pathways by a developed framework calculating minimum time trajectories between sequences of waypoints; the navigation framework is further integrated with the Robot Operating System (ROS).

Table 1 presents a critical taxonomy of selected studies regarding intelligent autonomous vehicles in precision agriculture which, along with its synopsis, could assist greatly in drafting the agenda for future research by first identifying the existing gaps and overlaps in current research. In general, despite the fact that there is a plethora of studies that examine the actual testing of physical UGVs, there is a lack of approaches describing the holistic application of conceptualization, simulation, emulation and physical implementation of intelligent vehicles in an agricultural setting.

Table 1. Intelligent autonomous vehicles in precision agriculture: a critical taxonomy.

Author	Analysis level				Publication analysis
	C	S	E	R	Algorithm - Benefits
Auat Cheein and Carelli [16]	•			•	SLAM – Minimised estimation errors in localization & mapping – Low cost localisation solution
Bengochea-Guevara et al. [21]				•	Annealing path planner – Simple – Travelled distance as optimisation criterion
Cariou et al. [17]	•			•	Bespoke, kinematic and back stepping models – Compensate for sliding effects during path tracking
Christiansen et al. [18]				•	DeepAnomaly – Human detection at long distances, using less training data and a small convolutional network – Low computation time & memory footprint.
Duggal et al. [22]			•	•	Way-Point Navigation – Minimum time trajectory
Eaton et al. [19]	•	•			Bespoke – Minimal amount of training data
Garcia-Perez et al. [20]	•			•	AGROAMARA – Concurrent agents' behaviour – Sharing of knowledge through a shared memory and by peer-to-peer messaging

Symbols: C for conceptualization; S for Simulation; E for Emulation, R for real-world physical system.

3   Agricultural UGVs: Emulation Framework

Generally, software tools that simulate UGVs are classified in the following categories [23]: (i) discrete event simulation software, (ii) robotics software, (iii) multi-agent software, and (iv) dedicated software from UGV's manufacturers. Simulation, offers a platform for developing algorithms and testing different UGV properties on various fields [24] and specifically ROS allows researchers to elaborate on their ideas and safely simulate vehicles prior to actual experimental tests on an agrifield level. In addition, ROS graph-based architecture eases the software developing procedures by providing methods for monitoring and even capturing real-time data and even executing high level procedures such as scheduling and decision-making activities with the use of the ROS Navigation Stack. A significant number of ready to use commercial and open hardware outdoor robotic systems, that are compatible with ROS could be used. Indicatively, two well-established ROS enabled, commercial research vehicles are the Husky UGV developed by Clearpath Robotics [25] and the Thorvald multipurpose agricultural vehicle by SAGA Robotics [26].

Emulation of agricultural UGVs allows for the simulation and 3-dimensional (3D) navigation of real-world vehicles in custom agricultural fields to perform related precision farming activities (e.g. seeding, spraying, and fertilizing). The proposed emulation framework basically suggests that a respective model consists of the following four (4) layers:

1. Field Layer – The field layer represents the landscape, the static objects (obstacles, trees) and all the geomorphological properties of the simulated environment.
2. Simulation Layer or Real-World Layer – The simulation layer represents the action agents, in our case the UGV that is a physical entity with kinematic and visual properties and performs precision farming activities in the 3D recreated environment [27]. Gazebo is an indicative tool for digitally recreating working environments.
3. Message Layer – The message layer represents the continuous transactions and the developed services between the system nodes to produce and manage raw data. The ROS has a plethora of tools (RVIZ, RQT etc.) that provide real-time monitoring and visualization actions to the simulation environment. Embedded sensors, actuators, motors and simulation results can be collected and processed in order to optimize UGVs' activities.
4. Application Layer – The application layer handles all the vehicle's activities including the action scheduler and the data acquisition block i.e. determining, prioritizing and scheduling the optimal navigation pathway of a UGV in the field based on any particular random obstacles or the geomorphological characteristics of the field.

The integrated emulation framework presented in Fig. 1 informs about the necessary development layers, as well as their inter-connections, that should be followed to provide a robust emulation tool applicable by relevant stakeholders.

ROS Tools   Objects/Actions

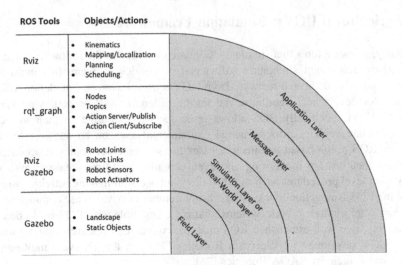

Fig. 1. Emulation framework: layers of development and related interconnections.

4 Agricultural UGVs: Software Emulation Tool

Emulation tools allow the implementation of multiple interfaces to replicate the functionality and interaction of physical machinery and/or equipment to the operational environment. In the present study we use the Gazebo simulation tool to recreate the virtual environment while ROS is used to simulate an autonomous vehicle's daily farming activities in an orchard field. It should be stated that Gazebo is fully compatible with ROS and thus we are able to use all the inherent ROS algorithms in order to control a UGV's movement and optimize its routing in the orchard field using the Simultaneous Localization And Mapping (SLAM) procedure. Notably, ROS is compatible with numerous third-party tools and relies on an extensive community of users and researchers that support it.

To apply the proposed emulation framework, we proceed to emulating an UGV's system in an orchard field. The representation of the field and the agricultural operations in the emulation tool are presented in the subsections that follow.

4.1 Agrifield Representation

Initially, a Digital Elevation Model region is examined through the open source Geographic Information System QGIS. The user selects the field's region and exports it as an image (e.g. in.png file format) with embedded altitude data for identifying the geometry of the landscape. The virtual world's landscape is created using the extensible markup language and the corresponding image file format. In particular, from a farm's geometrical area perspective, the devised system regards the most common area coverage practice involving a set of parallel field-work tracks, or trips, which start at one boundary of the field and terminates at the opposite boundary [28].

Afterwards, the landscape is imported in the Gazebo simulation software as a virtual world file (in a.world file format). The 3D model is the simulation environment for the UGV and an absolute 3D coordinate system is assigned to the model. Gazebo provides a gamut of tools for building the simulation environment as the user can add texture, colors and even static and dynamic objects for creating a near to the real-world model. Figure 2 depicts the experimental five-row orchard field where each tree model is manually inserted in the landscape. In the emulation demonstrator case under study, we consider a set of five -equidistant- parallel tracks. By convention, the Gazebo platform uses the right-handed coordinate system, with X- and Y-axes in the plane, and Z-axis increasing with the altitude.

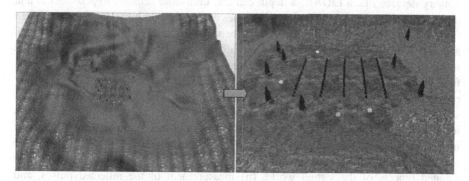

Fig. 2. The reference geomorphology of the emulated agricultural field.

Autonomous navigation techniques should be able to identify all the field-specific regions and objects and further provide a systematic area exploration plan. In the emulated orchard field, the entities include:

1. Orchard field boundaries – The UGV navigates in the field in order to map the field's layout and identify any static objects (i.e. regions of interest, obstacles, and landscape boundaries). It is worth mentioning that we could introduce the field boundaries by using pre-defined absolute coordinates, by building a fence around the orchard field property or by altering the landscape's morphology. In the proposed emulation model field boundaries are directly introduced within the landscape morphology as we created hills with intense slope around the orchard field. High hills with intense slope are considered as an impassable physical obstacle for the UGV and create a physical boundary for the vehicle.
2. Obstacles – In the emulated agricultural field we consider as obstacles the rocks and the non-orchard trees. The UGV identifies potential obstacles by using the Light Detection And Ranging (LiDAR) sensor, as a result of the mapping procedure. At this point all objects are identified as obstacles and the UGV does not distinguish obstacles from orchard trees.
3. Orchard Trees – Orchard Trees are considered as the points of interest. The UGV distinguishes orchard trees from obstacles with the use of a depth camera and image matching techniques.

4. Entry and Exit points – While the UGV navigates in the agricultural field it maps the orchard trees and several physical obstacles (i.e. rocks, trees and hills). The mapping procedure identifies the field's layout and the UGV can navigate to specific coordinates using a global optimum path. The entry and exit points of the orchard field could be recorded as arguments to the system using absolute coordinates in order to standardize the UGVs route.

4.2   Agricultural Operations Emulation

Operational data are collected while the UGV navigates in the agricultural field with the use of the vehicle's sensors. A UGV can be typically equipped with a range of sensory devices like a LiDAR, a depth camera, ultrasonic sensors, hyper-spectral and multi-spectral cameras. Data fusion techniques enable the combination of data gathered from different sources in order to increase the vehicle's sensing ability and operational accuracy. As an example, the use of a depth camera and data fusion techniques could result to the identification of points of interest (i.e. orchard trees) in the agricultural field. In our study the conceptual UGV is equipped with a LiDAR sensor that is further programmed and tested at the virtual agricultural field. The two-dimensional LiDAR sensor, with the ability of a 180-degree scanning angle, uses a laser beam which identifies geographically distributed points in the field that could represent points of interest (e.g. orchard trees) or obstacles. The functionality of the LiDAR sensor includes: (i) transmission of an initial laser beam to illuminate all the spatially distributed objects of the virtual world, (ii) measurement of the reflected pulses, and (iii) interpretation of the retrieved pulses into distances between the UGV and any detected obstacles. At a next step ROS identifies the obstacle's X- and Y-axes absolute coordinates and creates the orchard field's map. In case a linear distribution of sample points is captured, the mapping and routing algorithm recognizes a field-line of planted orchard trees. As the UGV navigates in the field (Fig. 3), the scanning angle of the LiDAR sensor constantly changes resulting in the identification of new sample points. This procedure continues until the final representation of the field's map that includes all the static objects present in the orchard field.

   In order to create the static map the UGV explores the agricultural field using either tele-operation methods or exploration algorithms until all unmapped areas in the field have been explored. During the UGV's exploration, a movement between two locations creates a global path from the starting to the ending point. Following that, a dynamic local path is constantly updated (Fig. 3) as the UGV tries to follow the global path but at the same time avoid all the dynamic obstacles. In order to keep a safety distance from the identified obstacles, the global and the local paths take into account the UGV's physical characteristics and the identified points are inflated using the UGV's actual dimensions. The final mapping of the field's layout is used by ROS to create a special matrix that is later used for calculating the optimized global path between two locations (global cost-map) and create the global UGV's navigation pathway in the field.

   As the UGV explores the field [29], the developed algorithm records the LiDAR's data in order to identify the static obstacles, the free space and the unexplored territories, as it gradually creates the map of the field's layout (Fig. 4). During this dynamic

Fig. 3. Agrifield mapping with inflated obstacles, global and local path generation.

mapping process, the created map is periodically saved as a snapshot of the working process and thus a sequence of consequent snapshots is generated. Each snapshot captures an "instance" of the map and is continuously compared with previews "instances" for comparing the unexplored regions with a predefined threshold using image processing techniques. This procedure determines the end of the mapping stage when the threshold criteria are met. The final map is identified and used as an input for the creation of the global cost map that will be used for calculating the optimized route of the UGV's movement.

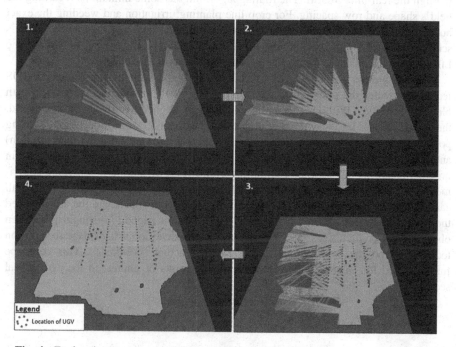

Fig. 4. Exploration process, the UGV's LiDAR sensor gradually creates the field's map.

At the first snapshot of Fig. 4 the UGV starts the exploration process and activates the LiDAR sensor in order to record the field's layout. At this starting point, the LiDAR beams are used to identify any unexplored areas and static obstacles in the field. White lines indicate free space where the UGV is able to move while the beams edge points are black and indicate the obstacle's contour. Unexplored areas have a gray color and should be further investigated. Gradually, as the UGV explores the agricultural field, more snapshots of the map are created until the final map is developed. The consecutive-aligned black points denote the orchard trees of the agricultural field and inform the UGV about possible movements around them.

5 Results

The emulation results demonstrate that the proposed software tool can be used for the efficient step-by-step scheduling of highly accurate farming tasks as the vehicle traverses through the trees' field tracks. More specifically, the UGV autonomously navigates and explores the orchard field using a LiDAR sensor for the mapping procedure. The UGV is always heading at regions that provide adequate free space for movement and maneuvers. The mapping and routing algorithm terminates in case the percentage of unexplored areas reaches a certain threshold and further optimization cannot be achieved. At this stage, the mapping procedure creates the final map and the UGV calculates a detailed routing schedule for visiting every tree in the orchard field while simultaneously avoiding static and dynamic obstacles present in every route, identified through the real-time SLAM. The routing algorithm has some limitations regarding the field's shape and row spacing. For crop line planting, irrigation and weeding the exact boundaries of the landscape could be pre-programmed and imported to the UGV's schedule. Figure 5 indicates the real-time SLAM of the UGV at the field level as the LiDAR sensor constantly scans for possible collisions in real-time.

The integration of the SLAM procedure combined with the implemented ROS features provides the potential to develop algorithms for optimizing the UGV's path planning activities. With the precondition of equally aligned tree rows within the field, the algorithm uses the entry point of the field at the upper left tree (indicates the starting position), the exit point of the field at the lower right tree (indicates the final position) and the field-work track's width and publish their coordinates using the ROS server in order to create the appropriate routing algorithm (Fig. 6). Furthermore, some experiments where contacted for real-time identification of the orchard trees using a depth camera and the Husky commercial UGV (Fig. 7). For a depth camera the authors used the Microsoft Kinect sensor on the Husky UGV, and managed to distinguish between obstacles and orchard trees. The orchard trees were identified using image recognition techniques and the depth camera captured their actual coordinates. This could be further tested for creating a knowledge base for points of interest in the agricultural sector.

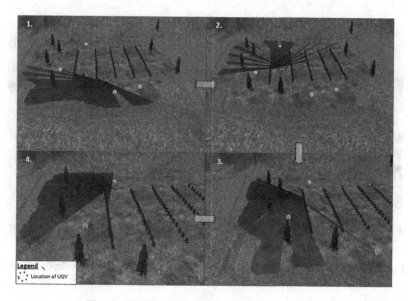

Fig. 5. UGV's navigation with real-time SLAM.

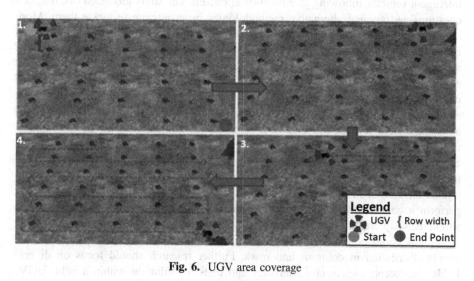

Fig. 6. UGV area coverage

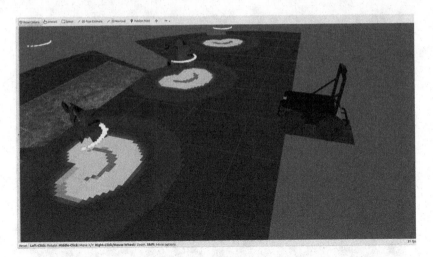

Fig. 7. Future work: dynamic region identification using Husky and a depth camera

6 Discussion and Conclusions

The paper addresses the issue of designing precision farming operations enabled by intelligent vehicles following an emulation approach. The study grounded two research questions and applied alternative methodologies in an attempt to tackle them. More specifically, RQ#1 concerned the identification of the main components of an emulation-based agricultural UGV system that can ensure the proactive assessment of the respective operations and it was answered with literature review and the authors' empirical experience in the field. Specially, an emulation framework comprising of multiple layers of development and related interconnections is provided. Moreover, an emulation software tool is developed and demonstrated through the conceptual case of an orchard field to answer RQ#2. Our findings are aligned with the insights gained from the literature review as they indicate that a UGV can effectively and efficiently execute precision farming activities. In this context, researchers and practitioners could use the proposed generic emulation tool for the ex-ante evaluation of UGVs' autonomous navigation in agricultural fields. Especially, the use of depth cameras' could perform a context aware SLAM where the UGV identifies points of interest while simultaneously creating the field's map. As discussed in Sect. 4, mapping and routing algorithms could be effectively applied in the common scenario where the trees are evenly distributed in columns and rows. Further research should focus on diverse fields' geomorphological characteristics and trees' distribution within a field. UGVs should constantly and dynamically identify new points of interest, determine their absolute coordinates and navigate in the field.

In this regard, the present study contributes to precision farming operations by providing an emulation framework and software tool for the real-time scheduling and control of UGV vehicles' navigation in custom agricultural fields under possible uncertainties. Overall, this research makes contextual/business environmental elements of operational management into more dominant elements of an operational system. More specifically, the low computational time requirements of the underlying process allow for the implementation of the proposed system as a real-time tool in agricultural operations. The developed system can be extended to capture multi-criteria optimization aspects and promote agrifood supply chain sustainability from an end-to-end perspective. The essential advantage of this algorithm is the low computational power that is required by the UGV in order to estimate and execute the anticipated path planning procedure.

Finally, the system is prone to be tested in real field conditions with the use of a custom or a commercial UGV. For enabling real-world, the vehicle should be equipped with the proper sensors (e.g. LiDAR sensors, depth cameras, inertial sensors etc.) and could either be a simple ROS node that exchanges information with the ROS core platform or a complete ROS enabled platform (with an embedded computer) that performs all the necessary computations.

Acknowledgements. The work was supported by the project "Research Synergy to address major challenges in the nexus: energy-environment-agricultural production (Food, Water, Materials)" - NEXUS, funded by the Greek Secretariat for Research and Technology (GSRT) – Pr. No. MIS 5002496.

References

1. Bechtsis, D., Tsolakis, N., Vlachos, D., Iakovou, E.: Sustainable supply chain management in the digitalisation era: the impact of automated guided vehicles. J. Cleaner Prod. **142**(4), 3970–3984 (2017)
2. Srai, J.S., Gregory, M.J.: A supply network configuration perspective on international supply chain development. Int. J. Oper. Prod. Manage. **28**(5), 386–411 (2008)
3. Bechar, A., Vigneault, C.: Agricultural robots for field operations: concepts and components. Biosyst. Eng. **149**, 94–111 (2016)
4. Tsolakis, N., Bechtsis, D., Srai, J.S.: Intelligent autonomous vehicles in digital supply chains: from conceptualisation, to simulation modelling, to real-world operations. Bus. Process Manage. J. (2018, In Press)
5. Walker, G.H., Stanton, N.A., Young, M.S.: Feedback and driver situation awareness (SA): a comparison of SA measures and contexts. Transp. Res. Part F: Traffic Psychol. Behav. **11**, 282–299 (2008)
6. Finomore, V., Matthews, G., Shaw, T., Warm, J.: Predicting vigilance: a fresh look at an old problem. Ergonomics **52**, 791–808 (2009)
7. Kaber, D.B., Endsley, M.R.: The effects of level of automation and adaptive automation on human performance, situation awareness and workload in a dynamic control task. Theor. Issues Ergon. Sci. **5**, 113–153 (2004)
8. Billings, C.E.: Aviation Automation: The Search for a Human-Centered Approach. Lawrence Erlbaum Associates, Mahwah (1996)
9. Ho, Y.-C., Liu, H.-C., Yih, Y.: A multiple-attribute method for concurrently solving the pickup-dispatching problem and the load-selection problem of multiple-load AGVs. J. Manufact. Syst. **31**(3), 288–300 (2012)

10. Zheng, H., Negenborn, R.R., Lodewijks, G.: Closed-loop scheduling and control of waterborne AGVs for energy-efficient inter terminal transport. Transp. Res. Part E: Logistics Transp. Rev. **105**, 261–278 (2017)

11. Tremblay, N., Fallon, E., Ziadi, N.: Sensing of crop nitrogen status: opportunities, tools, limitations, and supporting information requirements. Horttechnology **21**(3), 274–281 (2011)

12. Bochtis, D.D., Sørensen, C.G.: The vehicle routing problem in field logistics. Biosyst. Eng. **104**(4), 447–457 (2009)

13. Bochtis, D.D., Sørensen, C.G., Busato, P.: Advances in agricultural machinery management: a review. Biosyst. Eng. **126**, 69–81 (2014)

14. Wulfsohn, D., Aravena Zamora, F., Potin Téllez, C., Zamora Lagos, I., García-Fiñana, M.: Multilevel systematic sampling to estimate total fruit number for yield forecasts. Precis. Agric. **13**(2), 256–275 (2012)

15. Prieto-Araujo, E., Olivella-Rosell, P., Cheah-Mañe, M., Villafafila-Robles, R., Gomis-Bellmunt, O.: Renewable energy emulation concepts for microgrids. Renew. Sustain. Energy Rev. **50**, 325–345 (2015)

16. Auat Cheein, F.A., Carelli, R.: Agricultural robotics: unmanned robotic service units in agricultural tasks. IEEE Ind. Electron. Mag. **7**(3), 48–58 (2013)

17. Cariou, C., Lenain, R., Thuilot, B., Berducat, M.: Automatic guidance of a four-wheel-steering mobile robot for accurate field operations. J. Field Robot. **26**(6–7), 504–518 (2009)

18. Christiansen, P., Nielsen, L.N., Steen, K.A., Jørgensen, R.N., Karstoft, H.: DeepAnomaly: combining background subtraction and deep learning for detecting obstacles and anomalies in an agricultural field. Sensors **16**(11), 1904 (2016)

19. Eaton, R., Katupitiya, J., Siew, K.W., Howarth, B.: Autonomous farming: modeling and control of agricultural machinery in a unified framework. In: Proceedings of 15th International Conference on Mechatronics and Machine Vision in Practice, pp. 499–504 (2008)

20. García-Pérez, L., García-Alegre, M.C., Ribeiro, A., Guinea, D.: An agent of behaviour architecture for unmanned control of a farming vehicle. Comput. Electron. Agric. **60**(1), 39–48 (2008)

21. Bengochea-Guevara, J.M., Conesa-Muñoz, J., Andújar, D., Ribeiro, A.: Merge fuzzy visual servoing and GPS-based planning to obtain a proper navigation behavior for a small crop-inspection robot. Sensors **16**(3), 276 (2016)

22. Duggal, V., Sukhwani, M., Bipin, K., Reddy, G.S., Krishna, K.M.: Plantation monitoring and yield estimation using autonomous quadcopter for precision agriculture. In: 2016 IEEE International Conference on Robotics and Automation (ICRA2016), pp. 5121–5127 (2016)

23. Bechtsis, D., Tsolakis, N., Vlachos, D., Srai, J.S.: Intelligent autonomous vehicles in digital supply chains: a framework for integrating innovations towards sustainable value networks. J. Cleaner Prod. **181**, 60–71 (2018)

24. Farinelli, A., Boscolo, N., Zanotto, E., Pagello, E.: Advanced approaches for multi-robot coordination in logistic scenarios. Robot. Auton. Syst. **90**, 34–44 (2017)

25. Clearpath Robotics. https://www.clearpathrobotics.com. Accessed 29 Mar 2018

26. SAGA Robotics. https://sagarobotics.com/. Accessed 29 Mar 2018

27. Koenig, N., Howard, A.: Design and use paradigms for gazebo, an open-source multi-robot simulator. In: IEEE/RSJ International Conference on Intelligent Robots and Systems (IROS), pp. 2149–2154 (2004)

28. Bochtis, D.D., Sørensen, C.G., Green, O.: A DSS for planning of soil-sensitive field operations. Decis. Support Syst. **53**(1), 66–75 (2012)

29. Moisiadis, V., Bechtsis, D., Menexes, G., Vlachos, D., Iakovou, E., Bochtis, D.: Intelligent autonomous vehicles in industrial environments. In: 6th ICMEN International Conferences, Thessaloniki, Greece, pp. 207–2012 (2017)

Precision Poultry Farming: Software Architecture Framework and Online Zootechnical Diary for Monitoring and Collaborating on Hens' Health

Magdalena Stefanova[(✉)]

Department of Computing Systems, Faculty of Mathematics and Informatics,
Sofia University "St. Kliment Ohridski", Sofia, Bulgaria
stefanova.magdalena@gmail.com

Abstract. Livestock farming needs to reach superior productivity levels in an environmentally sustainable manner. In order to accelerate the development of the livestock industry, it is important to make optimal use of farming knowledge and provide farmers with adequate information technologies. This article describes the realisation of a precision livestock management information technology framework that can serve as a practical guide for the development of new and various livestock management software products. The business domain focus is on the egg industry with a detailed precision poultry farming example and real realization. The online platform specified hereafter as zootechnical diary delivers monitoring and collaborative capabilities to improve laying hens' health and welfare at industrial poultry farms. It connects egg and breeding farms through cloud technologies to provide continuous data recording, automatic comparisons between actual and expected production indicators, e-networking and integrated data-flow between the two parties. Breeding farms benefit from enhanced competitiveness, improved supplier-client relationships, while egg farms enjoy management precision, timely feedback on animals' health and economic benefits.

Keywords: Precision poultry farming · Precision livestock farming · ZooTechnical Diary · Software-as-a-Service · Production indicators · Health of laying hens

1 Introduction

According to the Food and Agriculture Organisation of the United Nations (FAO) farmers will need to produce 70% more food by 2050 in order to feed the rising global population (Food and Agriculture Organization of the United Nations 2009). Customers are looking for high quality and safe food products, at an affordable price. Moreover, both animal welfare as well as environmentally friendly animal production systems have turned into decisive factors when a consumer is filling up his shopping basket (Cumby and Phillips 2001). However, amidst these demands, livestock production must also be profitable if farming is to be chosen as a viable economic activity

© Springer Nature Switzerland AG 2019
M. Salampasis and T. Bournaris (Eds.): HAICTA 2017, CCIS 953, pp. 191–205, 2019.
https://doi.org/10.1007/978-3-030-12998-9_14

by future generations (Webster 2001). To fulfil these requirements simultaneously can be an overwhelming task for livestock producers (Schofield et al. 2002).

But given a thorough understanding of the process is developed and up-to-date control techniques are applied, even such complex processes can be described, managed and controlled (Gates and Banhazi 2002). To accelerate the development of the livestock industry, it is of vital importance to boost the spread of information and encourage the adoption of information technology applications in farming. The transformation of traditional animal husbandry through modern information technology is a significant and urgent task. If farmers do not adopt data collection, analysis and precise information, livestock modernisation will not happen (Huang et al. 2015).

The one tool that can open up real opportunities for animal production is precision livestock farming (PLF). In contrast to previous approaches, PLF systems aim to offer a real-time monitoring and management system that focuses on improving the life of the animals by warning when problems arise so that the farmer may take immediate action. Continuous, fully automatic monitoring and improvement of animal health and welfare, product yields and environmental impacts should become possible (Berckmans 2014). The Australian researcher Banhazi (2005) outlines that PLF involves establishing data acquisition systems, analysing the recorded information, triggering management actions and activating either automatic control systems and/or human intervention.

Also it is emphasised that the application of PLF practices in the Egg Industry can be framed as Precision Poultry Farming (PPF). PPF, in turn, has the potential to improve production efficiency as well as welfare and health of animals, and could also reduce the environmental impact of poultry production. In the same paper it is stated that implementing PLF technologies on poultry farms can improve profitability of these farms by improving technical efficiency. The Australian Egg Corporation Limited recognises (Banhazi 2005) that the development of an integrated data analysis tool for the egg industry is a potentially critical enhancement and can lift management standards on farms.

Research and examples of PLF tools have already been published (Berckmans 2004) for the pig, broiler, dairy industries. For instance, Daniel Berckmans discusses the nature of PLF and provides concrete examples of existing commercial hardware-based PLF technologies implemented in pig, broiler and dairy farms. Thirteen years later, as a result of the EU-PLF (2016) project the dedicated research team again describes analogous examples of several concrete implementations of PLF in the same types of farms - pig, broiler and dairy. The implemented technologies adopted by the participating farms have been already sold on the market by specific commercial companies. A high-level blueprint is outlined and it focuses on the PLF business models, economics and organization research. Some high-level requirements are provided for the hardware PLF equipment only - battery life of sensors, durability of the hardware given conditions in the farms (Guarino et al. 2017).

Even though the authors recognise that not only sensor, but also online technologies should be employed in PLF, and that a multidisciplinary approach is required in order to drive adoption among farmers, several aspects, which play a pivotal role for achieving the latter goal, haven't been identified. Firstly, instead of focusing on few examples by limited number of companies, there needs to be derived an overarching information technology framework that can serve as a practical guide for the development of new and various PLF information products. Secondly, PLF can include sensors, but more importantly, it should leverage online data availability, analysis and access for various stakeholders. Moreover, even though the egg farms are also large-scale productions like dairy, broiler and pig farms, both little example systems and applicable information technology frameworks have been presented for the egg industry in particular. Therefore, on the basis of industry value-chain analysis, interviews with experts, established companies, egg farmers, literature review, and interdisciplinary knowledge, this paper showcases an information technology framework for online platform that can serve as blueprint software architecture and design pattern for future PLF technologies. Furthermore, the business domain focus is on the egg industry with a detailed PPF example and real realization.

Specifically, the online platform is called hereafter a ZooTechnical Diary and it leverages cloud computing technology, statistical analysis, business intelligence principles and provides for integrated, real-time data and collaboration between breeding farms and egg farms. The Diary addresses a concrete market problem and leverages concrete egg industry use case. Namely, the capability to connect online breeding farms and egg farms, which allows them to realise improved animal health, improved supplier-client relationship and economic benefits.

2 Methods

In order to contextualise and ascertain the relatively new field of study of precision poultry farming, qualitative research methods were predominantly leveraged in this paper. The author employed semi-structured interviews with farmers in order to gather the specific use cases where veterinary data recording is most valuable and confirm the hypotheses for the benefits of the chosen software architecture. The questionnaire comprised 12 core questions and another 10 questions related to their farm or existing knowledge about precision livestock management. In addition, observation and on-site visits were performed as supplemental means for gathering more data and corroborating the research findings. Later, clickable software prototype, which consisted of user interface mock-up screens, was developed and provided to the farmers with the goal of validating the usefulness and practical market application of the zootechnical diary, test the proposed realisation and extract results.

A total of 6 egg laying farms and 2 breeding farms, which act as suppliers to the egg farms, were interviewed and visited in the course of 6 month period. The breeding farms as well as 5 of the egg farms were located in Bulgaria and one egg farm was based in Macedonia. The size of the egg farms ranged from 30 000 to 500 000 laying hens. All interviewees were farm owners. One egg farm asked to opt out from the research on the grounds that its farming practices were proprietary.

3 Technical Architecture of the ZooTechnical Diary

3.1 Cloud Tiers of the ZooTechnical Diary

The framework employs the three standard tiers of a cloud-based architecture -Infrastructure as a Service, Platform as a Service and Software as a Service. It follows the model of a software deployed on a public infrastructure as a service.

IaaS Tier. The IaaS level offers servers, networks and other fundamental computing resources. The main IaaS advantage for farmers, a.k.a end-users is that they don't have to buy and maintain cloud computing infrastructure, but they can readily use the corresponding resources anytime, anywhere.

PaaS Tier. PaaS provides a component-based architecture platform for supporting platform configurability and efficient development environment. Also the platform level arranges for the storage and maintenance of different service components such as authorisation, alerting, version management. The PaaS level results in reusability, saves development costs and shortens the development cycle.

SaaS Tier. The SaaS provides the end-user-oriented software and services. Farmers can access SaaS on common devices (laptops, desktop computers, smart mobile phones, etc.) through the client interface such as browser or web browser wrapper. SaaS has two abstract high-level layers - backend and frontend. The former is a user-oriented software application, which includes the ZooTechnical Diary business logic. The latter includes all user interfaces, which allow the farmers to manipulate and work with the software application.

3.2 Logical Architecture View of the ZooTechnical Diary

The ZooTechnical Diary is realised as a distributed application and it is decomposed into several logical layers. The layers are concerned with the logical division of components and functionality. Layers help to differentiate between the different kinds of tasks performed by the components and enable component reusability and scalability. The main advantage of this approach is that it allows to scale user presentation and computer-intensive processing independently of the data layer, which is harder to scale and handled by external IaaS provider.

Figure 1 shows a high level representation of these layers and their relationships with users, other applications that call services implemented in the ZooTechnical Diary within the metadata layer, data sources such as relational databases and shared data sources. The Database Layer is located on the IaaS physical tier, while all the other layers reside within the SaaS tier and their version deployment is orchestrated through the PaaS tier.

As shown in Fig. 1, the framework consists of the three basic layers widely employed by web-application professionals - Database Layer, Application Layer, Presentation Layer- along with two additional ones - Metadata Layer and Mediation Layer.

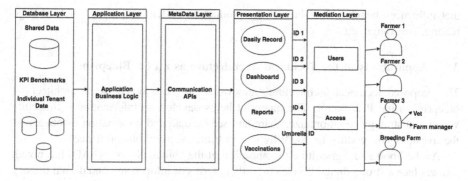

Fig. 1. Logical architecture view of the ZooTechnical Diary

Mediation Layer: This layer handles the transformation of user account details into specific IDs associated with certain roles and access permissions. It provides a solution to two key challenges – (1) farm employees different from the farm manager should have access to a restricted number of functionalities of the ZooTech Diary and (2) Users acting on behalf of the breeding farm should access only aggregated information and have read-only rights for the functionalities used by egg farms. In addition, breeding farms have additional functional modules available. Thus, breeding farm credentials are translated into the umbrella-type IDs.

Presentation Layer: This layer contains the user oriented functionality responsible for managing user interaction with the system, and consists of user interface modules such as Vaccinations, Reports, Dashboard, etc. that provide a common bridge into the core business logic encapsulated in the application layer.

MetaData Layer: Since the ZooTechnical Diary collects and stores valuable animal health data, it's advantageous to incorporate in its design a way for other external systems/applications to consume the business functionality and data results of the ZooTech Diary. This task is achieved through the MetaData Layer. The MetaData layer effectively provides an alternative view that allows clients to use a different channel to access the application. External clients and other systems can access the application and make use of its data by communicating with the business layer through Communication APIs. This allows to position the ZooTechnical Diary as a connected, integrated, single source of truth for animal health, egg production indicators and expose the functionality for integration with government veterinary and administrative systems.

Application Layer: This layer implements the core functionality of the system, and encapsulates the relevant business logic.

Database Layer: This layer provides access to data hosted within the boundaries of the system. The data layer exposes generic interfaces that the components in the business layer can consume. Each tenant a.k.a egg farm has a separate database to ensure data integrity and security across farms. Moreover, there is a separate shared data storage containing benchmark production indicators against which the actual egg farm production results are compared. The values for the benchmark indicators are specific to the laying breed offered to egg farms by the breeding farm. Another factor that influences benchmark values is the production system employed, such as cage rearing, free range, etc.

3.3   Applicability of the Technical Architecture as a PLF Blueprint

The proposed technical architecture framework can be adopted as an architectural blueprint in the PLF sector. The blueprint helps develop an information architecture vision and strategy to rationalize, share and secure data and information assets across the livestock and poultry farms. Why is a PLF architectural blueprint needed?

As the Food and Agriculture Organisation of the United Nations (FAO) has noted, farmers face a strong digital divide currently in terms of information and digital literacy skills, which prevents them from making use of the information technologies (FAO 2017). At the same time, the digital divide of farmers is also a challenge for the rest of the professionals such as consultants, animal science experts and IT professionals who are tasked with transforming the processes, providing the advice and developing the information technologies and software to be used by the farmers. As a result, a PLF architectural blueprint has the potential to bridge the divide by establishing guiding principles and standards for information as a resource in PLF. The PLF architectural blueprint is also instrumental for defining data governance best practices to ensure sustainable PLF implementations. Furthermore, the PLF architectural blueprint ensures business agility since it serves as standard information platform that makes it easier to conduct business activities across a wider range of customers, suppliers and partners. Specifically, thanks to the incorporated MetaData layer both the Zootechnical Diary and potential future PLF products can expose their data and functionalities to third party software applications. For example, a veterinary clinic working with a farmer can connect its own software product in a standardized manner (e.g. REST API) with the Zootechnical diary and monitor on-farm animal health in real-time. Alternatively instead of direct API calls, the MetaData layer can be technically realized with a distributed message streaming platform like Apache Kafka (The Apache Software Foundation 2017) More importantly, in the context of the overall PLF architectural blueprint, before exposing data and functionalities, it needs to be ensured that this data is reliable and due care is taken for its consistency and management. The latter is realized through the Database layer and thanks to the separation of data in an independent layer inherent advantages to database management are achieved such as insulation between programming logic and data, consistency of data during concurrent transaction processing, control of data redundancy, integrity constraints, backup and recovery mechanisms. During the research conducted for this paper, it was found out that data security and insulation are of utmost importance to the farmers. Thus, in the described PLF architecture framework it is outlined that each farmer a.k.a egg farm is allotted a separate database instance. The aforementioned design pattern of database separation per tenant can be abided by in future PLF solutions. Overall, a described PLF architecture blueprint/framework is a precondition for lower PLF IT operations costs since common information services, processes and tools are established as an enabling foundation.

4   The Main Functions of the ZooTechnical Diary

The ZooTech Diary functionally is separated into two main aspects: firstly, functional modules serving egg farms and secondly, read-only access to aggregated data along with a few additional modules dedicated to serving the breeding farm. The business value chain and supplier-client relationship between egg farms and breeding farms motivate such a software design. A single breeding farm is a supplier of parent eggs to its clients - multiple egg farms. The former provides guidance and knowledge to farmers for how to raise the chickens so that they become healthy, productive layers as prescribed by the breed production indicators. The latter, in turn, monitor the animal performance daily and rely on the breeding farm to provide know-how as well as scheduled new chicks deliveries.

4.1   Functionality for Egg Farms

The functionality for eggs farms includes the following modules:

Dashboard: The dashboard module shown on Fig. 2 enables the farmer to have a fast check of the most important actual production indicators for his flocks. These averaged indicators are compared with charts or UI control tiles against the prescribed values expected for the breed at a certain age in weeks. The farmer can receive instant verification for the liveability, egg laying rate, egg weight, animal body weight of a single flock. Also, he can evaluate the flock performance and detect any health problems by comparing expected egg grades to the actual egg grades the hens produce. The dashboard serves as an instant snapshot of the business and animal health.

Fig. 2. Dashboard with production indicators

New Entry: The new entry module as shown on Fig. 3 allows the farmer to input daily the actual production indicators per flock. In the tool the farmer enters raw value data, most of which has been already detected by the farm equipment and machines. Subsequently, the raw data is manipulated, calculated and associated with expected production indicator values in order to update the dashboard values, discussed above. Specifically, the farmers enters the number of dead chickens for the given day per flock and as a result the liveability indicator is calculated.

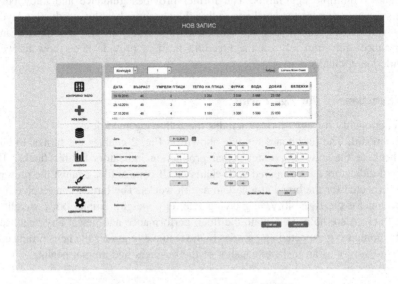

Fig. 3. New Entry module with available input

Subsequently, average animal body weight, water and feed consumption for the flock on the given day are also entered, which, in turn, are stored and used to recalculate and update the production indicators of the Dashboard module. As a last step in the New Entry module, the farmer types in the obtained number of eggs in specific grades given the flock is already a productive one. Both the common criterion of egg size for grading as well as the criterion, which classifies the eggs as grade B, are included in the scope of the New Entry module. Cracked eggs, eggs with dirty shells, and eggs with abnormal shape are all classified as grade B. The respective quantities of cracked, dirty shell and abnormal shape eggs are not detected automatically by the egg grading machine/s on the farm - these quantities are derived as a result of a manual inspection. The New Entry module is the single digital tool where the farmer can store the result of the daily manual inspection. Due to the fact that grade B eggs are sold at lower prices and often through a different market distribution channel, the total number of grade B eggs is calculated and maintained separately.

Data: The data module provides capability to inspect raw, detailed data per flock. As shown in Fig. 4 below, on the first screen of the Data module each flock on the farm is listed and summarized events such as flock age in weeks, number of birds in the

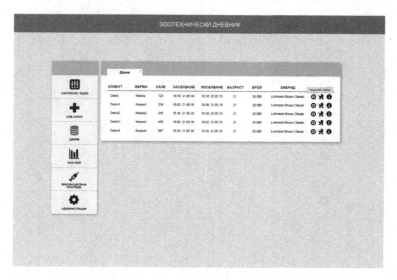

Fig. 4. Data module showing summary data per flock

flock, date of housing, etc. are displayed. The data is divided into rearing period and production period data and each of these has a separate button for expanded viewing.

As shown in Fig. 5 the expanded view of the production period reveals detailed daily data for all production indicators such as liveability percentage, hen day average, feed conversion ratio, egg mass, etc. For instance, if the farmer or the veterinary doctor wants to inspect each daily record they can do that through the module and also download the data in an electronic spreadsheet file format. The download capability allows for further flexibility in data analysis.

Reports: The reports module enables farmers to gain insights from trusted data in an understandable form and it provides actionable information at their fingerprints. The reports module leverages line charts and crosstabs as UI elements. Two levels for data exploration are offered so that farmers can slice and dice information to receive answers to animal performance questions. Users can filter visualizations on production indicator or flock level. The production indicator slicing level depicts a single production indicator over an extended period in weeks across all flocks. As shown in Fig. 6 the expected values for the indicator are shown as lines where the width of the line represents the acceptable range for variation. The actual flock performance values are depicted as lines with interactive tooltips. It allows the farmer to explore the animal performance of all his current flocks and detect trends or repeat problems. Each production indicator - hen day average, animal body weight, egg weight, feed consumption, feed conversion, egg mass, etc. has a dedicated report. For example, Fig. 6 depicts the animal body weight indicator across all flocks with both its expected values and actual ones. The flock slicing level depicts a single flock performance over a period across all production indicators. This visualization level enables the farmer to focus on a single flock and evaluate the overall flock status across the important indicators. Figure 7 depicts an example of the flock slicing level.

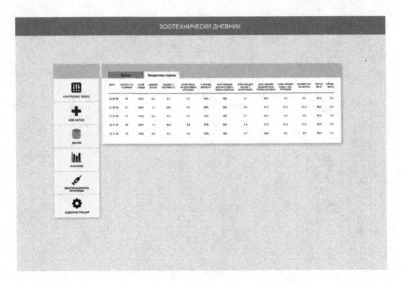

Fig. 5. Data module expanded view

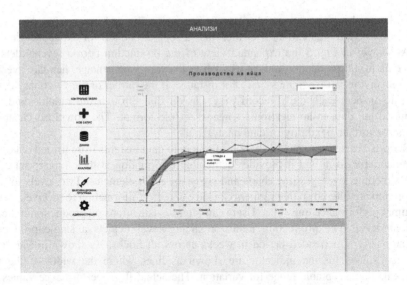

Fig. 6. Reports module - single indicator, animal body weight

Vaccination Schedule: The vaccination schedule module shown on Fig. 8 serves as a calendar and reminder for upcoming vaccinations for each separate flock depending on its age in weeks. It organises the vaccination activities and ensures preventive medication is applied on time and as prescribed by the breeding farm. Thanks to the Vaccination Schedule module the farmer is proactively notified for upcoming vaccinations and each notification specifically outlines the flock and the exact medication material needed for the vaccine administration.

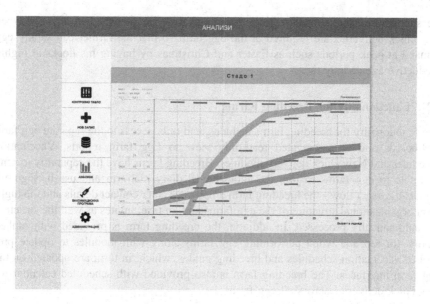

Fig. 7. Reports module - flock slicing level

Fig. 8. Vaccination schedule

New Chick Delivery: The new chicks delivery module is simply a form for farmers to schedule their upcoming chicks deliveries. From an IT perspective it is a simple implementation, but given seasonal variations in egg demand and the necessity to rely on highly productive flocks around demand peaks, this module has a major profit impact for the farmers. The New Chick Delivery module enables the improvement of the supplier-client relationship, since breeding farms are informed in advance when new chick deliveries are required at the egg farm so that the farmer can satisfy egg demand at peak periods such as Easter and Christmas by having his flocks at highly productive age exactly then.

4.2   Functionality for Breeding Farms

The functionality for breeding farms includes read-only access to the separate egg farm dashboards and an aggregated read-only view to Egg farm reports, Vaccination schedules and New chick delivery modules. Breeding farms have the capability to send an invite to egg farms to join the zootechnical diary platform and use it. Figure 9 depicts the exact flow - the breeding farm employees enter contact details and the high-level organizational structure of the egg farms and, in turn, invites as well the structure are automatically processed. In addition, the breeding farm is provided with ranked reports for top and worst performing egg farms along with modules to update pre-scribed vaccination schedules and breeding guides, which, in turn, are updated on the egg farm interfaces. The breeding farm is also provided with scheduled calendar for new chick deliveries across all egg farms.

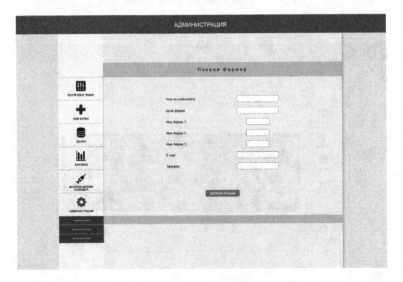

Fig. 9. Invite a farmer

Finally, if the breeding farm detects poor animal management at a given egg farm or reaches insight relying on the shared egg farm results, it can initiate online communication with the farmer via the tool. As a result, breeding farm benefit from customer loyalty, egg farms benefit from more productive laying hens and animals enjoy improved, closely-monitored health.

5   Non-functional Requirements

A system's utility is determined by both its functionalities and non-functional characteristics (Chung and do Prado Leite 2009). In this section the applicable non-functional requirements for farmers are identified and elaborated on. Throughout the research and interviews with farmers software characteristics such as usability, localization and language, performance were frequently brought up and cited by farmers themselves as decisive factors for software adoption.

Farmers identified ease of use and relevance of the information and workflow tasks to the actual farming setting as cornerstone characteristics. These requirements come as no surprise given the context of digital divide between farming and latest technologies and have been already outlined by other researchers (Rose et al. 2016). Nevertheless, in recent years the focus on usability has risen in the software industry as a whole and producing self-explainable, enjoyable PLF user interfaces should be a viable task. Given the importance of usability, the zootechnical diary mockups have undergone several iterations of usability testing and have been modified accordingly. Leveraging the principles of usability and conducting usability testing are best practices that can be adopted by future PLF solutions.

In contrast to the typical digital user, who freely uses English as a second language, farmers require that user interface is provided in their native language. As a result, all user interface designs have been developed with labels in Bulgarian, as shown on the figures. Furthermore, localization understood as the ability to achieve regulatory compliance by following the processes in the software tool was also a widely mentioned factor determining use. Farmers need to comply with various pieces of legislation. For example, poultry farmers are required to provide detailed record of the birds' health treatments and accurate bird count. Specifically, the zootechnical diary allows a farmer to export and submit to government agencies detailed reports for number of birds housed, breed, health status, vaccination treatments. Alternatively, these agencies are able to retrieve the data themselves through the MetaData layer.

Reliability and performance of a software tool were also frequently brought up by farmers participating in the interviews. Farmers expect to be provided with information quickly, even when they are on the field, and have their input reflected in the displayed data almost instantaneously. Although internet signal strength in rural areas is out of scope in this article, it is important for PLF tools to consider fast performance as a decisive factor and optimize it. The zootechnical diary has a target of one second response time after a user's input, for example.

In summary, the non-functional requirements applicable to PLF solutions are not surprising or PLF specific, but have already been addressed within the software development sphere. Thus, PLF software solutions should observe the software industry best practices.

6 Conclusion

Precision Poultry Farming offers new opportunities to increase the efficiency and sustainability of egg production, to improve the health and welfare of animals, and to support farming as a profitable activity, thus facilitating actual adoption by farmers. Research and examples of Precision Livestock Farming tools have already been published for the pig, broiler, dairy industries. The concrete contribution of this paper is that it describes an overarching software architecture framework and a market-validated example of application of information technologies in the egg production industry. The ZooTechnical Diary addresses the use case of supplier-client relationship between breeding and egg farms. Not only does it provide for continuous data recording and monitoring, but also allows collaboration and information exchange on animal health. Its software architecture caters to the need to ensure clear and concise farming data and offers possibility to connect farms with other systems and administrative, government institutions to ease knowledge sharing and red tape. Further research can be directed towards enabling automatic and autonomous transfer of actual production indicator values from equipment and machines to software tools and here specifically - the online ZooTechnical Diary. In addition, the collected historical data can be leveraged for predictive analytics and delivering insights for future planning to the farmer. For instance, as outlined by other researches, the linear programming can be beneficial to the poultry sector (Salampasis et al. 2003). Another area to investigate is how by leveraging the data, residing with the Zootechnical Diary, full egg production transparency can be offered to the final consumer at the grocery store.

Acknowledgements. The author wishes to thank the Sofia University and specifically Associate Professor Kamen Spassov for his continued support in structuring the author's research activities.

The developed system - ZooTechnical Diary- was implemented as part of the product portfolio of a start-up company known under the name CocoFarm Ltd. CocoFarm was founded and predominantly self-funded by the author herself. The rest of the funding was provided by the Climate - KIC Accelerator Bulgaria. The author wishes to thank Mr. Vasil Gichev and Mr. Martin Kirilov for their readiness to always lend a helping hand with technical advice, logistics, requirements.

References

Food and Agriculture Organization of the United Nations: Global agriculture towards 2050. Rome, Office of the Director, Agricultural Development Economics Division Economic and Social Development Department (2009)

Cumby, T.R., Phillips, V.R.: Environmental impacts of livestock production. Integrated Management Systems for Livestock, vol. 28, pp. 13–22 (2001)

Webster, A.J.: The future of livestock production: planning for the unknown. Integrated Management Systems for Livestock, vol. 28, pp. 113–118 (2001)

Schofield, C.P., Wathes, C., Frost, A.R.: Integrated Management Systems for Pigs- Increasing Production Efficiency and Welfare. Animal Production in Australia, vol. 24, pp. 197–200 (2002)

Gates, R.S., Banhazi, T.: Applicable technologies for Controlled Environment Systems (CES) in livestock production. Animal Production in Australia, vol. 24, pp. 486–489 (2002)

Huang, J., Guo, P., Xie, Q., Meng, X.: Cloud services platform based on big data analytics and its application in livestock management and marketing. In: Proceedings of Science, Guangzhou (2015)

Berckmans, D.: Precision livestock farming technologies for welfare management in intensive livestock systems. Scientific and Technical Review of the Office International des Epizooties, vol. 33(1), pp. 189–196 (2014)

Banhazi, T.: A National Workshop on "Precision Poultry Farming" in Australia, s.l.: Australian Egg Corporation Limited (2005)

Berckmans, D.: Automatic on-line monitoring of animals by precision livestock farming. In: International Society for Animal Hygiene, Saint-Malo, pp. 27–30 (2004)

EU-PLF: Smart Farming for Europe Value creation through Precision Livestock Farming (2016). https://cordis.europa.eu/docs/results/311/311825/final1-20170707v5-finalreport-gano311825. pdf

Guarino, M., et al.: A blueprint for developing and applying precision livestock farming tools: a key output of the EU-PLF project. Anim. Front. **7**(1), 12–17 (2017)

Food and Agriculture Organization of the United Nations (FAO): Information and Communication Technology (ICT) in Agriculture A Report to the G20 Agricultural Deputies. Food and Agriculture Organization of the United Nations, Rome (2017)

The Apache Software Foundation: Apache Kafka is a distributed streaming platform (2017). https://kafka.apache.org/intro

Chung, L., do Prado Leite, J.C.S.: On non-functional requirements in software engineering. In: Borgida, A.T., Chaudhri, V.K., Giorgini, P., Yu, E.S. (eds.) Conceptual Modeling: Foundations and Applications. LNCS, vol. 5600, pp. 363–379. Springer, Heidelberg (2009). https://doi.org/10.1007/978-3-642-02463-4_19

Rose, D.C., et al.: Decision support tools for agriculture: towards effective design and delivery. Agric. Syst. **149**, 165–174 (2016)

Salampasis, M., Kalentzi, E., Batzios, C.: Better Decision Making in the Broiler Industry by Integrating Linear Programming into the BRODESSYS Decision Support System (2003)

Author Index

Albuquerque, Teresa   64
Alegria, Cristina   64

Bechtsis, Dimitrios   177
Bochtis, Dionysis   1, 177
Bournaris, Thomas   51

Candela, Leonardo   20
Castelli, Donatella   20

Economou, Evangelia   51

Gentile, Aureliano   20
Giannelli, Annalaura   35
Giannerini, Gianfranco   110
Giuffrida, Salvatore   35
Gonçalves, Pedro   131
Gorelli, Giulia   20

Hakala, Teemu   164
Honkavaara, Eija   164

Kaivosoja, Jere   164
Kamariotou, Maria   97
Kappas, Thomas   51
Kateris, Dimitrios   1
Kitsios, Fotis   97
Kokkinis, Georgios   118
Kremmydas, Dimitris   84
Kriechhammer, Guenther   118

Madas, Michael   97
Malliapis, Michael   84
Mangiacrapa, Francesco   20
Manthou, Vicky   97
Marketakis, Yannis   20
Martello, Marco   110
Minadakis, Nikos   20
Moisiadis, Vasileios   177

Moulogianni, Christina   51
Mountantonakis, Michalis   20

Näsi, Roope   164
Navalho, Isabel   64
Nellas, Leyteris   84
Nóbrega, Luís   131

Pagano, Pasquale   20
Pedreiras, Paulo   131
Pepe, Antonio Gerardo   110
Perciante, Costantino   20
Petrellis, Nikos   148
Polymeros, Apostolos   84

Quinta-Nova, Luís   64

Roque, Natália   64
Rozakis, Stelios   84

Scheidl, Daniel   118
Smolka, Martin   118
Sørensen, Claus Aage Grøn   1
Stefanova, Magdalena   191

Taconet, Marc   20
Tascone, Fabrizio Luigi   110
Trovato, Maria Rosa   35
Tsiboukas, Kostas   84
Tsolakis, Naoum   177
Tzitzikas, Yannis   20

Viljanen, Niko   164
Vlachopoulou, Maro   97
Vlachos, Dimitrios   177

Wilfling, Bianca   118

Zucaro, Raffaella   110

Printed in the United States
By Bookmasters